LEARNING AND TEACHING WHERE WORLDVIEWS MEET

LEARNING AND TEACHING WHERE WORLDVIEWS MEET

edited by Rosamund Sutherland,
Guy Claxton and Andrew Pollard

Trentham Books

Stoke on Trent, UK and Sterling, USA

Trentham Books Limited

Westview House	22883 Quicksilver Drive
734 London Road	Sterling
Oakhill	VA 20166-2012
Stoke on Trent	USA
Staffordshire	
England ST4 5NP	

First published 2003

British Library Cataloguing-in-Publication Data
A catalogue record for this book is available from the British Library

1 85856 248 1

Designed and typeset by Trentham Print Design Ltd., Chester and printed in Great Britain by Cromwell Press Ltd., Wiltshire.

Contents

Part II: Professional and Disciplinary Cultures

Part III: Formal and Informal Cultures

1

Fishing in the fog: conceptualising learning at the confluence of cultures

Guy Claxton, Andrew Pollard and Rosamund Sutherland

Where currents meet there is fog,
but there is also the best fishing Ruth Campbell

'Show me something you find really beautiful', I say. A friend and I (GC) are standing in the vast foyer of the Tate Modern art museum in London. This is 'home' to her. She is a contemporary art curator, and I am entering a universe in which she is an experienced and respected insider, and I am a complete beginner and outsider. I want to understand – but I lack the perception, the expertise, even the vocabulary with which to articulate my questions convincingly. So I ask her to show me something she truly likes. She takes me to the gallery in which an enormous number of bits and pieces – fragments of wood, a bent watering-can, a headless doll, a twisted fork – are hung from the ceiling in a giant open see-through cube. It is a reconstruction by the artist, Cornelia Parker, of a garden shed which she has blown up and then meticulously reassembled as if frozen in the act of exploding. I think it is quite interesting...but 'beautiful'? I don't get it.

A year previously I would have been secure in my dismissal of much of contemporary art: pickled sheep, unmade beds, cans of excrement and so on. Now I am not quite so confident. I know that my companion is not a fool, a cynic or a charlatan, so I take her judgements

1

and her interests seriously. But I cannot see the world as she sees it. I have relinquished some of my old knee-jerk certainty, but am not ready or able – or indeed willing – to see and talk and value as she does. I feel clumsy and unsure. For the sake of the friendship, I sometimes read the art reviews in the Sunday papers more attentively than before. I try to be open-minded. And she, for her part, is mostly patient with my clumsy questions and cack-handed opinions, and tries to explain how Rubens and Cézanne and Tracey Emin fit together. We are 'teaching and learning where worldviews meet' – and it is not easy. It is not just a matter of acquiring knowledge or learning skills. I am slowly learning to experience and evaluate the world in a different way – without losing myself in the process. I am a cautious candidate for a culture that is very different from, and in some ways strongly dissonant with, the one with which I had been unthinkingly familiar.

As the world becomes more plural and interwoven, this kind of learning becomes more common, and perhaps more intense. We become enculturated into one group, and then find ourselves having (or choosing) to engage with people who do things in a different way, notice different things, organise themselves differently, and value different kinds of experience and achievement. We have to work alongside people from different disciplinary, professional and national cultures (Gibbons *et al.,* 1994). Electronic media enable daily interactions with people from around the world. Newspapers and television flood us with images of people going about their lives in ways that look, at first sight, strange or nonsensical. In the aftermath of Princess Diana's death, the British people engaged in heated debate about the 'correct' way to mourn: did the queen do it 'right', or Diana's brother, or Elton John? In the face of such escalating complexities, we may retreat into the reflex judgements that our own cultures provide – 'aren't they funny?', 'how could they believe such obvious tosh?' – or we struggle to expand, and maybe even question our own positions.

Such learning is, however, far from new. What must have been the experience of my (RS) father when he moved from the world of back-to-back terraces in the North of England to a 'posh' grammar school, a working class boy entering the world of the middle classes?

What sort of culture clash must my mother have experienced as she entered university in London, from a poor rural background in Norfolk? For myself I can still vividly remember the shock when at the age of 15 I spent my first summer with a French family. 'I don't get it' perfectly describes my multitude of experiences. How could it be possible to take body temperature from anywhere other than the mouth? Why did the family not know how to use a knife and fork in the 'proper' way? Why do they 'argue' and intellectualise with me all the time?

More recently I (RS) have taken up tango dancing, and in this new world have had to un-learn some of my propensity to anticipate and predict patterns (a core part of the 'mathematical me'). I have had to become, in a small way, a different person, perhaps partly by getting in touch again with a person I used to be. I resonate with the experience of Sally Potter, heroine of the film *The Tango Lesson*, as described by Davis, Sumara and Luce-Kapler (2000, p197).

> In the film Sally Potter is able to show how learning to dance the tango does not simply mean adding a new skill to one's bank of knowledge. Like all learning, mastering the tango means becoming involved in a whole set of interpersonal and intertextual relations that are new to the learner. These involvements alter the geography of the learner's past, present and imagined experience. As Potter learns to tango, she also learns to perceive, to remember, and to imagine in new ways. Learning, then, is not making deposits into one's data bank. It is more like mixing a new ingredient into the soup of perception and cognition.

In all my memories of moving between cultures there is, at the beginning, a physical sensation of shock and then, if I do not reject the new culture, a long period of 'making sense' in which I appropriate new views and values, and renegotiate my commitment to previous ones. I have begun to appreciate just how much, throughout my life, I have been formed by such processes of appropriation and renegotiation which the recurrent experience of meeting new cultures has forced upon me, and how these learnings have become an inextricable part of my lived experiences, an inextricable part of me.

Cultural complexity and education

Education systems have a responsibility, we could argue, to prepare people to handle cultural meetings and transitions as skilfully and productively as they can. But they cannot just 'teach' students about such things: they are themselves embodiments of and stimulants for all kinds of intercultural learning. As Bruner (1996) points out, 'Education is a major embodiment of a culture's way of life, not just a preparation for it' (p13). Here are a few examples:

• A four-year-old, in her first week at primary school, has to grapple with the complex ways in which her new class is both like and unlike her playgroup or her family. She has to learn the ropes of this new culture, of which much is not spelled out but are implicit in the rituals, structures and reactions which are dubbed and accepted as 'normal' (or 'good', or 'naughty', or 'cute' or 'silly'). She has to try to develop and negotiate new ways of 'being herself' that are adaptive and successful (Pollard with Filer, 1996).

• A nine-year-old, walking home from his music lesson through his working-class neighbourhood with his violin under his arm, may be teased and taunted by street-corner groups of teenagers. He feels himself positioned uncomfortably between the middle-class values of the school, which his violin symbolises, and the very different interests and priorities of the community in which he has grown up, and with whose values he is still imbued (Jackson and Marsden, 1966).

• A 13-year-old, being given a ticking-off by a teacher, follows the customs of his home culture by looking down at the floor, a gesture which, to him, denotes deference and respect – and is then puzzled and aggrieved when he is accused of showing 'dumb insolence'.

• A girl moves from Hungary to England at the age of ten and is constantly baffled because her teacher in England cannot make sense of her when she writes 3,45 instead of 3.45 – using a comma for a decimal point. The young girl and the teacher are stuck in different worlds, both believing that ways of writing mathematics must be culturally free and so both unable to envisage the other world.

- A university student, just arrived in Bristol from Papua New Guinea for his Masters' degree, may be completely thrown by an informally dressed 'professor' who says 'Call me Jane', starts the class by asking the students what their expectations are, and insists that they should criticise her pronouncements.

- A would-be teacher, arriving on her PGCE course with a 2:1 in Chemistry, is similarly flummoxed by the fact that her carefully honed skills of learning and studying no longer seem to count. She is being asked instead to learn in ways which are much more personal and reflective, and which she neither sees the point of, nor knows how to do.

- A mature student on a counselling diploma is introduced to a culture of 'assessment' which is formative, supportive and collaborative – but which seems in some ways more covert and confusing than the 'bad old world' of marks and grades.

- A senior teacher, appointed to his first headship, finds that the culture of 'education', in which he has been steeped for a dozen years, is now being challenged and superseded by the contrasting language, values and practices of 'management'.

In a whole host of ways, not far below the surface, the experience of education seems to be about negotiating the often turbulent interface between contrasting, even contradictory, views of the world. So 'teaching and learning where worldviews meet' is, we contend, not an arcane or occasional kind of learning, but is of core importance, both within education itself and in terms of the real-world social, cognitive and emotional demands of contemporary life. But there is little research that focuses directly on this topic. On the one hand, cognitive approaches to teaching and learning tend to concentrate on the organisation, transmission and assessment of specific bodies of content. On the other, sociocultural approaches to education have mainly focused on the small-scale interpersonal dynamics of 'scaffolding' and the 'zone of proximal development' (Vygotsky, 1978). Even cultural approaches such as those of Cole (1996) or Lave and Wenger (1991), which do view learning and teaching in terms of enculturation, have tended to see the learner as acquiring the habits, values, attitudes and identity of the target 'community of practice' *ab initio.* It is as if there were little or no inner conflict to be resolved or outer dissonance to be negotiated.

There are also deep clashes within the academic world about the meaning of culture. The idea of culture tends to be used in psychology to designate a group of people who 'belong together' by virtue of some shared feature (Valsiner, 2000) and this has been criticised by sociologists (Strauss, 1992) for creating an illusion of homogeneity. Early anthropological studies borrowed from behavioural psychology and defined culture as 'a mass of learned and transmitted motor reactions, habits, techniques, ideas, and values – and the behaviours they induce' (Kroeber, 1948, p8, quoted in Valsiner, 2000). By contrast, in contemporary anthropology culture has been viewed as the accumulation of knowledge and information together with 'core conceptual structures that provide a basis for an intersubjectively shared representation of the world in which the person lives' (Valsiner, p50). Socio-cultural theories and cultural psychology foreground the importance of humans' capacity to construct psychological and technical devices which mediate action and transform the here-and-now settings of human beings. This focus on the production of semiotic devices and other technologies has been highlighted by the advent of rapidly developing digital technologies (Pea, 1993, Perkins, 1993), although human beings have always produced technologies which shape and transform their action.

How to recognise a 'culture'
If we are to begin to develop a systematic approach to learning at the confluence of cultures, we have to start somewhere, however, and many of the explorations in this book take the neo-Vygotskean ideas of sociocultural theorists such as Cole, Lave and Wertsch as their jumping-off point. And the first move is to construct, if not a definition, at least a working set of ideas about what we mean by a 'culture'. Simply to get us going, therefore, we offer six facets in terms of which we might characterise, or even recognise, something that we might want to refer to as a 'culture'.

First and foremost, a culture reflects core understandings of a *group of people* who are in communication with each other, and who share, knowingly or not, some common sense of values and purposes. Sub-groups and internal differences remain important, reflecting the diversity within almost every element of modern societies. However, on the whole, the group still acts as if certain things mattered and others did not, and as if some things were 'obvious' or 'natural' and others 'ridiculous' or 'mad'. Animated debate may occur between sub-groups or about boundary issues, but core values, though often unarticulated, remain largely taken for granted.

Second, values are embodied in a variety of *psychological habits and processes*. Again, whilst manifesting patterns of variation, the members of a cultural group tend to think, feel and interpret in characteristic ways. They perceive the world in terms of a shared set of categories. They notice and attend to the same kinds of things. Their thoughts are shaped by the social evolution of their language. They approach problem-solving and decision-making in similar ways. They learn to tell particular kinds of stories in culturally recognised ways, and to agree about what makes a 'good' account. They value some ways of learning and knowing, for example scientific or intellectual ones, above others, for example intuitive, poetic or spiritual. They agree about what emotions are appropriate in different contexts, or for different sub-groups, and how they are to be displayed.

Third, the culture resides in a historically evolving set of *social structures and practices*. Despite internal diversity reflecting factors such as gender and social class, there is a degree of commonality in worldview. Activities such as agriculture, trade, education, making and enforcing laws, medicine, child-rearing and so on are carried on in some ways rather than others. Meetings are structured in culturally typical ways and tend to last a certain length of time. (There are cultures in which the length of community meetings is measured in days, and a wedding lasts a fortnight). There are normative rituals of birth, marriage and death; rites, habits and even dress-codes that distinguish the bereaved or the pregnant. Mapping these practices and structures is the delicate stuff of cultural anthropology.

Fourth, a culture's values, struggles and history are enshrined in the *material objects and environments* which it has fashioned, and the constraints or possibilities for thought and action that are afforded by these resources. Large-scale deforestation 'says' that the balance of power within a culture values cheap meat above biodiversity or global warming. Traditional classrooms with individual desks facing front 'afford' certain kinds of didactic, teacher-centred learning, and 'dis-afford' informal group work. Open-plan offices invite multiple, casual forms of interaction, and implicitly devalue privacy and solitude. Watching television may invite certain kinds of conversation (witness 'The Royle Family') and be less conducive to others. Reading a book exercises different kinds of mental skills and attitudes from watching a video. The values and beliefs of a culture can be read in the objects and spaces that it creates and inherits.

Fifth a culture shares a *language* and set of *symbols* which are conserved, elaborated and passed on from old-timers to new-timers, thus preserving the culture's identity and way of life. Becoming enculturated into the world of school mathematics requires students to learn to use words like divide, share and scale in ways which are different from the ways these words are typically used out of school. As we move between the world of educational research in anglo-saxon countries and countries in the Pacific Rim, for example, we have to re-examine what we mean by such words as teach and such phrases as rote learning which have evolved within distinct cultures of educational belief and value. The semiotic systems embodied within different cultures have profound mediating effects on thought and action.

Sixth, and critical in the present context, is the idea that cultures, whether tight or loose-knit, are almost inevitably *nested within or in contact with* each other, and these contacts generate disputes and conversations about the different values and purposes which their contrasting practices and languages embody. As we have indicated, any culture is rarely homogeneous. For example, within a typical school there are many 'sub-cultures', some in harmony and some in greater or lesser degrees of opposition to each other. Different classes and different corners of the staffroom may have quite distinct 'characters'. Each sub-culture may have other sub-cultures with which it is in open conflict or negotiation, and others whose existence it does not recognise at all. If you take a larger perspective, the school as a whole is itself nested within wider systems of value and belief that are political, commercial and sometimes global.

Seventh, we need to recognise that cultures are *rarely static*. Rather, they reflect dynamic processes of challenge, resistance, accommodation and assimilation. In these ways, their specific mediating affordances are adapted or renewed. The case of primary education in England is interesting in this respect. From the dominance of a 'child-centred' culture with considerable school and teacher autonomy during the 1970s, the introduction of a nationally supervised curriculum, assessment and inspection system brought dramatic changes by the 1990s. Initially, there was significant resistance, but new forms of accommodation later developed. Primary school cultures are now more concerned than they once were with attaining national targets and less attuned to issues in child development. Nevertheless, the legacy remains of primary school teachers' sense of moral commitment to young children in their care – and generates a particular quality within the cultures of these schools.

Finally we might remind ourselves, as we noted earlier, that individuals embody and reproduce the commonalities and differences of the range of settings into which they have become enculturated, whilst rubbing up against a multiplicity of others. Indeed, in today's educational and economic world, it is virtually impossible to live as a member of a single, stable, insulated, homogeneous society, whose worldview is accepted as universal, natural, unproblematic and uncontested. Instead, we can find ourselves at the turbulent interface of cultures, fishing in the fog, several times a day.

Responses to culture-clash

At these points of contact, both individuals and organisations find themselves under pressure to respond, and these responses can take a variety of general forms. Some of them are defensive – they are ways of coping with an alien set of cultural demands without, as it were, buying into it. One can, for example, attempt simply to *ignore* it, act independently, and carry on as if the demand did not exist. It is said, stereotypically, that military officers in the British colonies would insist that 'the Army does not adapt to local cultures; local cultures adapt to the Army' – a far cry, of course, from the diplomatic and negotiative skills that the armed forces now often aim to deploy in their modern role as 'peace keepers'.

Alternatively an individual or a group might, again more or less consciously, decide to *resist, oppose or subvert* another culture. Such resistance may be overt or covert, and may be fuelled by a complex mixture of emotions and motivations ranging from principled objection to personal apprehension. Where the alien culture is powerfully imposed, and explicit opposition carries significant dangers – as, for example, when people are enslaved or oppressed by totalitarian regimes – various kinds of pretence may be used. Holt (1982) has suggested that similar tactics may be adopted by some young people for whom school appears to be an alien and oppressive culture; an amiable dim-wittedness, for example, may be used to mask a total inner disidentification with the values and practices that are being imposed. Interestingly, opposition and subversion may be all the more effective, as military strategists suggest, if one is able to 'put oneself in the mind of the enemy'. Thus a degree of learning about the second culture – understanding it without 'buying' it – may be tactically useful. Such a possibility requires us to distinguish two kinds of 'learning', one that does and one that does not lead to personal assent, agreement or identification with the goals and values of a novel culture, even though both kinds may lead to a degree of mastery of its social practices.

If one allows oneself to become more personally encultured to the unfamiliar worldview, one alternative is to *adopt* it wholesale, and update or abandon old values and practices in the light of the new, with the uncritical and pervasive enthusiasm of the naïve convert. Though such conformity is seen most powerfully in, for example, religious conversion, where one may be almost literally 'born again', it can also be found in academic or educational circles, when practitioners 'fall in love' with a new worldview that seems to have 'seen the light'. Intense and romantic love affairs with fashionable concepts, new paradigms and their attendant discourses and practices, are not uncommon. The recent popularity of post-modern ideas might be seen in that light or, indeed, the interest being generated by socio-cultural theory – which this book reflects and reinforces.

Finally we might identify the approach of *negotiating*, in which new and existing worldviews are redefined and allowed to resonate in a more delicate, but often more uncomfortable, fashion, perhaps over a longer period of time, with previously held views. This is what we at Bristol have been attempting to do regarding the interdisciplinary study of culture and learning in organiations. Within our Graduate School's debates, psychological, sociological, political and linguistic perspectives are encouraged to co-exist and challenge each other. Of course, they each have different literatures, concepts and pre-occupations, but we have found that they also seem to have a different rationality, different ways of arguing and different ways of building knowledge. In such circumstances, instead of sticking resolutely to 'White', or uncritically espousing 'Black', one may allow one's experience to become more chequered, and to tolerate intermediate and shifting shades of 'Grey'. One may explore where precisely differing cultures are congruent or compatible, and where they are genuinely different, and what the pros and cons are of each perspective. One may begin to consider disciplines as comple-mentary rather than as opponents between which one is obliged to choose.

However, one should not make the mistake of assuming that such 'negotiating' and appreciative accommodation is always the pre-ferred or the optimal response to finding oneself at the confluence of cultures. Any of the broad range of responses outlined above may be the 'right' one, depending on a host of considerations. Do one's own personal (or institutional) values align more closely with one or other of the contrasting worldviews? In whose interests is it that one should accommodate rather than resist? What are the anticipated costs, benefits and risks of engaging with the new perspective as opposed to ignoring or opposing it? One's reaction may well be very different if the unfamiliar culture is imposed on one, or has been actively sought out. Does one feel free or coerced in the choice of how to respond? Do you see yourself as a pioneer, a refugee or a conscript?

Engaging with an unfamiliar culture is thus likely to cause some re-appraisal and amendments of existing habits and beliefs. One's dominant view of the world may become more subtle, differentiated or even compassionate as a result. But a different kind of learning may also be going on at a deeper level. In what some have called the growth of 'critical awareness', beliefs which had previously been unthinkingly dissolved in one's *modus operandi* now begin to become visible as beliefs. Instead of being presupposed by perception, thought and action, under the ultra-violet light of a contrasting worldview they become capable of being seen for the first time in their own right. Thus they can now serve as *objects* of perception, thought and action and so become capable of being scrutinised and interrogated.

This process of becoming more visible to oneself is potentially both liberating and discomfiting. It brings freedom to question values and practices that may have been bought, sight-unseen, from one's aboriginal culture. But the cost may be a reduced feeling of belonging: such critical reflection may leave one feeling at home in neither world. As Kegan (1994, p275) notes, educators who deliberately try to foster this kind of critical reflection in their students:

> are asking many of them to put at risk the loyalties and devotions that have made up the very foundations of their lives. We acquire 'personal authority', after all, only by relativising – that is, only by fundamentally altering – our relationship to public authority. This is a long, often painful voyage, and one that, for much of the time, may feel more like mutiny than a merely exhilarating (and less self-conflicted) expedition to discover new lands.

Learning and teaching where worldviews meet are thus, we argue, powerful, pervasive and profound aspects of 21st century global society. Such learning involves entering into a new culture that is necessarily more than the mastery of skills or the retention of knowledge. It involves the construction and re-negotiation of the fundamentals of individual identity and affiliation. And it reaches out beyond the realms of personal emotion and cognition into the structures, practices, languages, symbolisms and rituals of the cultures to which we belong. Rarely are these structures simple and homogeneous, any more (if they ever were); rather they are shot through with multiple threads that weave together in ways that are often confusing, jarring and hard to 'read'. Education is itself just such a complex tangle of visions and values. But in the midst of this internal plurality and complexity, it has the opportunity – some might say the responsibility – to work towards reconfiguring itself as a genuinely empowering apprenticeship in the arts and crafts of living in times that are, in Louis MacNeice's memorable phrase, 'incorrigibly plural.'

References

Bruner, J. (1996) *The Culture of Education*, Cambridge, Mass: Harvard University Press.

Campbell, R. (1988) 'Cognitive neuropsychology', in: G.L. Claxton (Ed) *Growth points in Cognition*, London: Routledge, pp153-72.

Cole, M. (1996) *Cultural Psychology: A Once and Future Discipline*, Cambridge, Mass: Harvard University Press.

Davis B., Sumara D., Luce-Kapler R. (2000) *Engaging Minds, Learning and Teaching in a Complex World*, Mahwah, New Jersey: Lawrence Erlbaum.

Gibbons, M., Limoges, C., Nowotny, H., Schwartzman, S., Scott, P. and Trow, M. (1994) *The New Production of Knowledge: The Dynamics of Science and Research in Contemporary Societies*, London: Sage.

Holt, J. (1982) *Freedom and Beyond,* Harmondsworth: Penguin.

Jackson, B. and Marsden, R. (1966) *Education of the Working Class, revised edition*, Harmondsworth: Penguin.

Kegan, R. (1994) *In Over Our Heads: The Mental Demands of Modern Life*, Cambridge, Mass: Harvard University Press.

Kroeber, A.L. (1948) *Anthropology*. New York: Harcourt and Brace.

Lave, J. and Wenger, E. (1991) *Situated Learning. Legitimate Peripheral Participation.* Cambridge: Cambridge University Press.

Pea, R. (1993) 'Practices of distributed intelligence and designs for education', in: Salomon G (ed) *Distributed Cognitions, Psychological and Education Considerations*, Cambridge: Cambridge University Press.

Perkins, D (1993) 'Person-plus: a distributed intelligemce and designs for education', in: Salomon G (ed) *Distributed Cognitions, Psychological and Education Considerations*, Cambridge: Cambridge University Press.

Pollard, A. with Filer, A. (1996) *The Social World of Children's Learning*, London: Cassell.

Strauss, C. (1992) Models and motives, in: R. D'Andrade and C. Strauss (eds), *Human Motives and Cultural Models*. Cambridge: Cambridge University Press, p1-20

Valsiner, J. (2000) *Culture and Human Development*, London, Sage.

Vygotsky, L. S. (1978) *Mind in Society: The Development of Higher Psychological Processes*, Cambridge, Mass: Harvard University Press.

Part I: National Cultures

Editors' introduction

We begin at the macro level, considering the influence of national cultures, international exchange and globalisation. This reflects the nature of the modern world, with the growth of powerful multinational corporations, deep penetration of local cultures by mass media, increasing levels of international travel and almost instant global communication. Whilst some have forecast the global dominance of US culture and sophisticated technologies, we also see reassertion of more local and regional cultures across the world. The gradual formation of significant alternative trading blocks, such as the Euro Zone, reflect countervailing forms of economic organisation; and new levels of enterprise and competition, in countries such as China, assert national aspirations to more diversified futures. However, amidst all this activity, some nations, regions (and even continents) struggle to compete internationally in economic, political and cultural terms. The tragedy of poverty and lack of influence may then be compounded by indignity and threat. In such circumstances, new challenges may emerge, as the September 11th 2001 destruction of New York's World Trade Centre tragically reminds us, from deeper cultural and religious traditions and from a profound sense of injustice.

Such events graphically illustrate the significance of the issues raised by this book. Cultures increasingly meet – and, where learning does not take place, they may well clash or collide. A socio-cultural analysis offers a way forward which is respectful and appreciative but at the same time can provide a foundation for attempts to build new understandings for the future.

The four chapters in this first part of the book offer snapshots and insights into some of the educational manifestations of these global issues, and model possible ways forward. Their foci are more specific to education – literacy, pupil learning, higher education overseas, mentoring. Such topics provide specific examples and settings in which world views meet and cultures are juxtaposed. Each chapter thus enables us to consider the confluence of cultures in respect of a tangible educational issue – and whilst we know from Bernstein and many others that 'education cannot change society', we also know that it is our responsibility to make whatever contribution we can.

David Johnson, Roger Garrett and Michael Crossley open the discussion in Chapter 2 with an analysis of the tensions between 'global cultures' and 'local cultures' and the ways in which these are played out in terms of literacy learning. There are struggles, they argue, over both the definition of literacy and curricular content, and over appropriate forms of teaching and learning. How far should Western notions of literacy be accepted as providing international standards? How should indigenous knowledge and cultural resources be drawn on in teaching and learning? In Chapter 3, Marilyn Osborn, Elizabeth McNess, Claire Planel and Pat Triggs offer us specific European examples of the schooling systems of Denmark, France and England. They highlight the aims and structural organisation of education in these countries and trace the underlying values, historical evolution and cultural traditions. The focus then shifts to secondary pupils and their experience of schooling. Cultural differences are revealed in the development of social identities and attitudes to learning – and the need for a 'social theory of learning' is argued. Here then, we see significant cultural differences even within the systems of proximate European countries. The chapter thus highlights the challenge across a wider canvas and also powerfully affirms the relationship between national cultures and individual identities.

Chapters 4 and 5 focus on two specific contexts in higher education, through which the confluence of cultures is played out. Arlene Gilpin considers the situation of students from regions such as the Middle East, Africa and Far East studying in the UK. As she graphically expresses it, they are 'out-of-service', 'out-of-culture' and 'out-of-language'. Further, unless they can adapt to UK expectations about processes in higher education, they also risk being 'out-of-learning'. The challenges that such overseas students face at this confluence of cultures is given added point by the high-stakes nature of each student's commitment. But there are also challenges for tutors and Gilpin helpfully suggests some ways of building understandings together. In Chapter 5, Elisabeth Lazarus and Shirley Tay reflect on the transfer, into the very different cultural context of Malaysia, of UK models of mentoring and direct observation of classroom practice in teacher education and professional development. Cultural mediation is shown to have considerable effects on such practices – making appropriate 'transformation' an essential element of any proposed cultural exchange.

In this section then, we have examples of cultural juxtaposition across national boundaries in the field of education. There are tensions, but there are also opportunities for learning exchanges and for the development of valuable new practices and understandings.

2

Global connectedness and local diversity: forging 'new' literacies at the point of confluence

David Johnson, Roger Garrett and Michael Crossley

Introduction

A common concern of many educational systems across the world is the perceived decline in literacy standards. While different countries have responded to the 'literacy crisis' by adopting strategies to raise attainment – for example, in Britain, schools have set aside an hour dedicated to the teaching of literacy – we have to ask ourselves the question whether the school-based literacy curriculum is sufficiently sensitive to demands for 'new' and different forms of literacies in late modern, culturally plural societies.

This chapter sets out to establish the premise that both globalisation and localisation have given rise to the need for new and multiple literacies which are essential to our working, public and private lives. On the one hand, the effects of globalisation on the world of employment has resulted in new work patterns and, concomitantly, has produced a new set of demands on the literacies we need to function adequately in an environment of global connectedness. Market societies have become so interconnected that what is produced in Britain will be on sale in America in a few days and vice versa. On the other hand, growing pluralism at the local level of society has produced its own demands for the literacies that we need in order to turn diversity into a productive force and to ensure that all communities, regardless of language preference, are integrated, productive citizens.

Assuming that these assumptions are correct, this chapter explores what kinds of literacies we are talking about, that will satisfy the demands of work as well as those needed to build communities based on the notion of productive diversity. It locates the role of the school in forging these 'new' literacies, so exploring how it might mediate between the demands of the global and the local.

Globalisation and the demand for new literacies

The most visible effects of globalisation are in the world of work. The structural re-organisation of big business which has been termed 'postFordism' (Piore and Sable, 1984) or 'fast capitalism (Gee, 1994) has brought about a significant changes in the practices, ethos, values and discourses of the world of work. The old 'Fordist' labour ethos which demanded a division of labour (some people planned and designed things, others worked on atomised tasks) is rapidly being replaced by one which demands that people work as teams and take responsibility for the whole production process including designing, producing and marketing. One of the consequences is a relatively sudden, if not yet institutionalised, change in the literacy demands of the wider community (Street, 1999). This demand operates at both a basic 'skill' level, such as the wide-spread need to operate computers and the use of multi-media devises to make presentations, but also at the level of learning new discourses such as negotiating, arguing a case, and discussing strategies in teams.

It is plain to see that the emergence of a new work order gives rise to demands for new forms of literacy which are different from the school-based, reading and writing literacies. The main difference between the literacies taught in school and those demanded in the new working environment lies in the way in which meaning is communicated and represented. In school-based literacies, emphasis is placed on representing meaning through the word, either spoken or written. Children read, recount and write stories, descriptions, instructions or persuasions and arguments and portray their understanding of various curriculum subject matter through these modes of representation. However, in the world of work and in various public spheres, we seem to rely increasingly on wider modes of representation than the word alone. Here meanings are made and represented through multi-modal forms of communication including the use semiotics. Semiotics, according to Kress (2001) is 'the science of the life of signs in society' and is 'concerned with an account of all meaningful systems in a culture' (23-24). Other modes through which we communicate meaning include linguistic representation (text, oral presentation, etc.), visual representation (colours, foregrounding, backgrounding, etc.) audio representation (sound effects), spatial representation (perspective) and gesture (New London Group, 1996). Thus, multimodality and multi-mediality appear, according to Kress (1998), literally to be 'pushing the word off the page'.

It is noteworthy that apart from in subjects such as Drama or Art, these forms of literacy are not taught in a systematic fashion in the school curriculum, much to the detriment of the literacy curriculum. According to Whitehead (1997)

> '...literacy itself will suffer if it is not established on a broad and deep foundation of worthwhile experiences of symbolising and repre-senting meanings through nonverbal communication skills, gesture, movement, dance, music, listening, talking, drawing, painting, modelling, building, storytelling, poetry sharing, scientific and mathematical inves-tigations, ritual and religious celebrations. Literacy in the written forms of a culture is only one form of literacy: the long list above represents the other 'literacies' (Whitehead, 1997, p177-8)

Globalisation, then, has produced new sets of working and social relations which demand that we communicate meaning in a multi-plicity of ways and through a multiplicity of modes. However, it seems that the school literacy curriculum continues to emphasise literacy as being a narrow set of skills to be acquired and learned.

Pluralism and the demands for new literacies

At the local level, cultural and linguistic pluralism has also brought about a demand for new forms of literacy which allow people to negotiate diversity within communities. In South Africa, for example, the post-apartheid language policy gives equal official status to eleven languages while several more make up the rich tapestry of communicative practices there. Similarly, in Great

Britain, Australia, the United States, the multiplicity of languages other than English in use in communities is testimony to the fact that cultural and linguistic diversity is now the norm rather than the exception. There is a growing recognition of the need for new and different ways for people to arrive at shared meanings. The sad events of 11 September 2001 have exposed how the use of language can fragment and divide communities, even those that occupy the same geographical space. At the same time, it exposed the extent to which culturally diverse communities could be united through a discourse, which contains shared values and common positions.

For most countries, finding ways in which to harness linguistic and cultural difference has become imperative to building citizenship and furthering social and political development. This means that there is a move away from the creation of a standard form of literacy to one which encourages people to learn a range of new discourses and modes of communication in order to deal with local diversity and the demands of local cultures. Thus, according to the New London Group (1996)

> The most important skills students need to learn is to negotiate regional, context; hybrid cross cultural discourses; the code switching often to be found within a text among different languages, dialects, or registers; different visual and iconic meanings; and variations in the gestural relationships among people, language and material objects. Indeed this is the only hope for averting the catastrophic conflicts about identities and spaces that now seem ever ready to flare up.

The role of the school in forging 'new' literacies at the points of confluence

Having made the argument that globalisation and pluralism both make demands on the need for new literacies, we turn to the role of the school in mediating the tensions between the global and the local. Basil Bernstein once remarked that schools cannot change the nature of society. But this is precisely the demand, rightly or wrongly, currently being placed on schools. It would seem then that the school finds itself faced with the challenge of revisiting the ways in which it thinks about literacy and its practices for developing it.

As Bruner (1996) points out

> Our changing times are marked by deep conjectures about what schools should be expected to do for those who are compelled to attend them – or for that matter, what schools can do, given the force of other circumstances. Should schools aim simply to reproduce the culture, to 'assimilate' the young into ways of being little Americans or little Japanese?..or would schools, given the revolutionary changes through which we are living, do better to dedicate themselves to the equally risk, perhaps equally quixotic ideal of preparing students to cope with the changing world in which they will be living? (pix)

The first problem appears to be, according to Kress (2001), the education system's inability to understand and make the link between school and society. It seems that there is no relation between what the school offers and the shape of the world young people occupy. There are two issues embedded in this thesis. Kress claims that schools in many countries continue to emphasise literacy skills which were once essential to the era of mass production for a mass society, despite evidence that the nature of society has changed, first, through the 'intensifying dynamics of globalisation' and second, in having become increasingly multilingual and culturally plural.

This lack of understanding on the part of the education system to the changing nature of society and its inability to respond appropriately is evidenced in the almost constant reviews of education policy, particularly language policy. Critically, this debate remains circular and sways from year to year between arguments supporting 'back-to-basics' methods for teaching literacy and arguments encouraging a more 'progressivist' stance towards the nature and content of the literacy curriculum (Johnson, 1994). The main problem with the this lack of advance on educational thinking in relation to the literacy curriculum is that it has the effect of excluding large sections of people from the worlds of work and social and political life. We will expand on this argument below.

The second problem is related to the first and is to do with current practices in the teaching and assessment of literacy. It stems in part from the way in which school-based literacy is defined. Pellegrini and Galda (1998) argue that school-based literacy is defined by what children can or can't do on a psychometric test. This, they suggest, results in a fairly narrow definition of literacy and one which does not recognise the wider context in which literacy is developed. The following quotation sums up their feelings about this matter.

> An all too simple definition of literacy in school is in terms of some performance outcome on a measure, such as a norm referenced 'grade equivalent score' or a criterion-referenced set of skills. While some tests can and indeed do measure early school-based literacy we suggest that defining literacy in terms of these scores on these measures are limited. It is limited, we think, because it confuses the directionality in defining a psychological construct such as literacy with the process used to measure it. Psychological constructs should be defined theoretically before they are defined, and measured, psychometrically. Psychometric definitions used to define literacy reverse this logic: it takes test scores or other discrete skills, which are indicative of literacy, and uses them to define the construct, literacy. Thus literacy becomes defined as the ability to recognise letters and produce their corresponding sounds. While phoneme-grapheme recognition is an important component in learning to read and write, it is only one small correlated dimension of the larger social cognitive process of learning literacy. This larger process is what needs defining. Then we can develop measures to assess it.

The argument here is that assessment procedures place pedagogy in a straitjacket. While there is a growing recognition for teaching and learning to include the development of creative and innovative abilities in the young, teachers are faced with the task of accounting for performance. It seems that creativity and innovation do not count as part of being literate.

A third problem is that there appears to be insufficient understanding on the part of the education system of the way in which literacy is developed outside school – in the social context of the home and the community. Street (1999) claims that the literacy curriculum is not driven by what happens in the real world. Apart from some work in the anthropology of literacy, such as that carried out by Scribner and Cole (1978), Heath (1982, 1983; 1991) and Freebody, 1998), there are few studies of everyday literacy practices. Thus literacy curricula are being developed in the absence of knowledge about literacy practices in the real world and literacy pedagogy appears to take little account of the way in which real life literacies are learned.

The danger of such a position is that school-based literacies remain disconnected from the real use of language and literacy in the community.

These three arguments are discussed more fully below.

1. Reconceptualising the literacy curriculum: the school as a site for negotiating multiculturalism and multilingualism

We have suggested that current debates about the nature of the literacy curriculum are circular. Because of the perceived decline in literacy standards, there is a strong resurgence of the back-to-basics movement which argues for the re-insertion into the curriculum of grammar and other traditional forms of learning literacy. Kalantzis and Cope (1993) describe the traditional curriculum as follows:

> Learning literacy in the traditional curriculum meant memorising spelling lists; doing exercises in traditional grammar like filling in close gaps or simply rote learning grammatical rules; 'compositions' marked according to its compliance with the conventions of 'standard' English; and testing 'correct' knowledge of spelling and grammar in formal examinations. Language learning became the 'art of speaking and writing in English correctly' based on prescribed absolute standards in which grammar amounted to a set of facts, fixed with no unresolved problems. (p3)

Those in favour of a more liberal approach to education argue that a curriculum which emphasises one 'standard' and 'correct' form of language and literacy is not taking account of multilingualism and cultural plurality. They adopt the stance that the literacy curriculum should recognise 'different voices' and 'different dialects' and this view has been realised in classrooms in which students are encouraged to 'write what they like'.

Progressivist stances towards literacy, however, are criticised for masking the real nature of literacy in society. Dixon and Stratta (1992) argue that to deny students, particularly those from disadvantaged backgrounds, access to a wide range of genres disables them socially. This view is shared by Christie and Rothery who argue that

> Without the capacity to handle the written genre in which information is processed and understood in the contemporary world, people will be truly left out, unable to participate in a world of increasing sophisticated information, construction and exchange. (1989:6).

It seems therefore that we need to reconceptualise the literacy curriculum so that it satisfies, on the one hand, a desire for profiling 'success', achievement and progress and on the other, the need to marshal diversity into a productive force which helps achieve this.

The need for literacies and discourses that enable students access to social, political and economic power need not erase diversity. According to Cope and Kalantzis (1993), diversity can be a resource for access. They suggest that as much as students from marginal cultural and linguistic backgrounds may be disadvantaged, they also have the potential to see things from two points of view: 'the self-evident need to live and work with an imminent epistemology of pluralism; and a linguistic and cultural positioning that can be a cultural resource for learning those theoretical, distancing modes of language and thought needed for successful (compliant or resistant) negotiation in or with dominant social discourses'. Thus dialect difference is neither something to overcome nor something to celebrate. Schools should be actively involved in 'nurturing different dialects to do different things'.

One practical example of how this might be achieved is from the work of Delpit (1988). She illustrates how students and teachers can 'work outwardly' from the language they know best, such as jointly analysing the structure of rap songs and then Shakespeare. Another practical example of how a reconceptualised literacy curriculum can recruit cultural and linguistic difference and turn it into productive use comes from one of the authors' own research in South Africa. We recently completed a study, funded by British Aerospace, into the possibilities offered by the Design and Technology curriculum for recruiting cultural and linguistic diversity into the literacy curriculum. In one example from this study, a teacher set up a 'design' task for a class of 12-year-olds from a wide range of cultural and linguistic orientations. Many were not conversant in English, which was used as the medium of instruction (and assessment) in this school. The design task demanded that learners, working in groups of six, design a 'vessel that is able to float, carry a cargo of two boiled eggs, is powered by some means or the other and is aesthetically pleasing'.

The groups set to work. One group was selected to be video recorded over a period of four days. During this time, the learners communicated with each other in a variety of ways, including 'gesture' ('it should be that big' said boy in halting English, holding his hands apart to demonstrate how long the ship should be). Another commented on the way in which the ship should be powered by drawing the sails. As the days passed, the groups used a variety of artefacts such as plastic Coke bottles, cardboard, string, sticks and so on, to design and make the ship. Each member of the group under investigation contributed, drawing on their own repertoires of knowledge and cultural understandings of what a 'floating vessel' should look like, how it should be powered and so on. These understandings were negotiated and represented through many modes of communication.

What we are proposing here is a pedagogical model in which schools use difference as a productive resource. Cultural and linguistic diversity should be seen as a powerful classroom resource. In this particular example, the school was contributing in a positive way by helping children to negotiate differences in such a way that they complement each other and creating opportunities for them to expand their cultural and linguistic repertoires so they can access a broader range of cultural and institutional resources (Kalantzis and Cope, 1993).

In short, the argument is that schools recruit into the curriculum the cultural and linguistic backgrounds of learners in order to ensure that literacy and learning are based on the ideal of productive diversity. In this, schools have an important role to play in shaping our social, political and working futures.

2. Providing opportunities for the design of new meanings for social and economic futures

There is, then, an expectation on schools to satisfy the demands of big business and industry and sometimes this is equated with producing measurable levels of skills. Also that success in these skills is taken to mean that a student is literate. There is constant pressure on schools by both government and parents for improving literacy standards and sentence construction, spelling and punctuation, amongst other things, are considered to be the indicators of achievement. Schools are constantly monitored in respect of their effectiveness in producing these skills. However, raising standards in terms of measurable skills is not the only pressure schools face. They are also expected to encourage 'creativity' and 'innovative practice' and, again, both the authorities and parents are keen that this should happen. The problem, however, is that creativity and innovation are not considered 'high stakes' as other literacy 'skills' are. How do we negotiate this dilemma?

We need to think of a theory of literacy and learning that goes beyond the presenting problem. In the presenting problem, literacy skills and dispositions are seen as two separate elements of the cognitive system. There is a need to recognise that a dynamic interaction exists between skill or competence and disposition. This belief leads Kress (1997) to abandon the term literacy for the notion of design. He argues that the notion of design assumes that competence in itself is insufficient. What is more relevant is 'competence in design of new, innovative forms, which are a response to the maker's analysis and understanding, and allows the designer to go beyond the forms which exist' (1997:155).

It is worth citing another practical example from South Africa here. A few years ago the Swedish Development Administration advertised a competition to attract the best design of a low cost water filtration system to be used in developing countries with poor quality drinking water. A 13-year-old South African boy from a rural area who used a mixture of cans and wire from his local environment won the competition. Indeed, visitors to Africa or Asia will not fail to notice the ingenuity of designs made from wire or other material often on sale along national roads or in the local markets. Some of these designs would represent in Kress's terms 'mere copying' – a design that is a representation of something, like a car or aeroplane. However, the example of the design made by the 13 year old represented an attempt to go beyond forms that currently exist, towards an appreciation of future needs. The design of the water purification system incorporated sensitivity to the problems in the social world and imagination of a new and different need for the future. It communicated meaning through incorporating a range of semiotic elements and represented a transformation of what the designer knew or had learned.

This issue of transforming knowledge or skills and putting them to use for creative and imaginative purposes which themselves are sensitive to the needs of the future, lies at the heart of my argument for a reconceptualisation of the literacy curriculum. An important element in the argument is the need to re-examine the basis upon which literacy assessments are carried out.

Most assessment concentrates on identifying what skills or competences have been internalised. The contention here is that we should move beyond internalisation to what Rogoff (1995) describes as participatory appropriation. Rogoff uses this term to describe the way in which people change and transform their own understandings through a continuous process of participation. She argues that the use of the term 'participatory appropriation' is different from the way in which the term 'internalisation' is used. While the latter assumes that children 'acquire' concepts, memories, knowledge, skills, etc., and store them for use in other contexts, the former involves a perspective where children and their social partners are constantly active and their roles and are dynamically changing. According to Rogoff, 'the specific processes by which they communicate and share in decision making are the substance of cognitive development' (p151). For her 'participation in sociocultural activities does not involve copying what is already invented or available in the thinking of participating individuals; it is a creative process' (p689).

The notion of design introduced by Kress helps us to see how learners might work with different modes and through different media to 'design' social, economic and political meanings for our futures.

3. Combining social contexts for the development of literacy

Our third argument is that the literacy curriculum and strategies for the improvement of literacy are being shaped in the absence of an understanding of real life literacies. By this we mean that schools do not have an adequate understanding of the variety of social practices in the communities they serve and are thus not privy to the literacies, which emerge as a result. We agree with Street's conceptualisation of literacy as social practice rather than as autonomous sets of skills or competences.

Moll and Greenberg suggest that communities, no matter what their historical origins, possess 'funds of knowledge' which are not dissimilar to other household funds (e.g., cash or crops). However, these funds of knowledge are not possessions or traits but characteristics of people-in-activity. By this they mean that funds of knowledge are manifested through events or activities and children who participate in community social activities acquire these funds of knowledge.

In their paper Moll and Greenberg discuss a number of case studies of families who possess such funds of knowledge as car mechanics or knowledge of soils and crops. Through participating in a social event like helping father while he repairs a cark, and by passing various tools to him, a child can learns a number of literacies, values and beliefs.

The theoretical origins of thinking of this kind are derived from socio-cultural perspectives on learning and cognition inspired by Vygotsky, Leont'ev and Luria, as well as the social interactional aspects of Piaget's work.

The cultural historical school of thought of Vygotsky, Leont'ev and Luria marked a departure from psychological explanations of cognitive development as processes occurring inside the heads of individuals. Vygotsky (1978) argued that an individual's development is a function of her participation in and her extension of the cultural and historical processes she is subjected to.

The most important claim of socio-cultural theorists is that learning and cognition is regarded as inextricably bound with the social and cultural activities that people engage in with others in mutually constituting relationships (Rogoff). Thus sociocultural theory shifts attention from the individual as a unit of analysis to sociocultural activity itself as the primary unit of analysis.

The challenge remains for schools to become more engaged with the communities they serve. For some, this immediately raises the possibility of home-school activities of which there are countless examples. However, many of the home-school programmes have been criticised for being uni-directional in their attempts to develop literacy (Gregory, 1999). Such programmes have for example encouraged parents or other members of the family to participate in reading activities. The aim was to improve children's attainment in school-based literacies. This is not the same as saying that schools need to become more familiar with the different kinds of social practices engaged in by the communities they serve so that they can develop literacy events in school which mirror the prior knowledge that children bring to school with them. According to Kress (1987) children are meaning-makers long before they come to school. The social events, which account for the shaping of their literacies in the home, tend to be ignored and often erased in the context of the school.

It is this that we should be guarding against in the re-conceptualising of the new literacy curriculum. In our view, the main thrust is to combine the contexts in which literacy is developed through knowledge exchange activities. The best examples we have of these are in the work of Greenberg and Moll. They have set up 'laboratories' in which teachers can glean insights into the complex organisational structures of working class families originating from Mexico and the extent to which certain social practices give rise to the opportunity for the development of literacy. Using this knowledge in class to build stronger links between the literacies of the home and school-based literacies seems to be the way forward in mediating between the demands of the global and the local.

We end with examples of what we can learn from countries elsewhere. In many communities of the developing world children play a more central role with each other than in Europe or the United States. In many Asian countries including Pakistan and Bangladesh where I have been working for many years, children as young as 10 serve as caregivers. They also work and play in mixed age groups. According to Rogoff, under such circumstances children develop skills in guiding other children but also opportunities for learning to take the perspective of others, collaborate in-group and engage in collaborative arguments. A lot of this is in evidence in the support street children in Brazil provide each other as they learn to become self-reliant (Groves and Johnson, 2000). Some other examples include child-to-child programmes, many of which have been recognised for their ability to promote literacies required to promote health and reproduction in developing countries. In such activities, children learn 'new' literacies for health and enterprise development or for community development, through involvement in community activities. They then pass these literacies on to older and younger members of the community.

Conclusions

This chapter argued that in a rapidly changing global context, we need to re-think the nature of the literacy curriculum. We need to re-define what we mean by literacy and review how it is currently taught and assessed. Literacy is more than reading and writing and the acquisition of technical competences and skills; rather it is a set of social practices and forms of knowledge that enable individuals to participate and function fully in society.

While the notion of globalisation is not taken for granted, we questioned what effect it has on the current literacy curriculum. We saw that different forms of globalisation produce new social situations and therefore demand new forms of literacy, new genres and discourses. The effect of this on schools has generated calls for a closer alignment of education with the demands of big business and industry and for measurable levels of skill. But there is also recognition that educational systems need to be socially responsible and responsive – responsive to the economic, social, political and cultural demands and needs of a pluricultural society with its own communication requirements.

These are some of the dilemmas that globalisation and pluralim place on schools and some of the possibilities for schools to meet Bernstein's challenge to remake the world.

References

Bruner, J. (1996) *Actual minds, possible worlds*. Cambridge, MA: Harvard University Press

Christie, F and Rothery, J. (1989) Exploring the written mode and the range of factual genres. In F. Christie (ed) *Writing in schools: study guide*. Victoria: Deacon University Press

Cope, B. and Kalantzis, M. (1993) (eds) *The powers of literacy: A genre approach to teaching writing*. London. Falmer Press

Delpit, L. (1988) The Silenced dialogue: Power and pedagogy in educating other peoples' children. *Harvard Educational Review* 58, 3 280-91

Dixon, J. and Stratta, L. (1992) New demands on the model of writing in education-what does genre theory have to offer? In M.Hayhoe and S. Parker (eds) *Reassessing Language and Literacy.* Buckingham: open University Press

Freebody, P., Ludwig, C. and Gunn, S. (1995) *Everyday literacy practices in and out of schools in low socio-economic urban communities.* Brisbane: Centre for Literacy in Education Research

Gee, J.P. (1994) New alignments and old literacies: from fast capitalism to the canon. In B. Shorthand-Jones, B. Bosich, and J.Rivalland (Eds.), *Conference Paper: 1994 Australian Reading Association Twentieth National Reading Conference.* Carlton South: Australian Reading Association.

Gregory, E. (1998) Siblings as mediators of literacy in linguistic minority communities. *Language and Education*, 12, 1, 33-54

Groves, L. and Johnson, D. (2000) Transforming Education for Street Children in Brazil, in T. Mebrahtu, M. Crossley and D. Johnson (Eds) *Globalisation, Educational Transformation and Societies in Transition.* Oxford: Symposium Books.

Heath, S.B. and Mangiola, L. (1991) *Children of Promise: literate activity in linguistically and culturally diverse classrooms.* NEA/AERA: Washington DC.

Heath, S.B. (1982) What no bedtime story means: narrative skills at home and at school. *Language in Society*, 11, 49-76

Heath, S.B. (1983) *Ways with words.* Cambridge: Cambridge University Press

Johnson, D.F. (1994) The effectiveness of a genre-based approach to the academic literacy of teacher trainers and trainees in Zimbabwe. Unpublished PhD Thesis. University of Bristol.

Kalantzis, M. and Cope, B. (1993) (Eds.) The power of literacy and the literacy of power. In B. Cope and M. Kalantzis. *The powers of literacy: A genre approach to teaching writing.* London. Falmer Press

Kress, G. (1997) *Before writing: Rethinking the paths to literacy.* London. Routledge

Kress, G. (2001) 'You've just got to learn how to see': curriculum subjects, young people and schooled engagement with the world. In J. Cumming and C. Wyatt-Smith. *Literacy in the curriculum: success in senior secondary schooling.* Melbourne: ACER Press

Leont'ev, A.N. (1978) *Activity, consciousness and personality.* Englewood Cliffs: Prentice-Hall

Luria, A. R. (1976) *Cognitive development: its cultural and social foundations.* Cambridge, MA: Harvard University Press

Moll, L. and Greenberg, J. (1992) Creating zones of possibilities: combining social contexts for instruction. In Moll, L. (ed) *Vygotsky and Education.* Cambridge: Cambridge University Press

New London Group (1996) A pedagogy of multiliteracies: Designing social futures. *Harvard Educational Review*, 66, 1, 60-92

Pellegrini, A. and Galda, L. (1998) *The development of school-based literacy: a social ecological perspective*, London: Routledge

Piore, M., and Sable, C. (1984) *The second industrial divide.* New York: Basic Books

Rogoff, B. (1990) *Apprenticeship in thinking. Cognitive development in social contexts*. Oxford. Oxford University Press

Rogoff, B. (1995) Observing sociocultural activity on three planes: participatory appropriation, guided participation, and apprenticeship. In J. Wertsch, P. del Rio, and A. Alvarez (eds.) *Sociocultural Studies of Mind*. Cambridge. Cambridge University Press

Scribner, S., and Cole, M. (1981) *The psychology of literacy*. Cambridge, MA: Harvard University Press

Street, B. (1999) *Multiple literacies and multilingual society*. NALDIC Working Papers. NALDIC. Waltford

Vygotsky, L.S. (1962) *Thought and Language*. Cambridge, MA: MIT Press

Vygotsky, L.S. (1978) *Mind in society: the development of higher psychological processes*. Cambridge

Whitehead, M. (1997) *Language and Literacy in the Early Years*, 2nd edn. London. Paul Chapman

3

Culture, context and policy: comparing learners in three European countries

Marilyn Osborn, Elizabeth McNess,
Claire Planel and Pat Triggs

Introduction

As Claxton, Sutherland and Pollard reflect in the introduction to this book, culture resides not only in the core understandings of a group of people and in a variety of psychological habits and processes but also in a historically evolving set of social structures and practices. In this chapter we explore the significance of a particular set of structures and practices, national educational cultures and the resulting school organisation and pedagogical practices for pupils' different patterns of engagement with learning. We draw upon a research project: Education, National Culture and Attitudes to Secondary Schooling (ENCOMPASS) which was designed to explore the significance of the cultural context in which learning occurs by examining the perspectives of pupils in three European countries, England France and Denmark, on the purposes of schooling and on themselves as learners.

We have chosen to compare these three contrasting national education systems because, despite a common European history, they illustrate three fundamentally different approaches to the provision of compulsory education and schooling and enabled the team to investigate the effect of cultural context on pupil experience. We argue that, though similar in many respects, national education systems, as illustrated by Denmark, England and France, have differences in their basic values and aims because they are the products of the specific cultural and historical environments from which they spring. They are both informed by, and help to reproduce, the deep socio-cognitive and cultural patterning of a particular nation state. This, in turn, has an impact on the organisation of the three systems, and consequent implications for the pedagogical environments created, and the learning experiences of pupils.

Previous studies led us to hypothesise that, although students in the three countries would be likely to share many concerns associated with their age and with global youth culture, they would also have very different attitudes to and expectations of themselves as learners, of their teachers and towards school. Thus the broad aim of the research, drawing upon a socio-cultural theoretical perspective (Bruner, 1996, Wertsch, 1993) was to explore the social reality of schooling for students and the relative significance of the factors that influence the development of learner identity in the three national settings.

The research used an innovative comparative methodology which was designed to look beyond the powerful statistics of the large comparative studies carried out by the OECD and others. Such studies seek to measure the efficiency and value of different education systems by attainment outcomes as defined, largely, by one-off, academic achievement. The ENCOMPASS research, on the other hand, sought to understand the lived experiences of pupils and the effect such experiences had on their attitudes to teaching and learning.

The methods employed included a large scale questionnaire survey of 1800 pupils in the three countries, follow-up interviews of selected 'target' pupils, classroom observations, focus group discussions, teacher and head-teacher interviews, performance data and the collection of institutional and national policy documentation. These methods are reported in more detail elsewhere (Osborn, 1999, Osborn and Planel, 2000). For the purposes of this chapter the data are drawn from the documentary analysis and from the individual and focus group interviews of pupils in a matched sample of three secondary schools serving a mix of socio-economic backgrounds in each country.

Some commonalities across the three education systems

Education systems around the world have two main intentions. The first is to introduce a new generation of pupils to the existing knowledge base of their culture and, in European education systems, this is usually made explicit through a curriculum which is split into discrete 'subject' areas. The knowledge and skills gained are intended to equip youngsters for a future economic role. The second intention is to introduce a new generation of future citizens to the cultural norms of a community and equip them to take their place in society. Issues of equity and social cohesion are also important and the balance between these elements can change over time and from culture to culture.

Drawing on the analysis of Green *et al* (1999) six common aims of compulsory education can be identified in all fifteen European Union Member States:

• to attempt to develop equality of opportunities

• to offer as many young people as possible a sound basic education

• to promote both change and social stability and integration

• to prepare young people for all aspects of adult life: work and leisure, family and society

• to motivate young people to learn and prepare for a changing world

• to nurture the well-being of young people while they are in education

Consequently, it is not surprising that, at first glance, there are many similarities between the schools and classrooms of our three target countries. All three systems provide free, compulsory, comprehensive education for pupils for ten or eleven of their formative years. Pupils begin school at around 5 to 7 years of age and continue through to approximately 16 years of age. The education systems initially provide instruction in the basic skills of literacy and numeracy and later help to prepare students for employment or further/higher education. All three systems also have a commitment to national cultural transmission and the social development of individuals.

Cultural and historical influences

However, we also found marked cultural and historical influences which have given rise to differences in governance, administration and operation. These differences are mediated through successive regional, local and individual school levels and have far reaching implications for the work of teachers and the experience of pupils in their classrooms. We analysed a selection of policy documents – from national Education Acts to School prospectuses – to try to understand more clearly what the fundamental aims of the three systems were, as stated in the official discourse, and identified some fundamental differences in perspective. The following three extracts from the INCA database, which describes different European education systems, encapsulate some of these:

The English system

The basic principle underlying statutory [school] education is that it should provide a balanced and broadly based curriculum which is suitable to the child's age, ability, aptitude and to any special educational needs the child might have ...The Department for Education and Employment's aim is: to support economic growth and improve the nation's competitiveness and quality of life by raising standards of educational achievement and skill and by promoting an efficient and flexible labour market.

The Danish system

As far as compulsory education is concerned, the general objective is to give the individual pupil the opportunity to develop as many of his/her talents as possible... The focus is on the development of personal qualifications: independence, independent thought, ability to co-operate and communicate, and a desire for learning throughout one's life span.

The French system

Every child and young person in France has a right to education and training, regardless of his/her social, cultural or geographical background... education's main objective is: to educate an entire age group to at least the level of the vocational aptitude certificate or vocational studies certificate and 80 per cent of the group to Baccalauréat level within ten years.

[Source: INCA CD-ROM, NFER/QCA, June 1998]

Historically the English education system has grown out of a *laissez-faire*, liberal tradition, and has been associated with voluntarism and local autonomy in educational provision. It has promoted an individual, child-centred pedagogy which has, historically, regarded pupils as having individual needs and abilities which traditionally have required different types and levels of schooling.

The Danish system, in contrast, has a strong tradition of communitarianism which places less emphasis on professional autonomy and relies more on a powerful folk tradition of local democracy and social partnership, It has traditionally integrated with, and been accountable to, the local community. The Danish schooling system also stresses the importance of education for democracy and values the affective dimension encapsulated in the close relationship between the class teacher and one particular group of pupils.

In France, the educational system has developed constitutionally and been organised according to the republican ideal. The state is seen as having a duty to provide a universal education, which promotes equality for all. To treat pupils differentially has been regarded as morally unacceptable. It is underpinned by an integrative notion of citizenship and nationality and based on rationalist traditions of knowledge which must promote national values and social solidarity.

However, there are tensions within all three systems as they struggle to keep pace with the changing demands made upon them. The 'cultures' from which they spring are not static but evolve as society evolves. National concerns have called for reforms which, though similar, are coloured by the cultural context in which they are set. Concerns over standards, efficiency and accountability have driven many of the policy initiatives in all three countries. The most significant of these are encapsulated in the 1988 Education Reform Act in England and the multiple innovations which followed it in the 1990s, the 1989 Jospin Reform in France and the 1993 Act of the Fokeskole in Denmark. In England, such recent reforms have combined increasing central regulation over curricula and assessment with greater school autonomy, at least in financial terms. This has overturned a tradition of professional autonomy in matters of educational content and pedagogy and established a quasi-market which defines education as a consumer service.

In Denmark, the state plays a regulating and co-ordinating role and recent changes have both retained local power, within a national framework, and encouraged the ideal of school democracy and the importance of student rights and parental involvement within education. Issues of parental involvement, in particular, are far more central to the Danish system than they are to either of the other countries studied. During the late 90s and afterwards, increasing concerns that Danish schools are not being as effective in terms of the underperformance of their pupils in international tests have prompted a call for differentiated teaching which puts each child and their abilities at the centre.

In France, a growing awareness of social pluralism within French society has resulted in recent changes which have begun to create the opportunity for some limited devolved power. Regionalisation has involved both devolution and '*déconcentration*', which has delegated powers to regional tiers of central government by making use of locally placed civil servants who may be better informed of local conditions than centrally placed bureaucrats. The increasing incidence of violence in some French schools has also prompted calls for the enlargement of the role of the teacher to include affective concerns.

Cultures and context

From the beginning of the project, researchers from the University of Bristol worked with nationals from both France and Denmark to pose questions, design research instruments and to analyse data. This enabled the team to gain 'outsider' insights into each national system as members of the extended team were asked to write about, and comment on, the schools and classrooms involved in the study from a country which was not their own. The following three extracts illustrate those differences which, though familiar to nationals, take on more significance when viewed from different national and cultural perspectives.

These following three extracts highlight, from a largely social and anthropological perspective, important elements of schooling in the three countries which are so much part of a particular national culture that they can be overlooked when reviewing policy in relation to raising standards. The strong identity of English schools can

Figure 4.1 A French impression of English Comprehensives

A French visitor to an English secondary school is immediately struck by two impressions, both of which relate to the English school context. On entering a school the visitor comes upon an entrance hall of varying proportions and modernity, which serves to express the school's individual identity. The history of the school, the portraits of its senior members of staff and the school's main claims to fame are presented at a glance. English school entrance halls are like miniature museums in the way in which they summarise the past and outline the school's individuality. English schools display their identity, show that they have a past, give evidence of their existence as a social organisation and thus stake their claim to an individual reality. The individuality of the school is further enhanced by not only the display of the names of former headteachers but also often those of former head boys and head girls. These displays emphasise the importance of 'belonging' to a school.

The second impression given by English schools to the French visitor is the feeling of space. English school buildings may be dilapidated and not adapted to pupil needs but the school grounds are always impressively vast. Although generalisations from only three schools need to be treated with caution, each school visited had good sports equipment and extensive playing fields. This feeling of space is important as it gives firstly the impression that schools are places designated as much for living as for learning. Secondly, it gives the illusion that schools are not enclosed places bounded by four walls, but that they are places open to their surroundings. This impression is particularly strong in rural schools where the school's boundaries are not always immediately apparent to the visitor's eye.

The visitor's attention is then drawn to the way in which English schools are organised. What strikes the French visitor above all is the sense of belonging imparted by schools to school users. This idea is communicated in different ways by many small details: teachers remain on the site throughout the school day; during free periods they stay at school, planning lessons and taking part in meetings. Pupils wear uniforms (more or less prescriptive depending on the school) which sport the school's emblem. Headteachers have an ownership and authority which is schoolwide and can run counter to an individual teacher's professional autonomy.

With regard to pedagogy, English schools appear to be simultaneously more selective and less competitive than their French counterparts. Most schools use some form of setting or banding by achievement level but, because selection can occur earlier on in a pupil's school career, there appears to be less uncertainty and, therefore, less competition. Another difference is concerned with the relationship between academic and affective education where there is less of a distinction and all staff have responsibilities in both domains. This, together with the extended responsibility for pupils both inside and outside the school premises, the requirement to wear a uniform, and a pastoral system which provides a tight network through which pupils' behaviour is constantly monitored and controlled, provides English pupils with an educational environment which has more constraints but which is also more clearly defined.

Figure 4.2 A Danish impression of French Colleges

French schools, viewed from the Danish perspective, convey several ideas about learning and the role of teachers and pupils in France, which differ from those in Denmark. These include: a greater distance between pupils, teachers and school administration; more disconnection between cognitive and affective education and less consideration for the pupil as a person; more disconnection between pedagogy and pupil experience; stronger and more direct and open control over pupil learning and physical mobility; more limited parental input in school; and finally a stronger emphasis on the class as a unit rather than the school.

What first strikes a Danish visitor to a French school is its clinical and strictly functional environment. From the exterior the buildings could be mistaken for an industrial unit. Internally there is an impression of space with wide, bare corridors which are kept clinically clean. There is no evidence of learning outside the classroom. Nor is there any evidence of pictorial decoration or space for pupils' to hang coats and leave personal effects. Classrooms, which are kept locked, are also strictly functional. The outside area provided for pupils during recreation, which includes a covered section for inclement weather, is very limited in size. Pupils are sometimes reduced to standing or sitting in groups as there is insufficient space for physical games. Pupils are not allowed access to the interior of the school during recreation. They are also not allowed access to the staff room. Before lessons pupils line up in class groups, either in the recreation area or outside the relevant classroom, and await their subject teacher.

Lacking a home base, French pupils appear not to 'belong' anywhere. There is much movement between lessons from one similar classroom to another. Pupils are obliged to carry their school bags and outdoor wear with them during the school day. Pupils do not have the opportunity to create their own physical space where they can express and stamp their individuality. As in Denmark, classes appear to be composed of heterogeneous groups, although class composition is not, as in Denmark, based on shared residential location.

Unlike in Denmark, where pupil control operates through a 'co-operative' system with greater reliance made on pupil responsibility for learning and good behaviour, pupil control in French schools is more direct and overt. Sanctions such as detention or written work are common. There is a clear and strong difference in status between French pupils and most of the school staff. This distance between teacher and pupil and the priority given by teachers to instruction and the academic domain may contribute to the apparent disassociation between pedagogy and the experiences of French pupils both inside and outside school. Home school links are more formal than in Denmark and apart from parents' evenings and the representation by parents in the class council, parental visits to French schools tend to be limited to when parents are summoned for specific incidents or problems.

Figure 4.3 An English impression of Danish Folkeskoler

When visiting a Danish Folkeskole, the English visitor is reminded more of a large English primary school than a secondary comprehensive school. Pupils range from 7 to 16 years and both urban and rural schools are set within, and serve, a relatively local community. The average size, in terms of pupils is about half that of a typical English comprehensive and pupils usually live within easy walking or cycling distance.

School buildings are relatively compact, with only one or two storeys, and are kept in good repair. Close to the main entrance is a suite of administrative offices which are well-staffed, well-equipped and easily accessible for pupils, parents and teachers. A teachers' room contains a comfortable mix of tables and easy chairs, where teachers can socialise over tea or coffee, or eat together at lunchtime. There is a sense of investment in decent working spaces for all the people in the school. In more urban situations, the older school premises are similar in scale and design to English urban primary schools built by the Victorians. Conditions are less spacious and well-equipped but they still give the impression of being well cared for by the local community.

The school buildings are usually set in grounds which have seating and equipment on which the children can play during their short breaks. Communal spaces are also provided within the school buildings, close to classrooms, where children can socialise informally, often within grouped age bands. Close to, or even physically attached to, the main school building is often the after school club [School/ Freetime Organisation] where younger children go to play and relax when school finishes, until they are collected by their parents.

However, it is perhaps within the classroom that there is the greatest noticeable difference for the English visitor. Each classroom 'belongs' to the class group in it. The pupils remain in their class for most lessons and have a close and long-standing relationship with the class teacher [klasselærer]. This reduces fragmentation in curriculum, temporal and spatial terms and negates the need for whole classes of pupils to move around the school building, carrying their books with them, when a lesson finishes. Pupils appear to regard the classroom as 'their' space and are required to take it in turns to sweep the floor at the end of school day. As well as desks and chairs, there may also be different areas within the class where pupils can relax, read or work with a friend on a particular project. Classrooms, which in England may accommodate 30+ children, would accommodate perhaps as many as 20, but sometimes as few as a dozen pupils. This gives a feeling of space, reduces noise levels and allows a more relaxed approach to teaching and learning. Pupils do not wear uniform, as they would in England, and there is a lack of overt discipline, with teachers and pupils referring to each other by their first names. The relationship of parents to the class is closer and more informal than that which exists at English secondary level. Parents often arrange parties and social outings which involve not only pupils but also their parents.

engender feelings of belonging but can also be socially divisive and learning opportunities can be restricted by an 'historical reality' which tends to move pupils along particular learning paths. This is reflected in current policy which encourages schools to foster particular strengths and compete with neighbouring schools to attract pupils. It is shaped by a view which regards education as a consumer product that should be regulated by market mechanisms.

The emphasis on democratic values in Denmark can lead to concerns from both social and academic perspectives. The need to conform can be difficult for both parents and pupils from ethnic minorities. The relaxed and informal atmosphere in the classroom and the concentration on relationships within the group can lead teachers to be reticent about challenging the more able pupils as this could cause social divisions within the class. Teachers feel more comfortable about putting their energy into bringing the slower children up to an 'average' performance.

The French system places great emphasis on the equality of the national system but its separation of the cognitive from the affective is currently recognised as being unhelpful in addressing the needs of some sections of the population. Violence is a problem in some French schools and has prompted reformers to call for a more extended role for the teacher, to include the affective as well as the cognitive development of their pupils.

As we argue in the next section, these different emphases in the national education systems, and in the consequent organisation of schools and teacher roles, have definite implications for the way in which pupils position themselves in relation to schooling.

Constants and contexts in pupil experience

Part of the value of cross-cultural research is the extent to which it is able to identify both 'constants' and 'contexts' in educational experience (Broadfoot and Osborn, 1993). Cross-cultural comparisons of pupil experience identify pupil responses to learning which are more universal to the situation of 'being a secondary school pupil' (referred to as 'constants') from those which may be more culturally specific (referred to as 'contexts'). Pupils in England, Denmark and France have to engage with school contexts and teacher mediations which relate to cultural, philosophical, political and historical differences between the three countries. These in turn are mediated by pupil concerns and perceptions of schooling and learning and will ultimately affect behaviour and learning outcomes.

Thus this section draws upon the individual and group pupil interviews in order to illuminate understanding of the relationship between social and cultural influences and cultural practices, and to explore how these might affect pupil behaviour and ultimately pupil learning. Using the pupils' own voices as far as possible, the key concerns of the pupils are considered under three headings: the teacher pupil relationship; social identity; and pupils' perceptions of learning.

The teacher-pupil relationship

There were notable differences between pupils in the three countries in how they perceived the teacher pupil relationship. Pupils in France expressed a strong perception of distance between teacher and pupil. There was a strong difference in status relating to a concept of adult (and particularly teacher as the fount of all knowledge) superiority and pupil inferiority. Adults were '*grands*' (teachers were particularly '*grands*' as their role was to form children), children and pupils were '*petits*': '*Des êtres incomplets, encore naturels, parfois dangereux, et qu'il convient de dresser*' ('Incomplete beings, sometimes natural, sometimes dangerous, who need taming') (Dubet, 1996, p31). French pupils were well aware of their perceived inferiority:

> '*Un prof c'est plus grand que nous, il nous apprend des trucs*' (Teachers are bigger (more important) than us, they teach us things).

French pupils thought that teachers used their perceived superior status to maintain their distance from pupils:

> '*Les professeurs, ils méprisent les élèves. Nous on est des enfants et ils ne considèrent pas vraiment ce qu'on dit. Ils disent que ça nous concerne pas*' (Teachers look down on pupils. We're children and they don't pay much attention to what we say. They say it's got nothing to do with us).

Pupils used terms like *esclaves* (slaves), and *robots* to describe their position in relation to teachers. There was also a distance between French teacher and pupil in terms of time and social class. Pupils, whether high or low achieving, from middle class and working class backgrounds, of French or ethnic minority parentage, thought that many teachers had not changed with the times and did not understand the needs of the new generation. They thought that teachers were out of touch with their lives:

> *'Un professeur qui est dans les cinquante ans, c'est plus son temps. Lui quand il était jeune, les élèves il étaient comme ça ... mais évidemment c'est plus comme ça, ça a complètement changé'* (A teacher who's in his fifties is out of step. When he was young children were like that ... but obviously it's not like that anymore). (High achieving girl from Paris)

> *'C'est pas le même environnement que quand eux ils ont grandi. Eux quand ils ont grandi on leur a toujours dit ..., mais nous on est livré à nous même, c'est dehors qu'on apprend. Il faut comprendre que nous on est jeune, on est d'une autre génération. Il faut qu'ils se renseignent sur ce qui se passe. Ils nous voient pas quand on est dehors ce qu'on subit'* (It's not the same world as when they grew up. When they were little they were always told what to do, but we bring ourselves up, we learn outside school. They have to understand that we're young and that we're from a different generation. They need to find out what's happening now. They don't see us outside school, what we endure). (Low achieving, half Arab boy from Paris)

The distance between French teacher and pupil was traditional and institutionalised. English pupils were far less conscious of the difference between teacher and pupil status although in some cases they acknowledged that there was an imbalance of power: 'Some teachers think they are higher than you', and there was some awareness of time and social distance: 'They're still back in the seventies', 'They have to realise there's drink and drugs ... they don't want to believe that's going on; but it is.' But it was not an issue which overtly pre-occupied them. Instead English pupils were in most cases more concerned with negotiating their own individual status with their teachers. The strong emphasis on individualisation and differentiation in the English context of education made the teacher pupil relationship far more open to negotiation in England than in France and, arguably, more significant in the learning process.

Danish pupils, like English pupils, referred to, but did not dwell on, the time distance between teacher and pupils. They were concerned that their teachers be relatively young and up-to-date – as one pupil expressed it: 'modern teachers, fairly young teachers who have modern views on teaching and learning'. However, like English pupils, they were more concerned with their personal relationships with teachers which were perceived by them as playing an important part in the learning process. Relationships between teachers and pupils were again open to negotiation and negotiation itself was institutionalised.

The concept of a teacher as a friend was particularly difficult for French pupils to comprehend. Indeed, the idea horrified many French pupils. English pupils had less difficulty with the idea but were reluctant to identify teachers as 'friends' in any real sense: 'They're just teachers', 'Not someone you would go out with at weekends', 'When you're in trouble they can't forgive you; they've got to punish you'.

Danish pupils, although held back (in this respect like English and French pupils) by the concern that teachers should not be too friendly in case this led to interference with their private lives, did acknowledge in some cases that teachers could almost be friends: 'Not a real friend, but someone who knows something about you .... with whom you feel good'.

An important common concern for pupils from all three countries, which prevented them from regarding teachers as real friends and confiding in them, was their anxiety about their teachers' personal and professional ability to keep confidences.

Another significant similarity between English, French and Danish pupils was their common belief that there should be mutual respect between teachers and pupils before learning could take place. The word 'respect', or its equivalent, was used by pupils in all three countries. In the English context 'respect' was not perceived as automatic for either party. Teachers could earn their pupils' respect by a combination of listening to pupils and giving them a voice. Pupils felt that they were more likely to gain respect from their teachers if they were perceived as having a positive work attitude. English pupils in particular seemed to be caught by contradictory pressures: the need to negotiate a good working relationship with their teacher by earning his/her respect through their positive work orientation, as against the need not to be too positive towards their work for fear of losing their peers' support.

An important cultural difference was clear in the pupils' responses to their teachers and their schools' demands in relation to the presence or absence of a sense of solidarity within the class. In the English context of classes with changing pupil composition because of banding, setting and streaming, there was little evidence of classroom solidarity or even of solidarity with the school as a whole. Internal classroom social relationships were more pertinent to English pupils' sense of social identity. However there were similarities between France and Denmark in the pupils' attitude to solidarity and commonality. In the Danish cultural context of consensus and where the school practice is for pupils to remain in the same class for all subjects over many years, pupils had a strong sense of commonality in their class 'because that's where you spend most of your time'. The class was a collective unit: 'The class holds us together not the school'.

In the French cultural context of universalism and republicanism and where pupils remain in the same class for nearly all subjects on a yearly basis, pupils seemed to use classroom solidarity as a positive strategy for mutual support:

> '*La classe c'est un ensemble' 'C'est à nous de les aider, nous sommes un groupe*' (The class is a group. It's up to us to help them, we make up a group).

> '*Il faut se tenir la main pour que ça marche ...il faut se tenir à l'écoute, il faut s'entre aider*' (We've got to stand together to make things work .. you've got to be ready to listen, you've got to help each other).

Teachers were aware of pupil solidarity: '*La classe c'est un groupe, c'est tout un groupe, ils font un bloque*' (The class is a group, one group, they're one entity). Occasionally solidarity seemed to be con-trived rather than reflecting reality: '*Il n'y a pas de groupes (dans la classe), il n'y a qu'un seul groupe*' (There aren't any separate groups, we're all one group), which suggests that pupils were res-ponding to the relatively harsh learning environment of the French context by presenting a front of solidarity; in accordance with the French saying, '*L'union fait la force*' (There's strength in unity). Perhaps the strategy of solidarity and the pupils' exploitation of the institutional distance between French teacher and pupil enabled French pupils to protect themselves from entering into more indivi-dual relationships with teachers. In the face of relatively high nega-tive teacher assessment, such individual relationships might have had negative consequences on pupils' 'real' identities

Social identity

In all three countries pupils were, to a greater or lesser extent, con-cerned with establishing their social identity. To many pupils, parti-cularly English pupils, social identity dominated and determined learner identity. There was some evidence to show that English pupils divided their classes into groups of three different types of pupils on the basis of their academic achievement: 'One group works really hard, another group doesn't, they mess around in class. Another group works sometimes and messes about sometimes' (English pupil). English pupils' school experience seemed to be dominated by these academic and social groups and English pupils' social identity was defined by membership of such groups. At one school where high attainment was more evident there was a gloss on working hard. 'Keeners' were described as 'not necessarily clever but very interested': 'they work hard, do extra work'. They were dis-tinct from pupils who generally did good work, tried hard and con-formed, and from 'people who don't bother doing their work and behave badly', who 'had a bad attitude to work', 'often they don't do well with school work and don't try hard', and 'they can be nasty to other pupils.' In the inner London school, pupils expressed an even more finely-tuned version:

> 'There's boffins – really brainy, always quiet, always answer the question, always do their work. They know what they're doing, they push hard with their work ... don't talk when they're work-

ing, never stop to enjoy themselves, put their heads down in their books even when everyone else is laughing.'

'Some (other) people talk and mess about in their lessons but they still do their work as well.'

'There's 'bad' boys – they're popular, like to joke.' 'Some people smoke, drink, bully, get on report for being late and for bad behaviour'.

Group identity in the English schools involved codes for behaviour as well as social and learning identity:

'Everything perfect – not just work. The right uniform – not hipsters, not thick soles or jewellery, not a polo shirt, no make-up'

'Top of the class, always do work, set their pencil cases out tidily, would bring a briefcase if they had the choice'

As might be expected, the description of these groups depended on who was doing the describing and their relationship to this particular sub-set. Something of the flavour of the speaker's own positioning is detectable even in the short extracts above. For pupils in all three English schools the epithet of 'boffin' or 'keener' was not particularly complimentary, though not always unwelcome. For many average and low achievers it was a way of categorising 'the other' as someone undesirable. Pupils like Simon in Year 7 did not want to be seen as a keener: 'People think you are really good and they don't want to be with you'. Pupils in 'top sets' were often characterised by pupils in lower sets as: 'Clever and boring ... they don't have much of a social life'. They were said to be: 'nerdish', 'sad', and 'they don't have a good time at school'. However, for some pupils there might have been an element of jealousy in their attitude to high achieving pupils. As one English pupil explained: 'You can use it to tease people because you're a bit annoyed that they have done better.'

The link between social and learner identity was a strong one for English pupils. Boys were in a particularly difficult position as it was more acceptable for girls to work hard: 'For boys there is an image to keep up about not working hard'. The negotiation of social identity required boys to make people laugh, mess around or confront teachers. Such behaviour was thought to be a particular asset for boys who wished to make themselves attractive to girls. A boy observed: 'Girls would say they liked a hard worker but they would really like one who had a laugh'. Boys with natural charisma could afford to be 'laid back'; others had to establish their credibility by: 'having a big mouth', 'being loud', 'being hard', 'doing the opposite of what the teachers tell you', and generally establishing an anti-work reputation.

There was less evidence in France and Denmark of this division of classes into social groups, although some French pupils also acknowledged the existence of friendship groupings which followed a rough division into low, average and high achievers. The French term 'intello' matched the English 'keener' and 'boffin': 'C'est quelqu'un qui passe ses weekends à la bibliothèque' (It's someone who spends their weekends in the library). 'C'est quelqu'un qui a tout le temps de bonnes notes, jamais de zéros, jamais au dessous de la moyennne' (It's someone who always gets good marks, never a zero, always above the average mark). 'Intello' also had negative connotations: 'C'est en général un terme plutôt perjoratif' (It's generally rather a pejorative term).

Despite these similarities with English pupils, there was evidence that French pupils tended to play down the importance of learner and social differentiation. They too tried to convey the idea of unity and lack of competitiveness. Lower achieving pupils stressed that intellos were not discriminated against by the rest of the class. Pupils claimed that anyone could be friends with intellos. A boy explained, 'Ils sont avec nous' (They're with us).

Success in academic performance played an even smaller role in the social identity of Danish pupils. They appeared to be more preoccupied with social behaviour: 'School is not just academic', 'You should behave well and be a good friend'. As one pupil put it: 'You are allowed to do well and be a bit of a keener, but you also have to be nice towards others.' Competitiveness in the classroom was perceived by pupils and by many Danish teachers as something to be avoided.

In the Danish cultural context of a philosophy of 'consensus' and a school context of small classes, small schools and classes where pupils remained together for seven years, maintaining good social relationships and behaving well were perhaps important survival skills as well as learning skills. For Danish pupils, it was personal interests, fashion (also important in England and France) and the degree of freedom allowed to pupils by their parents which seemed to dictate group composition, rather than academic achievement.

Attitudes to learning

Pupils in England, France and Denmark were in considerable agreement over what constituted effective teaching and learning. The first requirement was that pupils should be 'active': 'doing something' (English pupil), '*si on faisait que parler et copier sur le cahier personne apprendrait*' (If all that happened was (the teacher) talking and us copying it down no-one would learn anything) (French pupil), 'mixing the dry reading stuff with a film and the like ... makes you feel more engaged' (Danish pupil). Pupils from the three countries all decried teacher monologues and copying. The second requirement was that learning had to be interesting. 'Interesting' was defined in the three countries as a lesson which had an element of 'fun' or humour: '*Monsieur Giroud est rigolo tandis que Madame Bonnard ... elle raconte, elle raconte ... elle dicte, elle dicte*' (Mr Giroud is funny whereas Mrs Bonnard goes on and on and on, she endlessly dictates). '*C'est endormant, c'est toujours 'ha hein ha hein ha hein ha hein'. On dirait qu'ils ravagent toujours les mêmes choses, c'est sur mëme ton, toujours monotone*' (It puts you to sleep, it's always blaa blaa blaa. They always seem to go over the same things, with the same monotonous tone of voice). 'He goes on and on ... reads it out' (English pupil).

Pupils in all three countries appreciated teachers who, 'have a laugh', 'can make a joke', liven it up'. In the event of the teacher not being able to fulfil these conditions it was pupils who provided the interest. As a French girl explained: '*Dans le cours il y a toujours quelqu'un là pour mettre de l'ambiance*' (There's always someone in the lesson who'll make it interesting) and that role was generally occupied by a boy. Pupils from the three countries also thought that they learnt more when teachers brought in themes from contemporary life.

Danish pupils differed from English and French pupils in that they felt they had a considerable degree of choice in the content and organisation of their lessons and that this helped their learning. For example, Danish pupils reported having a say in the history issues they wanted to work on, the form a biology report was to take, or whether pupils wanted to work in groups or as a class. One German pupil told us: 'It's almost up to us to decide what to do'. Two Danish pupils summarised their degree of choice: 'To my mind we have a say in learning in this school', 'We can choose to say if we want or not .... if we don't want, the teacher can't do anything.'

Thus, effective teaching and learning in Denmark was perceived by pupils to be linked with a certain amount of pupil choice. A Danish pupil explained: 'There is no reason for the teacher just to go on in one particular way'. Whereas many English learners would have liked more choice than they felt they had, French pupils did not expect much choice and indeed, frequently said that they felt it better if their teacher chose. They did not make the same link between effective learning and 'choice'.

French pupils also differed from English and Danish pupils in their criticism of how their teachers differentiated between low ('*mauvais élèves*') and high achieving pupils ('*bons élèves*') in the same class. French pupils of all levels of achievement thought that many of their teachers neglected lower achieving pupils with negative consequences for their learning:

> '*Les professseurs ils s'occupent que des élèves qui travaillent, mais les élèves qui travaillent pas ils les abandonnent*' (Teachers only relate to hardworking pupils, they don't do anything with those that don't work). (Low achieving girl in a Paris school)

> '*Les professeurs ils mettent les mauvais élèves à part. Ils n'essayent pas tous. Il y en a qui les laissent à part. J'avais une prof de français et franchement elle mettait ceux qui ne travaillaient pas au fond de la classe et elle les laissait dormir, elle ne faisait pas d'efforts.*' (Teachers put the weak pupils to one side. They don't all try to help them. They leave them out. I had a teacher of French who quite honestly put those that didn't work at the back of the class and she let them go to sleep. She made no effort). (High achieving girl from Bordeaux).

This common criticism of French teachers and their perceived un-equal treatment of pupils was another expression of French pupils' expectation of solidarity in the classroom. It had strong echoes of the French national policy rhetoric in which social solidarity and equal treatment for all was strongly emphasised and in which dif-ferentiating between pupils was regarded as morally unacceptable.

Conclusions

The findings from these individual and group interviews suggest that pupils in the three countries had many common concerns which remained constant regardless of the national educational context. Some pupil responses appeared to be universal to the situation of 'being a secondary school pupil'. These included the importance of teacher respect for pupils and of pupil-pupil respect. All pupils were equally concerned that learning should be active and involving for pupils and that teaching should be interesting, including lessons that had an element of fun or humour. There were clear differences bet-ween boys and girls in perceptions of schooling in all three countries.

However, pupils in England, France and Denmark have to engage with different contexts at the level of national educational system, school and teacher mediations which relate to cultural, philo-sophical, political and historical differences between the three countries. In many respects these different contexts appear to lead to significant differences in the way pupils define their relationship to school. Some of the more detailed quantitative findings from the study are reported elsewhere (Osborn, 1999). These also support the argument that pupil perceptions, filtered as they are through the mediation of teachers and the particular interpretations which pupils bring to school with them, do nevertheless resonate fairly closely with the particular emphases of the goals of the national systems.

Thus the Danish emphasis on collaboration and consensus and the concern with education for citizenship and democracy emerged strongly in the pupils' responses. Danish pupils saw school as help-ing them to fit into a group situation rather than emphasising the development of the individual. English pupil concerns reflected to some extent the dual emphasis at national level on the affective dimension of education as well as the cognitive, and the stress on individualisation and differentiation. In contrast the French emphasis on universalism and social solidarity and the separation of the academic and the personal was reflected in pupil concerns, although it was clear that teachers' practice did not always support this.

In terms of pupils' own perceptions about effective learning there was striking unanimity about the definition of an 'interesting' lesson and a 'good' teacher, despite the national and institutional differences in pupils' school contexts. However, what still needs to be explored more fully is the relation between pupils' contrasting national, social and cultural responses to the school context and actual pupil learning. Does the French pupil response of solidarity help to motivate pupils, particularly lower achieving pupils? Does the English pupil response of complex social interactions and negotiation of group identity divert and de-focus English pupils from academic objectives? Does the Danish pupil response of downplaying academic objectives in favour of social relationship objectives have a negative effect on pupil achievement?

What is clear from the research, however, is that the policy priorities, institutional arrangements and classroom processes of a national education system do have an impact on the way in which pupils position themselves in relation to school and to learning. Thus pupils' developing identities as adolescents and as learners are negotiated within a larger cultural patterning related to the above. This in turn helps to determine their personal and learning priorities and their expectations of their teachers and themselves as learners. French, English and Danish pupils could be located on a continuum representing respectively: the extent to which they were seen within the educational system as 'pupils' or as 'persons'; the degree of distance seen as desirable in the teacher-pupil relationship; the nature of the inter-pupil relationship and the balance of pupils' negative or positive feelings about school. It was striking that the inherent ambiguity of adolescents' emerging identities was most marked in the English system, with its culture characterised by the most fragmentation and differentiation in school. The study suggests that the much deplored and significant differences in English pupils' attitudes to achievement appear to be far from inevitable since, in different ways, they are much less marked in the other countries studied. Notably, there was a relative absence of adolescent disaffection with school in Denmark and a relatively high level in France. Thus the study highlights the institutional and cultural, rather than biological, origins of youth disaffection.

The implications of this are clear for policy makers who need to be sensitive to both the constants and contexts in pupils' learning identities as revealed by such comparative studies if they are to introduce policies which are to be successful in raising the aspiration to learn. The study suggests that there is a need to understand how schools develop a positive learning culture – where pupils feel that it is 'cool to learn' and to identify the cultural factors that militate against academic achievement. The research highlights the need for a 'social theory of learning' (Broadfoot, 2000) which links the broader socio-cultural setting of the education system with the individual socio-cultural biographies and identities of teachers and pupils.

References

Broadfoot, P. (2000) Comparative Education for the 21st Century: Retrospect and Prospect, *Comparative Education* Vol 36, No 3, pp357-371

Broadfoot, P., and Osborn, M. (1993) *Perceptions of Teaching – Primary School Teachers in England France*, and British Library Cataloguing-in-Publication Data

Bruner, J. S. (1996) *The Culture of Education*, London, Harvard University Press

Dubet, F. *et al* (1996) A sociology of the lycée student in Corbett, A. and Moon, R. Education in France: *Continuity and Change in the Mitterand years, 1981-1995*. London: Routledge

Green, A., Wolf, A., and Leney, T. (1999) *Convergence and Divergence in European Education and Training Systems*, London: Institute of Education, University of London

INCA CD Rom – *International review of curriculum and assessment frameworks archive Qualifications and Curriculum Authority* (QCA) (1998) QCA Publications, Hayes

Osborn, M. (1999) National Context, Educational Goals and Pupil Experience of Schooling and Learning in Three European Countries, *Compare*, Vol. 19, No. 3

Osborn, M. and Planel, C. (2000) Life in School: Constants and Contexts in Pupil Experience of Schooling and Learning in Three European Countries in *Educational Research in Europe*, Yearbook 2000, pp291-309, Garant Publishers and EERA

Wertsch, J.V. *et al* (1993) 'Continuing the dialogue: Vygotsky, Bakhtin and Lotman' in Daniels, H. (ed) *Charting the Agenda: Educational activity after Vygotsky*. London: Routledge

CULTURE, CONTEXT AND POLICY • 57

Acknowledgement

This chapter is based on the ESRC funded ENCOMPASS project. ESRC's support for this work is gratefully acknowledged. The ENCOMPASS project team were Birte Ravn and Thyge Winther-Jensen, University of Copenhagen, Olivier Cousin, CADIS, University of Bordeaux II, Marilyn Osborn, Patricia Broadfoot, Elizabeth McNess, Claire Planel, Pat Triggs, University of Bristol.

4

Overseas students and their tutors at the confluence of cultures

Arlene Gilpin

Introduction

In 1999, the Prime Minister unveiled bold new targets for UK universities to 'attract a quarter of the world's share of international students by 2005. International students represent one of the fastest growing revenue streams for UK universities, bringing an estimated £1.5 billion annually into academic coffers' (Guardian, 15th August). This was a bold ambition, and one which has been strongly endorsed by universities, anxious to earn the revenues that such students can bring in.

No groups are more sharply at the confluence of cultures than international students and their tutors. For these members of the educational community there is a wide range of cultural uncertainties inherent in all their interactions. Failure to recognize such uncertainties may lead to frustration on both sides: lecturers may complain that the students are deficient in this or that, while students give covert negative reports on the teaching they experience.

International students present characteristics that are both similar and different to other mature students. They are similar in that they may have initial anxieties about undertaking a higher degree or diploma after being away from formal education for longish periods; they are becoming students again when they are used to being the teacher or the manager. They are different because they are entering a cultural context with well-established mores that may be initially opaque, and the assumptions behind the scholarly work to which they are exposed are likely to be overwhelmingly western. Yet they are here for professional development to improve professional practice in some way in their cultural homes and, unlike home students, they have to live in a socio-cultural setting which may be very different from their own.

Consequently, a focus on international students provides an exemplary site for discussing issues of cultural confluence and dissonance. Such a focus also has a strong ethical dimension, since a concern to explore how to make their experience of studying in a foreign culture more beneficial would appear to be of major ethical importance, given the benefits that accrue to the host institutions.

For many postgraduate international students their period of study is culturally unfamiliar in at least four ways. They are out-of-service (Gilpin and Reis Jorge, 1995) and in-student role, in spite of the misnomer 'in-service courses'. They are out of culture in terms of their own personal cultures. They are out of language, in that they are almost certainly studying in what may be their second, third, or even fourth acquired tongue. Most crucially, they may be out of a familiar learning culture, where even their subject cultures may be very differently construed.

Out of service

Home students can be said to be in-service even when they are undertaking full-time study, since they are likely to remain in contact with the world of work socially, and much of the reading they do is located within their professional culture. This is not the case for the international student, who is geographically distant from the world of work, and may find relatively little in the academic literature that relates to their background.

Reflecting on practice may be quite difficult for two reasons. Tutors are probably unfamiliar with students' backgrounds, and so cannot draw them readily into the discourse of classes. Current practices and research in the west may depend on different historical and philosophical approaches to teaching and learning, and so the parallels may be far from explicit to the students.

Within this last difficulty lies a psychological as well as a philosophical problem: approaches to professional practice in the west, where cultures are largely individualistic, may be genuinely unacceptable to those students who come from predominantly collectivist cultures. The mode of teaching where students are expected to participate individually in plenary discussions, notions of questioning received authority (being critical), even familiar modes of address with tutors, may all create initial dismay. The professional practices which are the focus of discussion (teaching and learning theories and techniques) may also be unacceptable within the educational and wider cultures of the students. This can cause at best incomprehension and, at worst, rejection and alienation (Holliday, 1992), unless these dilemmas are addressed as part of the programme.

Out of culture

Many international postgraduate students are awarded scholarships because they are experienced professionals who are sponsored to enable them to contribute to national priorities. They thus have status, a position in society. This is reflected in a comfortable lifestyle at home, emotional and financial security, high self-esteem, and respect from others for their professional knowledge and competence. In many countries around the world, family structures are still based on the extended model, where people belong to large social groups of kinship and neighbourliness.

This background can create anxiety for the international student abroad in two different ways. The first results from the kinds of unhappiness anyone can feel when away from home in a strange environment: loneliness, homesickness, dissatisfaction with basic student accommodation, and so on. In addition, however, the pressures for these students to succeed are very high indeed: their professional colleagues, sponsors, and the wider social groups to which they belong are all aware of the scholarship, and await the student's success as indicative of their own success.

It may be argued that such pressures are true for all mature students. This may be so, but they are especially salient for many international students, where the pressure for success may be much more keenly felt, and where failure would result in a major loss of face not only for them but for others.

For international students there is also the wider sense in which they are foreigners in this society, and they may have anxieties about being discriminated against. There is some evidence that generic anxiety is associated with increased stereotyping (Stephan and Stephan, 1985) e.g. if you are anxious about being the victim of racism, you are more likely to interpret actions as racist. Popular culture in England in the first years of this century seems to be becoming more stridently xenophobic, and international students will not be unaware of this.

Out of language

Learning the discourses of postgraduate study is a challenge for all students, but the international student living abroad for the first time has to learn multiple discourses, of which those of academic study are only part.

> Everyone's use of language is based on cultural presuppositions about the kinds of language behaviour that are appropriate for particular situations and the expectations people have regarding effective structuring of information. These presuppositions are taken for granted and are usually at a low level of awareness. (Smith, 1987: 6)

Yet these students are often mature professionals, used to managing a wide range of discourses, both social and professional, intuitively. To find oneself in a milieu where one's every utterance has to be considered, and where the ways one writes is corrected and criticized, is perhaps the biggest culture shock of all. Since the tutors are operating within their own culture, they may be unable to notice difficulties with discourse management, let alone offer assistance in ways that adults can accept as adults.

Out of learning

Since the pioneering work of Marton and Saljo in 1984 there has been a steadily growing body of research exploring student learning, usually, but not always, focused on undergraduate learning in the west. Much less attention has been paid to international students' learning in formal contexts, although the work of Kember is a notable exception. 'Good' students are those who develop a relational view of knowledge, learn to be critical, and use their own schema to understand new material.

There is also a growing body of research into university teaching (see Kember, 1997 for a review). A continuum exists between tutors who see teaching as transmitting knowledge, and those who see it as facilitating learning. Most tutors in schools of education would espouse a constructivist view of learning, in which critical reflection plays a major role, placing them at the facilitating learning end of the continuum. Implicit in constructivist learning are a number of assumptions. It pays particular attention to the learner's prior knowledge: 'the learner is an active builder of her/his knowledge' (Limón, 2001). This is a strongly individualist approach to learning, which may conflict with the students' own preferences. A constructivist approach may also lead to what Vermunt and Verloop (1999) call 'loose teacher control', a facilitating role which leaves many learning decisions to the learner. This sounds as though it would be ideal for multicultural classes. However, unless all the students know the script, it is unlikely to be successful.

International students may come from different points on these continua, and encounter an approach to teaching, and expectations of how they will have to learn, quite unlike what they are used to. Many come from a cultural background that has different views of how learning and teaching should be conducted (which are different, not worse). This situation must create anxiety and uncertainty, certainly for the students, but also for thoughtful tutors. Gudykunst (1993) posits two major factors that constrain effective communication – uncertainty – a cognitive construct; and anxiety – an emotional construct. Both of these fluctuate (often independently) over time in contact, and an excess of either can prevent learning. For example, at the outset of a programme in a foreign culture both uncertainty and anxiety are likely to be high; as the course progresses parts of it will become more familiar and uncertainty will decrease, while pressure to perform well in exams or assignments will cause high anxiety at any point in a course.

Gudykunst's concept of 'mindfulness' as a mitigating force to control anxiety would seem to be *similar* to what others call consciousness, awareness, open-heartedness, paying attention (but further away from noticing only, since the idea of mindfulness seems to encapsulate both noticing and knowing – and perhaps being able to do something as a consequence, i.e. both knowledge and skills are involved). Three main conditions contribute to lack of mindfulness: familiar scripts (in the Abelson sense); emotionally driven states, or stereotyped intentions and attitudes.

These conditions create lack of mindfulness in different ways for students and tutors. For the students the highly emotional states (e.g. anxiety), perhaps in the face of scripts so unfamiliar as to be virtually impenetrable, will be the major factor. For tutors the very familiarity of the script means they may be unaware that the situation is difficult for the students. The scripts are controlled by the tutors (although we have no idea to what extent these have been consciously or unconsciously moulded over the years by successive groups of incomers) and are almost certain to be unfamiliar – and possibly unexplained.

The paradox is that it is within these conditions that the student is expected to be critically reflective.

Implications

If universities have a genuine concern for the persons who come from overseas to continue their professional development, implicitly or explicitly we are saying that we wish them to develop their potential to grow within their own cultures through a formal period of learning in ours. The issues outlined above are therefore of central concern, because we may be unintentionally obfuscating the learning culture students find themselves in or, at least, failing to elucidate it. This may have a number of consequences.

• *Growing alienation/anomie of incomers – and insiders*
Students may withdraw into strategic or surface learning behaviours that allow them to pass their assignments adequately while failing to engage with the culture of education in which they find themselves. Tutors may also withdraw towards the transmission end of the teaching continuum, feeling that effort in preparing interactive classes is a waste of time because the students do not appear to benefit from them.

- *Reinforcement of narrow category width, i.e. cultural stereotyping on all sides*

Anxiety can lead to the reinforcement of stereotyping and exacerbate withdrawal and mutual misunderstanding.

- *Reduced learning because of script clashes*

In educational settings (and others) there is a question of power – real or perceived – which may be differently true for different participants. For example, if tutors are teaching within a well-tried script, they may be utterly unconscious of any conflicts with other scripts the students may bring to the class and, vested with the authority of the institution and the subject, they may take the view that students have to be initiated into the institutional mores and that a deep-end approach will do this most effectively.

- *Lack of professional growth*

All parties may continue to act *as before*, the experience having failed to engage with their contextual realities in conscious ways.

In a truly reflective learning environment, both tutors and students learn together. Howell (1982) pointed to four stages of growth in (communication) competence, which has also been applied to other competences: unconscious incompetence >conscious incompetence > conscious competence > unconscious competence. What level of competence would be the target for lecturers in a department with many cultures in contact? If the international students are encouraged by circumstances to take a strategic learning stance, they are likely to achieve as a ceiling conscious competence to pass their assignments. The reflective model of teaching and learning, however, aims, through a stage of conscious competence, at unconscious competence which can make a real difference to the ways we think and behave. For the student this would make 'tissue rejection' less likely. For tutors the trajectory through conscious competence to unconscious competence would be focussed on learning about the students and their backgrounds. For them, too, reflection includes mindfulness and a stage of conscious competence.

- *International students may be discriminated against*, whether consciously ('poor writing skills' which may actually have their roots in much deeper cultural differences) or unconsciously (through miscommunications).

What can we do?

- *Research our own teaching, and challenge taken-for-granteds* (Johnson and Badley, 1996 p4)

Many teaching and learning innovations are introduced following considerable research into content, approach, resources and procedures. Relatively few of these innovations are then subjected to systematic evaluation of a fundamental kind. All universities now obtain student feedback and require annual reviews of programmes and units of teaching, but most of this evaluation is fairly shallow. Biggs (2001) points towards the depth real evaluation should attain. Quality teaching means that institutions and individuals need to clarify and be explicit about the theory of teaching and learning they espouse. Review of design and content of courses should be based on systematic evaluations that take into account new knowledge, changing student populations, changing conditions in the institution and society. The impediments to quality teaching and learning need to be evaluated, and these will include not only institutional policies and procedures but also lacunae of knowledge about the students. This process has the tutor at its centre; mindful tutors, researching their students' learning, may discover that their taken-for-granteds about international student learning are not founded on the evidence uncovered.

- *Find out about the students' backgrounds*

There exists a fairly substantial research literature into how learners from Confucian heritage backgrounds prefer to work (e.g. Kember 1996, Kember and Gow, 2000, Biggs, 1996). This is part of a much wider literature on student learning. Knowledge of this scholarship would appear to be as essential a part of good teaching as subject expertise.

We could introduce the concepts and practice of needs and wants analysis into teaching and learning approaches. For example, teaching teams can also do much to find out essential information about the background of students before the programme begins – from application forms, for example. One simple technique is to draw up a template from application forms as they are processed, listing educational background, professional experience and so on, and when the cohort is finalized to make sure that the tutorial team meet and discuss this background data. This information can then be explored further during an initial meeting of personal tutors and students and the results again shared among the teaching team. As part of the process of teaching students can be asked to provide examples of concepts and issues, perhaps after initial modelling by tutors. In Vermunt and Verloop's (1999) 'shared structure' of teaching, the tutor elicits professional examples from students, and does not simply provide what may be culturally inappropriate ones from his or her own experience.

Discussion of such issues should be on the agenda of course committees, much of whose business is too often taken up with procedural matters.

• *Make discussion of learning and teaching part of the course*
Kember (2001) suggests that for students to move towards a transformative approach to learning they may need to change their beliefs about learning. This can be both traumatic and lengthy. Change in belief can be facilitated by teaching, but is unlikely to be altered by short study skills courses. 'To cause a developmental shift in beliefs it does appear necessary to confront students with the incompatibility of their current beliefs. They cannot come to appreciate a facilitative/transformative model of the teaching and learning process unless exposed to teaching based on these principles'(p218). He points out that rather than having confrontation happen accidentally, leading to confusion and anxiety, it would be better to design this deliberately. Most study skills courses focus on a narrow range of activities: academic writing, reading, and so on. Integrating discussion of teaching and learning into normal subject teaching need not be a time consuming activity, and doing so will enable students and tutors to clarify each other's taken-for-granteds.

• *Listen*
This does not mean listening only to spoken comments, where culturally constrained power distance beliefs may prevent international students from being frank. A simple technique for tutors to elicit the views of the class is to ask for short evaluative comments, questions, impressions at the end of each session. These are written on 'post-it' notes about three inches square and are anonymous. The tutor then types them out, perhaps with responses (this takes about half an hour

for a class of thirty) and returns the collated list to the students in the next session. Slips have a number of advantages. They provide detailed additional knowledge of the class's priorities and wishes; they can build up a good picture of what problems students are facing; the sharing of the collected list allows students to see that they are not the only ones who have a particular difficulty; they allow the tutor to see what has not been understood, and they form the basis for discussion of a range of issues, including reflection. It is important to do this after each session so that students develop both confidence in the acceptability of a range of comments, and skills in making them. I have used this method for many years now, and it has proved to be highly effective as a listening device.

- *Root new concepts in familiar contexts*

It is helpful to students if new concepts are based on practical examples from their own environments. For example, before discussing with a class of overseas teachers the fairly complex concept of 'context of situation', they were asked to work in small groups and describe their classrooms and pupils. The tutor elicited the results of the (brief) discussion, putting their accounts on the board. These were then categorized by the students, allowing the tutor to use their naïve categories to build the topic.

- *Explain what technical terms really mean*, rather than expecting the students to learn this by osmosis

Student handbooks could deal with substantive issues as well as procedures and regulations. Many technical terms to do with the learning process are used in student handbooks and by tutors, especially in connection with assignments. We must both explain what they mean and create opportunities for students to come back to them and refine their understanding and ours. Critical analysis is one example of a frequently used term which is seldom explicated, as is the term 'reflective'.

- *Observe and observation practice*

I believe that if students are to be able to analyse anything, they must first be trained to observe and describe. It is fairly straightforward and takes little time to build small episodes of student observation into teaching sessions, ensuring that over time all students have opportunities to observe and report. What they observe is the processes of teaching and learning they and the tutor engage in. (Gilpin, 1999) observes that reflection consists of a number of elements:

- noticing, that is, observing some discrepancy between what occurs and what is taken for granted

- reasoning, that is, articulating what has been observed, and analysing it, drawing on a wide knowledge base

- change of some kind, whether conceptual or practical

- questioning of whatever has hitherto been taken for granted

- an element of affective involvement

Noticing requires the skills of observation. The most important element in observation is to learn to discriminate between seeing and judging: all too often there is no borderline between these, and observation is false: a matter of judging without having a factual basis

Careful noticing enables the tutor to facilitate various dependent activities, e.g. analysis techniques such as categorizing, consideration of the differences between judgement and evaluation. Such observational activities develop the key academic skills of describe, analyse, evaluate – skills which are also key life skills.

Finally...

The aim of having a quarter of the world's international students in the UK by 2005 was described above as bold. If it is for money alone the policy is indefensible; if it is for influence it is marginally less so. Whatever the policy, it is university teachers who will be at the interface of this cultural encounter, not politicians or senior managers of institutions. They will be the people who will have to guarantee the real ethical propriety of this ambition.

References

Abelson, R. (1976) Script processing in attitude formation and decision making. In Carroll, J. and J. Payne (Eds) *Cognition and Scocial Behaviour* (33-45) Hillsdale, Lawrence Erlbaum

Biggs, J. (2001) The reflective institution: assuring and enhancing the quality of teaching and learning *Higher Education* 41: 221-238

Gilpin, A. (1999) A framework for teaching reflection. In McGrath, I. and H. Trappe Lomax (TO BE SENT)

Gilpin, A. and Reis-Jorge, J.M. (1995) Professional Development: How Diaries can Bridge the Gap *Journal of Teacher Development* Vol. 4/3: 22-28

Guardian 15th August 2000 Lee Elliot Major, 'Slipping Abroad'

Gudykunst, W. B. (1993) Toward a theory of effective interpersonal communication. In Wiseman, R and J. Koester 1993 *Intercultural Communication Competence* (33-71) London, Sage

Holliday, A. (1992) Tissue rejection and informal orders in ELT projects: Collecting the right information, *Applied Linguistics* 4: 403-424

Howell, W. (1982) *The Empathetic Communicator* Belmont, Wadsworth.

Johnson, R. and Badley, G. (1996) The competent reflective practitioner Innovation and Learning in Education: *The International Journal of the Reflective Practitioner* 2/1:4-10

Kember, D. (1997) A reconceptualizing of the research into university academic's conceptions of teaching *Learning and Instruction* 24: 109-124

Kember, D. (2001) Beliefs about knowledge and the process of teaching and learning as a factor in adjusting to study in higher education *Studies in Higher Education* 26: 205-201

Kember, D. (2000) Misconceptions about the learning approaches, motivation and study practices of Asian students *Higher Education* 40:99-121

Limón, M. (2001) On the cognitive conflict as an instructional strategy for conceptual change: a critical appraisal *Learning and Instruction* 11 357-380

Martin, E., Prosser, M., Trigwell, K., Ramsden, P., Benjamin, J. (2000) What university teachers teach and how they teach it *Instructional Science* 28:387-412

Marton, F. and Säljö, R. (1976) On qualitative differences in learning I: Outcome and process. *British Journal of Educational Psychology*, 46, 4-11

Marton, F. and Säljö, R. (1976) On qualitative differences in learning II: Outcome as a function of the learner's conception of the task. *British Journal of Educational Psychology*, 46, 115-127

Smith, L.E. (Ed) (1987) *Discourse Across Cultures: Strategies in World Englishes*, Hemel Hempstead, Prentice Hall International

Stephan, W.G. and Stephan, C.W. (1985) Intergroup Anxiety *Journal of Social Issues* 41 157-177

Vermunt, J. D. and Verloop, N. (1999) Congruence and friction between learning and teaching *Learning and Instruction* 9 257-280

5

Transfer and transformation: developing mentoring in Malaysia

Elisabeth Lazarus and Shirley Tay

Introduction

Mentoring is now a well-established practice for professional development and support in many Western educational settings (Lazarus, 2000). This chapter tries to explore what happens when such an educational concept is transposed to a different country and into a different socio-cultural setting such as Malaysia. Why is there a perceived need for mentoring? How is the concept defined and modified to make it suitable for different contexts? The authors are a lecturer from the UK charged with implementing courses on mentoring in Malaysia and a course participant, a senior teacher, who is introducing aspects of mentoring in her secondary school in Kota Kinabalu, Sabah, Malaysia.

The chapter focuses on developments of mentoring and classroom observation and the perceptions that mentors and protégés hold about the nature of mentoring for professional support and enhancement. It tries to explore how cultural influences, such as the long established spiritual tradition behind the word 'guru' (teacher), shape the way Malaysians understand and exemplify the role of the mentor. In many Asian societies the concept of 'preserving face' (*jaga maruah* in Bahasa Malayu) is a strongly embedded cultural phenomenon and we try to highlight how one needs to be sensitive to such views and aware of how they can impact on educational practices such as mentoring. We argue that an educational concept such as mentoring cannot just be transferred from one context to

71

another but needs to be transformed, taking into account local beliefs and attitudes, contexts and practices in order to gain acceptance and to be of benefit to teachers, learners and school managers.

Findings from a number of small-scale empirical studies in Malaysian schools and colleges, carried out by other participants in the first author's mentoring programmes, are used to illuminate these experiences. Surveys and discussions conducted in Sabah with teachers, lecturers and student teachers provide additional information. These studies were carried out at a time of significant educational change and innovation in the Malaysian education system. The country was also experiencing a period of economic downturn, which meant that in-service training was being drastically curtailed and some of the planned cascade mentor training programmes were reduced or frozen.

Mentoring in the Malaysian Context

In Malaysia the trends towards mentoring in teacher education and professional development in other countries were noted with interest. In 1996 the introduction of a new teacher training course leading to a Diploma in Education (*Diploma Perguruan Malaysia – DPM*) provided the platform to move teacher training and education forward from a clinical supervision model to a mentoring model, as a result of which schools and teachers were expected to carry out a much more significant role than before in supporting, training, collaborating with and assessing students. This move was supported by a pilot project sponsored by the Ministry of Education, Malaysia and the ODA of the United Kingdom which focused on primary English teacher education, the so-called PETEP project (Ministry of Education, 1996). In 1996 a number of workshops were held to introduce the changes in the DPM to key personnel. These workshops were intended to be the vehicle for a cascade model of dissemination.

Representatives of the teacher training colleges and regional and key personnel were targeted first. They in turn were to run workshops in their own colleges for lecturers and for school representatives, typically school principals. Finally, these head teachers or other school representatives were to introduce the concept of mentoring and greater school involvement in teacher education and training in their schools. The intention was to start with mentoring in the primary schools and then develop this further in secondary schools.

To facilitate the dissemination of mentoring in Malaysia, the Ministry of Education supported a twinning programme between the Malaysian Institute of Educational Management, Institut Aminuddin Baki (IAB) and the University of Bristol. The Bristol Masters of Education programme carried a significant specialisation in mentoring and professional development for teachers. The Universiti Malaysia Sabah (UMS) on the island of Borneo also organised a number of workshops for head teachers, lecturers and student teachers. These sessions were facilitated by the lecturer from Bristol and were intended to act as a catalyst for the local development of a mentoring programme suitable for Sabahan conditions.

Why is there a perceived need for mentoring?

Malaysia is a country of great contrasts and rich cultural and geographic diversity. The population is racially, linguistically and culturally diverse. National and local needs determine the posting of teachers to schools. Teachers may be transferred from the generally more affluent urban areas to remote rural regions where villages and schools are only accessible by boat, plane or helicopter, where different languages or dialects are spoken and different religions practised. These transfers, however sensitively executed, can present challenges for teachers on a scale which many colleagues in the West are unlikely to experience. Teacher shortages can mean that unqualified and untrained personnel have to be employed and that student teachers stand in for absent colleagues during their practicum. In the past, the role of the supervising or 'co-operating' teacher was often limited to offering student teachers a class to practise on, resources and some advice but rarely included providing opportunities for observing established teachers. Student teachers felt that they were expected to sink or swim and that support and advice was available from their training institution only via the occasional visits by lecturers and not from the schools. In recent years, however, it became widely recognised that a more systematic application of mentoring principles could help the newcomers, both student teachers and those transferring from other schools, adapt to the new demands or conditions. Mentoring was seen as a crucial support mechanism for their professional learning and adjustment.

Transferring the concept of mentoring

Anderson and Lucasse Shannon (1995, p29) provide a useful and frequently quoted western definition of mentoring, as:

> a nurturing process in which a more skilled or more experienced person, serving as a role model, teaches, sponsors, encourages, counsels and befriends a less skilled and less experienced person for the purpose of promoting the latter's professional and /or personal development. Mentoring...(is) carried out within the context of an on-going caring relationship between mentor and protégé.

Mentors in western educational settings are frequently involved in a range of inter-related tasks and behaviours such as modelling, observing, supporting, listening, discussing, analysing, challenging, negotiating, encouraging and assessing their protégés. These different role dimensions require mentors to react and respond to their protégé in a variety of ways and to use their expertise, planning skills, interpersonal skills, professional judgement and intuition as part of their mentoring role (Lazarus, 2000).

Such a definition of mentoring explicitly or implicitly presupposes that an openness can be established between mentor and protégé which can be further fostered through observation and professional dialogue. It also implies that both partners need to be clear about roles and relationships and that there is a willingness by the mentor to carry out his or her role. A key feature of mentoring is allowing student teachers access to the 'craft-knowledge' of mentors. This can be difficult for mentors as they may not have needed to talk about their beliefs and implicit views of teaching and learning for some time and their classroom practice has become so intuitive that articulating what they are doing or why is quite a challenge (Tomlinson, 1995).

Visits to schools, colleges and universities and discussions with teachers and lecturers indicated early on that observation of mentors by protégés would be a likely hurdle in Malaysia. The prediction that mentors might be reluctant to act as role models in their classrooms was born out by a number of small-scale studies in 1997-8 and by responses to questionnaires by head teachers, lecturers and student teachers attending INSET courses on mentoring in March 2001. The studies indicated that although the *guru pembimbing* (the mentors) profoundly agreed with the importance of observation in principle, they generally did not allow beginning teachers access to their classrooms in practice (Nur Anuar, 1997; Mohd. Abd. Razif, 1997; Lee, 1998). These discrepancies between espoused views and practice echo earlier findings by Choo *et al* (1996) and Filmer and Chandran (1996) (see review by Leila Herani, 1998). The fact that trainees were rarely welcomed into mentors' lessons or encouraged in team teaching was explained by one student in the following way: the mentor '*was not happy that I had to observe her as she thinks that she is not perfect*' (D'Silva, 1998, p89).

The mentors' reluctance to be observed can be easily understood when one considers past practice, when observation was equated with assessment (Saleena, 1998) and with cultural sensitivities, as expressed by one respondent but shared by many: '*Asians are shy people. We are not open to criticism. They think that if you go and observe them you're trying to find out the mistakes, their weaknesses*' (D'Silva, 1998, p84). The importance of the affective domain in the development of beginning teachers and in the mentoring process cannot be overestimated, in our opinion. One Malaysian novice teacher made this abundantly clear when she wrote: '*It is very difficult to ask teachers. I am very shy to ask. Scared afterward they say how come you don't know? You never learn in college? So I just try and do it on my own and sometimes I do it right. But sometimes it was no good*' (Goh, 1998, p83).

Asma Abdullah (1993), a specialist in Human Resource Development, is of the opinion that Malaysians are deeply rooted in their cultural values, customs and traditions and bring these differing systems of values into the workplace. She contends that these different values need to be understood by those in managerial positions so that 'shared values and shared practices can contribute to enhancing group morale and productivity' (1993, p39). Cultural values such as collectivism, hierarchy, relationship, face, religious orientation and pursuit of success are values held by the various Malaysian cultural groups, but not necessarily shared by all these groups. She believes that these values need to be allowed to 'co-exist with modern managerial values of goal clarity, co-operation, decisiveness, commitment, achievement, accountability, shared wisdom' (*ibid*). We consider an understanding of the different value systems motivating different teachers to be significant when one is trying to develop mentoring strategies in Malaysian schools too.

In a western setting, it has been shown that beginning teachers hold strong beliefs about teaching and teachers. These views often arise from personal experiences (John, 1996) and hence mentors need to provide not only models of 'good practice' but opportunities when such views can be challenged or questioned in a supportive environment. The process of questioning and probing is a mutual process, which is closely linked to mutual observations. Both partners in the mentoring relationship have the opportunity of observing the other teach and, in a dialogue which follows the observation, trying to make sense of what they have seen. Questioning the more experienced teacher or colleague is a fundamental aspect of western mentoring and it can help both partners interpret actions in the classroom, rather than relying on espoused theories. Questioning or challenging the views of more senior teachers and elders may be an area of particular difficulty in Malaysia and mentoring needs to take account of cultural sensitivities. In discussions with teachers, lecturers and students in various parts of Malaysia, there appeared an easy acceptance of the idea of mentors as guides and leaders. One participant explained this in terms of Malaysians being used to turning to a spiritual guru, imam or family member to guide and lead the individual on a personal or spiritual level and hence the role of the mentor was one that she thought most Malaysians would feel comfortable with. But she considered that allowing protégés to question the *guru pembimbing* or to critique observed practice would be difficult to implement. If the *guru pembimbing* could be persuaded that asking questions about practice could lead to better learning for the protégé (whether a student teacher or peer) and ultimately for the pupils in the classroom, then attitudes might be more flexible.

Concern was also voiced that promoting a protégé (as used in the definition by Anderson and Lucasse Shannon above) could be misconstrued to mean some sort of favouritism which might operate along racial, religious or cultural lines and would be highly resented in a Malaysian setting. Mentors in a western setting can be seen as promoting the welfare of their protégé by providing advice and ideas, sharing resources and information and by offering a real or a metaphorical shoulder to cry on. Mentors of new colleagues may point out the key players within the school organisation, the right person to turn to if you need a specific task to be done. Such information, highly valuable to the newcomer but often not explicitly available, can, in the hurly burly of a school setting, pass the protégé by unnoticed. Hence the mentor's intervention can be invaluable.

Mentors can also promote the professional development of their protégés by encouraging them to attend relevant courses or introducing them to colleagues who could help them. Mentors keep an eye on their protégés, watching out for signs of emotional or physical stress and promoting their well-being. Mentors in Malaysia would need to remain scrupulously objective so that the 'promotion' of their protégé could not be misconstrued. It is part of Malaysia's heritage for racial, cultural, religious and family groupings which provide strong support to its individual members. Some linguistic barriers exist which are difficult for the individual to overcome. Fairness would have to be demonstrated so that mentors could not be accused of supporting and promoting only the protégés who are members of their own cultural or religious group. However, if the full role dimension of mentors can be communicated to protégés and colleagues alike and mentors engage in an open and constructive dialogue with teachers, then the misinterpretations and misunderstandings can be reduced. The spiritual support that a imam, guru or priest provides and which benefits both the individual and the wider community is widely accepted in Malaysia. If, as one participant pointed out, the *guru pembimbing* can be seen to offer professional support and advice, not dissimilar to that of a spiritual leader, mentoring has a chance of becoming firmly established.

Challenges in introducing mentoring in Malaysia – a case study

When Shirley Tay took the first steps to introduce aspects of mentoring in her school, she was well aware of the existing cultural expectations and the delicate balance between different ethnic or religious groups. The school population is predominately Chinese but members of all the other main ethnic and religious groups can be found amongst pupils and staff. As in many Malaysian schools,

teachers can appear quite passive, waiting for change to be introduced top-down by the senior management teams and supported by
ministerial decrees. In her school, like many others, classroom
observations were rare and, when they did occur, were predominantly used for assessment or inspection purposes. Initially, Tay
took on the role of mentor to new student teachers in her school and
set about designing an experience which she deemed appropriate for
her school's students. She acted as a role model by demonstrating to
other teachers a willingness to be observed by student teachers but
she offered members of her department the opportunity to observe
her too. By tapping into their own training experiences she was able
to convince colleagues that the observations of experienced teachers
was important for the novice and opened doors which had been previously shut. In return, she regularly observed student teachers and
teachers who were newly posted to the school and provided them
with detailed feedback. The quality of professional dialogues that
these interactions stimulated and the positive evaluation she
obtained from students encouraged Tay to seek to extend the
observation process across the school. In this endeavour she had the
active support of her head teacher.

She drew on the findings from colleagues in Malaysia and from
other countries when she developed her mentoring programme.
After the initial focus on mentoring for student teachers, she decided
that the next step was to prepare a training day for all teachers, when
discussion focused on areas such as:

- the purpose of classroom observation for new and experienced
  teachers

- what can be observed during lessons

- the process of observation

- instruments that could be used and the advantages and
  disadvantages of each

- how to select a mutually beneficial focus for observation

Being aware of the close equation of observation with assessment in
many teachers' minds, Tay stressed the importance of developing a
truly non-judgemental manner of observation. She felt that teachers

agreed with her that the key purpose of the observation was for examining and improving teaching techniques, as a tool for mutual learning and for building a stronger team for the benefit of the learners at the school. As in many other countries, educational change is normally introduced in a top-down fashion through directives from the Ministry of Education or the State Education Departments in Malaysia. Accordingly, Tay decided to invite more senior members of the school to observe more junior colleagues first.

In training sessions during the twinning programme at IAB and in Bristol, Lazarus used video clips from a variety of classrooms from Malaysia, the UK and Sweden extensively. Observation techniques were practised in depth and a wide range of different observation schedules were trialled. Simulation activities included role-plays on providing feedback to different colleagues and in different situations and activities that highlighted the differences between verbal and written feedback were also included. Tay used similar strategies when working with her teachers.

Following these sessions, the observers met the teachers they were going to observe, discussed the focus and process of observation and agreed on a procedure for giving feedback. This pilot initiative received overwhelmingly positive responses from observers and teachers about the value of the exercise. Although some teachers had initially felt uneasy about being observed by their heads of department, this was outweighed by the sense of *improving together*, being *very useful in improving the teaching and learning process* and leading to greater collaboration. Only one teacher in the survey felt unhappy, and that was because she received no feedback after the observation. The observation process was endorsed by all. Some teachers felt such observations should take place on a regular basis and there was a strong feeling that such observations should be mutual and involve all teachers, so creating a true peer observation cycle. Tay's pilot study indicates that teachers were looking for a more egalitarian approach where observations are carried out in a collegial fashion and where the focus is on professional development rather than critical assessment within a hierarchical top-down model. These suggestions are now being implemented.

Mentoring for student teachers and new teachers and regular mutual observations have also been successfully introduced in a secondary school in another part of Sabah in Sandekan (Ngiam Eng Hong, 2001, personal communication). As in Kota Kinabalu, the head teacher implementing these innovations in Sandekan was a participant of the IAB/Bristol twinning programme. Both teachers commented that their senior positions in the school and the fact that they had learnt about mentoring practices during a higher degree course had facilitated its implementation in their schools. Their status was important but even more so was their willingness to act as role models, to open themselves up for observation and discussion. Their willingness to act as role models when demonstrating mentoring approaches and mutual observations was considered fundamental to implementing the process. In other words they were breaking the mould of the role of senior teachers and were even prepared to break cultural taboos. By taking risks with their status they were making it safer for other colleagues to follow. They drew heavily on the discussions they had had with their Malaysian counterparts during the mentoring course and on the local literature, which they were able to access through IAB or the EPRD in Kuala Lumpur. Their success can also be attributed to the discussions they had with colleagues and the targeted training sessions they held for staff.

In a cultural context where age and experience is revered and teachers enjoy high social status, it is no doubt difficult for the protégés to articulate directly to the mentor or observer how they are feeling, what they perceive their needs to be or how they would like the mentoring process to operate Tay's colleagues appreciated. The opportunity to provide group and anonymous feedback was appreciated by Tay's colleagues. It would go against cultural conventions to voice views or criticism of her endeavours directly, but teachers found it easier to express their views publicly through explicit invitations and via anonymous questionnaires. Tay responded publicly to concerns and points raised in the questionnaires but ensured that the source of the concern could not be identified. She encouraged individuals who wanted to discuss issues further to see her in confidence. Providing such opportunities for anonymous feedback about the mentoring and observation experience was strongly supported by Tay's teachers.

Challenges for the future

Developments in Malaysia offer the western mentor important lessons. Choosing one's words with great care, being sensitive and courteous, considering change with a certain amount of scepticism can all contribute to establishing a healthier mentoring environment. But, as with all change, the early phases of moving from supervision to mentoring can be problematic, especially as one is requiring individuals to adapt to new roles which make demands.

Some of the teachers in Tay's school did not necessarily want to participate in observations, mentoring for student teachers or peer mentoring. As in other schools, they considered that providing feedback or listening to feedback would add to their already heavy workload. The top-down nature of the introduction of change meant, however, that teachers had no choice but to comply. In only one case did the reluctance manifest itself in one partner not receiving any feedback from the observer and strongly resenting this. Teachers already overloaded with new initiatives may well buy into change on the surface but show no significant change in their practice. Only time and careful monitoring will tell Tay whether the change she has tried to implement has really taken root in her school, and that this mentoring initiative, like so many others, does not follow a road into oblivion.

Malaysian studies have shown that one central difficulty encountered in redefining the role of the mentor and distinguishing this from that of the co-operating teacher was maintaining the same term in Bahasa Malayu for co-operating teacher and mentor. Retention of the term *guru pembimbing* for the more extensive role of mentor could lead individual teachers, principals or lecturers to believe that in practice no paradigm shift was needed and cause confusion about what the new regulations were requiring of the mentor (D'Silva, 1998). A new term may need to be coined and agreed between schools, colleges, universities and the Ministry. It could be helpful to have different terms for the mentor who works with student teachers, for the induction mentor who supports new teachers and for the colleague who acts as mentor for a peer who is at a particular point of change in his or her career.

Asma Abdullah noted that 'there is a tendency for Malaysians not to be too expressive in conveying their frustrations upwards unless it is collectively done and assured that the information is received objectively and for the purpose of making continuous improvement' (Asma Abdullah, 1993:36). As we have seen, Tay was aware of this and her preparedness to take risks and sensitive handling of feedback and questionnaires meant that she was making inroads in gaining the trust of her colleagues.

College and university tutors in Malaysia have commented that although they monitor the mentoring and supervision experience of their student teachers, this information is rarely shared with mentors. It could be very helpful to mentors to obtain feedback from a particular cohort of student teachers, which could be both anonymous and constructive, as was the case in Tay's school. Mentors and observers invest a great deal of time and energy with student teachers and colleagues and deserve to know that their work is appreciated, but they also need to become aware of how their practice could be improved. A collective and anonymous summary of how mentoring is working within a particular college/university and school partnership could possibly provide this. Mentors need to see that their time is well spent and it would seem fair that their efforts should at least be rewarded with some feedback.

It is important that mentors and protégés are made aware by college or university tutors that they might experience conflicts of perceptions and clashes of views which can be both debilitating and a source for learning (Mazlina, 1998). Both good and questionable practice in mentoring could be highlighted by training institutions using examples from other schools or by creating fictitious case studies. Examples of how mentors work effectively with protégés could be collated and disseminated via mentor training meetings at the training institutions or through mentoring networks within the school or farther afield.

The fact that Tay has actively asked for comments and feedback from her colleagues and has been seen to be acting on their suggestions bodes well for the continuing process of developing mentoring practices in her school. Mentoring relies heavily on the development of professional and personal relationships, as most work is carried out on a one-to-one basis, so can be time-consuming and requires a great degree of trust and understanding. Implementing mentoring in a culturally sensitive manner is clearly possible and appears to us to the right way forward for Malaysia.

As Nagendralingan Ratnavadivel notes in his review of twenty years of teacher education in Malaysia, 'change takes time. It involves a period of destabilisation and restabilisation. It involves experimentation and the taking of risks' (Ratnavadievel, 1999:209). If a school truly wants to develop into a 'learning school' it will not be able to avoid engaging in this process. However a gradual and progressive move from clinical supervision to mentoring, which can be adapted to the pace needed by teachers for educational change in Malaysia, would seem most appropriate. Rapid and bewildering change can leave teachers feeling frustrated and disengaged. The dialogue between training institutions and schools and between colleagues in schools will be crucial in making the implementation of mentoring a success. Good communication and clear role descriptions will be vital.

Critically, educationalists, teachers and students need to be introduced to the concept of observation as a tool for professional growth and development and not as a means of finding fault with, critiquing and assessing teachers. Only then will classroom doors be willingly opened.

References

Anderson, E.M. and Lucasse Shannon A. (1995) Towards a conceptualisation of mentoring in Kerry, T. and Shelton Mayes, A. *Issues in Mentoring*, London: Routledge.

Asma Abdullah (1993) Leading and motivating the Malaysian workforce, *Malaysian Management Review*, 24-41.

D'Silva, M. (1998) A survey on the role of collaborative teaching during the DPM practicum 3: Perceptions of school mentors and student teachers in Malaysia, unpublished Master of Education dissertation, University of Bristol.

Goh Lay Huah (1998) Perceived concerns and needs of newly qualified English language teachers, unpublished Master of Education dissertation, University of Bristol.

John, P. (1996) Understanding the apprenticeship of observation in initial teacher education: exploring student teachers' implicit theories of teaching and learning, in: G. Claxton *et al* (eds.) *Liberating the Learner – Lessons for professional development in education*, London: Routledge.

Laila Hairaní Bt.Hj. Abdullah Sanggura (1998) The roles of English language college tutors in the school-based teaching practicum: a case study in Malaysia, unpublished Master of Education dissertation, University of Bristol.

Lazarus, E. (2000) The role of intuition in mentoring and supporting beginning teachers, in: Atkinson. T and Claxton, G. (eds) *The Intuitive practitioner,* Buckingham: Open University Press.

Lee Thum Eng (1998) A survey of the relationship between the needs of newly qualified teachers and their experiences of induction in selected secondary schools in Malaysia, unpublished Master of Education dissertation, University of Bristol.

Mazlina bt. Azhar (1998) Conflicts between school mentors and student teachers during the 1998 KDPM practicum 3 in Malaysia, unpublished Master of Education dissertation, University of Bristol.

Ministry of Education (1996) PETEP Mentor Training for School-College Partnership, Kuala Lumpur: Ministry of Education.

Mohamed Abdul Razif Abd. Razak (1997) The Reality of Mentoring in Primary Schools in the State of Pahang: Perceptions of Mentors and ESL Student Teachers, unpublished Master of Education dissertation, University of Bristol.

Nagendralingan Ratnavadivel (1999) Teacher education: interface between practices and policies – the Malaysian experience 1979-1997, *Teaching and Teacher Education*, 15, 193-213.

Nur Anuar Mutalib (1997) The perceptions of ESL co-operating teachers on classroom observation responsibilities during the teaching practicum, unpublished Master of Education dissertation, University of Bristol.

Saleena Chang Abdullah (1998) The reality of classroom observations and feedback discussions during the 1998 Diploma Perguruan Malaysia Practicum 3: Perceptions of student teachers and school mentors in Malaysia, unpublished Master of Education dissertation, University of Bristol.

Tomlinson, P. (1995) *Understanding Mentoring – reflective strategies for school-based teacher preparation*, Buckingham: Open University Press.

Part II:
Professional and Disciplinary Cultures

Editors' Introduction
In this section of the book we examine the experiences of professionals and students who practice on the boundaries of different cultures. These practises are situated within institutional settings, structured by both explicit and implicit demands, such as national policy, curricula, ethical practices, textbooks, graduation ceremonies and examinations. Moreover, diverse and possibly conflicting professional cultures are likely to be represented within any institutional setting, such as the professions of counsellors, teachers and educational psychologists. It is important to recognise that professional cultures change over time, structured by a particular socio-historical and political system. Within this complexity students are agents in the construction of their own culture, although they may not be aware of the ways in which they are being positioned by cultural artefacts such as textbooks and other media. What then do the authors in this section of the book have to say about these issues?.

In Chapter 6 Eric Hoyle and Mike Wallace focus on organisations at the level of school, a major structuring constraint which impacts on what is possible in the classroom. They suggest that 'the cultural turn', which occurred in the educational management of UK schools in the 1980s, relates to whole-school approaches to school improvement and school effectiveness and emphasises a school culture which is prescriptive, holistic and instrumental. Tracing the history of change in British schools from the 1960s to the present day they argue that improving school leadership and management 'came to be seen as the golden road to improving the quality of education' (p93). This involved focusing on the culture of an organisation, and this, they argue, 'is underpinned by an assumption that school leaders can create a common culture for their school'. They maintain that the climate created by this 'cultural turn' can lead to strategic compliance and ambiguity because of the limits to which the professional work of teachers can be controlled by management procedures.

Tim Bond in Chapter 7 explores the relationship between ethical discourse and professional culture at the interface of school counsellors and teachers. By analysing the similaraties and differences between ethical codes for both professions he shows that both are 'aware of the inescapable moral pluralism of contemporary society'. He argues that the process of developing an ethical code makes explicit the implicit moral commitment and cultural norms within an institution or professional body. He discusses some of the tensions between person-centred institutions which place the individual at the focus of the moral purpose of education and institutions which view the relationship between morality and education as passing the values of one generation to the next, independent of the learner. Finally, he argues that in preparing young people to become citizens institutions should support them to take an active and critical stance towards ethics as a social construction.

In Chapter 8 Alec Webster and his colleagues explore the relationship between the two 'cultures' that are contending for the territory known as 'educational psychology'. Beginning with a review of the emergence and current context of educational psychology, they analyse how educational psychologists have historically constructed their professional identity which centres around the culture of the 'clinician'. They argue that the existence of educational psychologists as a profession has tended to locate problems with individual pupils outside the classroom and outside school. They suggest that educational psychologists have always been uncomfortable with the view that they can diagnose problems without reference to the social contexts which generate them. New roles will mean crossing established boundaries between teachers and educational psychologists and will provoke psychologists to work with teachers to find solutions within the whole system. This implies new types of professional training which, the authors argue, should involve a research-orientation which focuses on both individual difference and the social context which constructs this difference.

In Chapter 9 Laurinda Brown and Alf Coles focus on the importance of students' developing their own voice when immersed in new and possibly conflicting cultures. They suggest that the whole experience of entering secondary school involves endless boundary crossing between subject cultures, such as history, science and mathematics. Focusing on the case of learning mathematics, they argue that teachers can draw on pupils' powers to see similarity and difference so that they can develop a voice which allows them to participate in the emerging culture of creating mathematics. 'We believe that learning in unfamiliar contexts takes place through the use of our powers of discrimination, seeing difference and similarity. What seems important is that as we enter a new culture, we are present in our perception and are able to say what we see' (p145).

Whereas Brown and Coles' chapter focuses on student voice as a constituent part of creating a culture, Molyneux-Hodgson and Foner's chapter centres around the way in which scientific texts construct a specific scientific culture for undergraduates, which may or may not support them to identify with the world of being a scientist. They raise questions about the likelihood of particular groups of students making the transition from 'you' the scientific community to 'we' the scientific community. 'Just as scientific language is socio-culturally constructed, so it is important to underline, is the construction of scientific community preferred by the textbook' (p?). This suggests that more attention should be paid to the often overlooked artefact – the textbook. We would also argue that as textbooks are increasingly becoming web-based it is even more important for educationalists and students to become aware of the ways in which the culture of a particular practice is represented within educational settings through a variety of different media.

6

Management and teaching: two cultures or one?

Eric Hoyle and Mike Wallace

The implicit aim of the educational reform movement which emerged in Britain in the 1980s was to transform the culture of education. This entailed a two-pronged strategy. Central government took to itself through a raft of policy initiatives a greater direct responsibility for the delivery as well as the structure of education. It also devolved to individual schools greater managerial responsibilities for effective and efficient education at the point of delivery. Thus for the first time central government concerned itself with the management of schools and particularly with fostering a culture of managerialism. The central cultural theme of these policies was *instrumentalism*, a pre-occupation with means and with specified ends. This theme of *instrumentalism* was extended to include the culture of teaching via the 'new professionalism'.

It is our purpose here to take stock of this policy of cultural transformation. The first part of this chapter considers the culture of teaching prevailing in the 1960s and 1970s, a growing criticism of which precipitated the reform movement. The second section explores the 'cultural turn' in management theory and its impact on educational management. The third part identifies characteristics of the 'new professionalism'. The fourth section examines the prospects for the development of school cultures as unified cultures embracing both managerialism and professionalism. The final section returns to the question posed in the title of this chapter.

The convention in academic writing of beginning with a consideration of the key concept, in this case *culture*, is not one we will be
observing. Raymond Williams famously wrote that 'culture is one of
the two or three most complicated words in the English language';
the anthropologist Adam Kuper has proposed that the concept
should be abandoned because it is 'hyper-referential'. We will treat
culture as a somewhat diffuse concept which refers to a configura-
tion of values, beliefs, norms, behaviours and rituals and their symbolisation which is relatively distinctive to some social institution –
the educational system, the teaching profession, the school.

The culture of teaching

The culture of teaching *may* have universal properties but it certainly
varies over place and over time. The material reported in the Bristaix
study vividly illuminates the differences between the cultures of
primary school teaching in France and England (Broadfoot *et al.,*
1993). We are here concerned with the culture of teaching in Britain
during the 1960s and 1970s. Although the culture of teaching has
many dimensions we focus on two: the culture of teaching as an
occupation and the culture of teaching as practice. These two dimensions of teaching interpenetrate.

The culture of teaching as an occupation embraces values, beliefs,
norms and their symbolisation which centre on such factors as
status, role and workplace. The central cultural theme in the culture
of teaching as an occupation in the 1960s-1970s was *autonomy*.
Achieving and enhancing autonomy in relation to the state had been
one of the major projects of teaching as an occupation. The degree
of autonomy and the conditions of its negotiation have been explored by Ozga and Lawn (1981), Lawn (1987) and Grace (1987).
The 1960s saw perhaps the apotheosis of the autonomy project. The
teachers' associations were highly effective in sustaining relative
autonomy in the face of, for example, governmental attempts to set
foot in 'the secret garden of the curriculum' (Manzer, 1970).

Teacher autonomy was also a key theme in the occupational culture
at the school level. Organisationally schools were loosely coupled.
The headteacher's domain was policy, administration of routine
matters and external relations. The teacher's domain was the
classroom. There was a strong cultural norm of non-interference in

a teacher's classroom activities. And although teachers expressed a desire for greater participation this was a desire for participation in policy-making in only certain areas, particularly those which impinged most directly on classroom practice. It may be interpreted as a desire to participate in order to protect the conditions of their individual classroom autonomy. The desire for autonomy comes out quite clearly from existing research as one of the major factors affecting teachers' work satisfaction. Its significance is also brought out clearly when teachers talk about their work (Nias, 1989).

It can be noted, however, that some students of the culture of teaching take a somewhat negative view of autonomy. The alternative conceptualisation of this cultural theme is *individuality*. Lortie (1975), for example, wrote: 'Teacher individualism is guarded and cautious... [it] is not cocky and self-assured; it is hesitant and uneasy... the individual teacher is shielded' (210-211). Lortie also argues that individualism inhibited the development of a shared *technical culture* amongst teachers to the detriment of the status of teaching as a profession.

If we turn to the culture of teaching as classroom practice there were perhaps three strong cultural themes in the 1960s-1970s:

- *developmentalism* refers to the significance which teachers attach to fostering the development of individual children over time, the development not only of cognitive capacities but also social, emotional or physical development – in sum, the development of 'the whole child'

- *child-centredness* is related to developmentalism and refers to teachers' belief that the 'needs' of the individual child should take priority over the expectations of other groups such as employers, the state

- *progressivism* is used here to refer to a set of beliefs that learning occurs most effectively where discovery, experiment and creativity are encouraged.

These terms symbolise a culture of teaching which became the focus of change from the late 1970s. Of course, the culture of teaching is more complex than can be captured in a few terms. We do not know to what extent these themes represent simply the espoused values of teachers or the extent to which they were internalised. The evidence of external inspection reports implies that full commitment to developmental, child-centred and progressive practice was found in only a minority of classrooms (eg DES, 1978). Some critics of the culture of teaching in the 1960s partly exonerate teachers and put the blame on teacher education and other components of the 'educational establishment' who peddled 'trendy theories' (for a discussion see Hoyle and John, 1998). To the cultural themes listed should be added the theme of *pragmatism*. We use this term here in its everyday sense (as opposed to its technical philosophical usage) to indicate teachers' preference for what appears to work in the classroom over theory-led solutions to their perceived pedagogical problems.

Nevertheless autonomy, developmentalism, child-centredness and progressivism became the emblems of a culture of teaching which the reform movement sought to change. The perceived excesses resulting from the existing culture of teaching were to be offset by the development of the culture of managerialism.

The cultural turn in educational management
Before the 1960s schools were not 'managed', they were 'run'. 'Management' was not part of the educational discourse; management was what occurred in business organisations. Schools were not businesses and to apply to them the term 'management' was to strike a jarring note. Schools were run by headteachers with the help of a deputy head and a secretary. In secondary schools subject responsibilities would be delegated to specialists. The administrative apparatus was relatively simple compared with current complexity of contemporary school management. The few promoted posts made available to teachers during this period were introduced to serve several potentially contradictory purposes over which headteachers had considerable leeway (Wallace, 1986):

• to reward past performance in the classroom

• to attract teachers of shortage subjects

• to retain teachers with scarce expertise

• to legitimate the delegation of administrative responsibilities.

A wider range of differentiated posts was introduced incrementally as a result of further negotiations over the next two decades, being awarded for all these purposes depending on local school circumstances.

The late 1960s saw the emergence of an interest in the improvement in what came to be termed 'school administration' – 'school management' did not become a term of art until the early 1970s. The sources of this interest were headteachers themselves, local education authority (LEA) advisers, union leaders and academics in a number of departments in higher education institutions. There was very little in the way of central government initiative on school management before the 1980s. LEA advisers and academics developed courses which were designed to improve the 'normal' management of schools and also to equip school staff to cope with emergent innovations in curriculum and method which increasingly entailed a whole-school approach to implementation. But the increasing focus on management generated little change in the *culture* of the school. The change began in the 1980s with the onset of the accountability movement where greater responsibilities were placed in the hands of headteachers. Improved school leadership and management came to be seen as the golden road to improving the quality of education and central government ministers introduced a number of initiatives to improve its quality.

The new central government interest in school management connected with the 'cultural turn' in management theory. There had been in North America an earlier interest in the administrative *climate* of schools. 'Climate' referred to the tone of the work relationships between teachers, particularly the impact of the leadership style of the principal, and was thus a measure of collective job satisfaction. The 'organisational climates' identified or 'invented', as he put it, by Halpin (1966) are widely known. But he noted that the work on climates was very much in the human relations tradition and the conception of leadership was that of 'transactional leadership' based on leaders' exchanges and trade-offs with followers deemed necessary for task achievement (Northouse, 1997). The model of leadership was the maintenance of a contingent balance between the emphasis on tasks and an emphasis on people and their needs.

The 'culture' of an organisation came to be seen as somewhat wider than its 'climate' and included values, beliefs and norms and particularly their symbolisation. The cultural turn was linked to an emerging view of 'transformational' leadership (Burns, 1978), leadership orientated to a longer term mission, leadership creating a vision which organisational members were led to internalise. The work of Schein (1985) was highly influential but the cultural turn was given a considerable boost with the publication of *In Pursuit of Excellence* by Peters and Waterman (1982). This became an 'airport bookstall' best-seller, as did the work of Ouchi (1981) and Deal and Kennedy (1982). This genre of publication purported to illustrate how the difference between highly successful and less successful companies could be explained by differences in culture and leadership. As Schein (1985:317) put it, 'the unique and essential function of leadership is the manipulation of culture'.

The cultural turn in educational management was influenced by this industrial-based literature. Theories of educational leadership favoured the transformational pattern and stressed the importance of a 'strong' culture. Caldwell and Spinks (1992), key contributors to the cultural turn in educational management, wrote: 'A strong culture will emerge when a shared culture has been achieved and there is a high degree of consistency among the tangible manifestation of their core values' (89).

The point here is that developments in leadership and management have created a *culture of managerialism. Management* is a set of processes and procedures accorded primarily instrumental value as a means to a worthy end. *Managerialism* is a set of beliefs which endow these procedures with intrinsic virtue. The central themes of the managerialist culture are as follows:

* *instrumentalism* – it may seem odd to apply this label to an approach to leadership and management which takes the transformation of values as its aim, but the ultimate value is seen as effectively institutionalising educational policy. Much is made of the need for educational leaders to have 'vision' but their scope for choosing the content of their educational vision is narrowly delimited by the imperative to implement central government reform policies (eg Wallace and Huckman, 1999)

• *integrationism* – the aim of leadership is the creation of a strong, shared culture for a school. The structural response to the perceived problems of the 1960s and 1970s is to tighten the coupling between components. The cultural response is to achieve a homogeneity of values and beliefs centred around national policies. Thus the current orthodoxy in educational management holds that school improvement and effectiveness are the outcome of the capacity of a transformational leader to use symbolic means to create a strong culture as an expression of shared values, guided by a clear vision, encapsulated in a distinctive mission, and internalised through a programme of professional development centred on creating a committed and collegial staff.

The culture of managerialism is particularly symbolised in language. The new management discourse is pervasive. It is marked by such key words as *quality, performance, delivery, efficiency, targets, results.* These are 'harder', 'masculine' terms adopted from the discourse of industrial management, as are such metaphors as *re-engineering, zero-defect* and *right-sizing* and terms from the management literature such as *management-by-walking-about* and *management-by-exception.* The discourse also includes job titles which have proliferated over the past twenty years – the titles sometimes preceding the conception of the job to be performed. The culture of managerialism is also symbolised in procedures, especially those entailed in accountability procedures – committees, documentation, inspections, validations or published league tables of test results.

Management and teaching came to be conceived as discrete activities linked through accountability procedures. 'The new professionalism' was seen as integrating the two cultures.

The culture of the new professionalism

The new professionalism can only be understood in relation to an older concept of a profession. To tell briefly a familiar story: the established professions had attributed to them by functionalist sociologists, and attributed to themselves by themselves, a set of distinguishing characteristics including practitioner autonomy, a body

of theory and research which underpinned practice, a lengthy process of higher education and professional socialisation, a self-
governing body and a code of client-centred ethics. Critics of this
idea of a profession argued that these were not so much objective
characteristics as manifestations of an ideology supporting self-
interest and self-aggrandisement. These alleged characteristics
nevertheless constituted benchmarks for aspiring professions seeking to meet these criteria through the efforts of their unions and
associations. The pursuit of professional status can be termed *professionalisation*. However the rhetoric of professionalisation claimed
that meeting these criteria was in the interests of clients since their
achievement would improve the quality of service by enhancing
knowledge, skill, commitment and judgement. These improvements
can be termed *professionalism*. The rhetoric conveys the view that,
in the terminology used here, professionalisation and professionalism proceeded pari passu.

The 'growth of professional society' (Perkin, 1959) reached its
highest point in the 1960s. This was true of teaching which had
achieved a high degree of autonomy from the state, had maximised
practitioner autonomy, had become an all-graduate profession and
was building a body of theory and research. To the political left
criticisms of the professions were added the criticisms of the New
Right, for whom the professions constituted vested interests which
were a constraint on the market for services. Thus began a movement
termed, depending on theoretical perspective, *de-professionalisation*
or *proletarianisation*. The essence of the political response was to
deter professionalisation and to enhance professionalism through a
variety of procedures rendering professionals much more accountable to immediate clients and to the state as client. This marked the
new professionalism.

It entailed a set of policies whose implicit purpose was to change the
culture of the professions. We can identify some of the cultural
themes which emerged:

*   *client-orientation* – this was a theme in the rhetoric of profes-
    sionalisation but legislation and accountability procedures have
    ensured the actuality that clients' needs are central to practice

- *standards* – the new professionalism entails working towards pre-determined standards rather than, as in the older concept of profession, exercising judgement with errors or misconduct subject to the sanctions of professionals

- *efficiency* – this cultural shift is signalled by a semantic shift which de-couples professional as noun and, particularly, as adjective from the honorific term profession. 'Professional' connotes a no-nonsense, practical, efficient, detached delivery of a service. One does not have to be a member of an elite profession to be professional

- *collaboration* – the older conception of the autonomous, individualistic practitioner is becoming replaced by a more collaborative approach to professional practice – and to management

- *skill* – new professionals will have acquired specific skills during the course of initial training and through subsequent in-service training. The older nexus of knowledge-skill, or of theory-practice, is now being disaggregated with a growing emphasis placed on assessable skills.

It is noteworthy that a congruence between professionalism and managerialism is implicit in a delineation of the new professionalism by two influential contributors to new conceptions of educational management (Caldwell and Spinks, 1998) who include in their list of characteristics such elements as:

Working within frameworks established for the profession; incentives, recognition and reward schemes will be developed at the school level that are consistent with the needs of the workplace ...

Schools will advocate, support and participate in programmes of unions and professional associations that are consistent with the new professionalism in education.

Staff will seek recognition of their work that meets or exceeds standards of professional practice...

There is little doubt that many of the practices condoned in the culture of the old professionalism are now seen to be indefensible – a response reinforced by recent cases of medical malpractice, and criminality, which remained undetected for many years. There is also little doubt that the cultural change brought about within the reform movement in education leaves little room for the 'unprofessional' teacher. On the other hand, increasing managerialism has undoubtedly led to the early retirement of heads and teachers who were judged to have been effective within the older culture.

Schools as unified cultures

The school is the unit of accountability. It is the school on which OFSTED reports. It is the school that is listed in league tables. It is the school which is put into 'special measures' to bring its educational performance up to the minimum standard as determined by inspectors. Recent policy has been based on the assumption that schools can become more effective to the degree that they strengthen their organisational cultures. In this section we explore the idea of school culture.

There has been an interest in this topic at least since Waller's (1932) classic which described 'the separate culture of the school'. Waller portrayed the school as having two major subcultures, that of teachers and that of pupils, which he saw in endemic conflict. Most early studies of school culture focused on the characteristics of the pupils forming the catchment of the school, the groups which they formed in school, and the activities of those groups as constituting the school culture. The view developed that it was the social background, abilities and interests of pupils which overwhelmingly determined the culture of schools and therefore that 'schools make no difference', meaning that the 'output' of schools on a variety of indicators could be predicted from the 'input', the characteristics of pupils. This view was challenged by the pioneering work of Rutter *et al* (1979) which showed that where the nature of a school's catchment was held constant, variations in their 'output' on a variety of indicators varied according to what was termed 'ethos'. This ethos, or culture, centred on the relationship between teachers and pupils, the expectations regarding work and behaviour which underpinned these relationships and the symbolisation of these expectations. This culture was a property of an individual school. Rutter's study did not explore the relationship between this culture and the management structure of the school or the leadership styles of the headteacher.

With the cultural turn in educational management greater interest was taken in the role of management in creating a school culture and the 'school effectiveness' tradition of research attributed a key role to school leadership.

Within a school there are many subcultures. No attempt to map them is made here (see Firestone and Louis 1999 for probably the best current review of school culture). But if we broadly distinguish between the management subculture, the subculture of teachers, and the pupil subculture, we can see that the reform movement is underpinned by an assumption that school leaders can create a common culture for their school. The culture of management will incorporate the culture of teachers, via the new professionalism, and the pupil culture through its acceptance of the value of individual academic achievement as symbolised by academic credentials.

Contemporary organisation theorists generally identify three major 'frames' for understanding the fundamental characteristics of organisational cultures: the *integrationist*, the *differentiationist* and the *fragmented* (see Martin and Frost, 1996).

The *integrationist* frame is focused on the features of an organisational culture which gives it a shared quality, its coherence and its 'strength' ('strong' cultures are always assumed to be beneficent cultures, although this may not always be true). It is the integrationist frame that is the organisational theory correlate of the management theory of 'values engineering'. Dissent, anomaly and ambiguity are viewed as forms of aberration rather than as endemic to organisations and are seen as being amenable to being 'managed away'.

The *differentiation* perspective conceptualises organisations as sites of the conflicts which characterise the wider society. Organisational culture is 'a nexus where environmental influences intersect creating nested, overlapping sets of subcultures with a permeable organisational boundary' (Martin and Frost op cit: p 604). The differentiation frame includes a variety of approaches but an important element focuses on the symbolic significance of such structural aspects as hierarchy, procedures and task allocation. A related element focuses on the cross-cutting cultures of gender and ethnicity. The differentiation frame is orientated not towards management but towards policy issues and macropolitics.

The *fragmentation* frame is outlined thus: 'the relationships among the manifestations of culture are neither clearly consistent nor clearly inconsistent; instead, the relationships are complex, containing elements of contradiction and confusion ...consensus is not organisation-wide nor is it specific to a given subculture. Instead consensus is transient and issue-specific...' (Martin and Frost op cit: p609).

By far the most interesting empirical data on contemporary school cultures come not from organisational studies but from studies which have focused upon a substantive issue, particularly teachers' responses to the policies generated within the reform movement. Of these the work of Helsby (1999) and Osborn *et al* (2000) is particularly significant. A broad and necessarily oversimplified interpretation of the results of these studies suggests that they conform to the *fragmentation* frame – which, because the metaphor of *fragmentation* is not wholly appropriate, we would prefer to term the *ambiguity* frame. (Note here the telling metaphor of the school as a 'mobile' as used by Nias *et al* (1989) in their study of primary school cultures.) On the evidence of these and other studies, there is no doubt that the culture of managerialism has been influential but appears not to have achieved hegemony. Nor is there evidence of concerted resistance, though there is some of unobtrusive subversion (Wallace, 1998). Osborn *et al* (op cit.) report a range of responses including *compliance, incorporation, creative mediation, retreatism* and *resistance* (see also Pollard *et al.,* 1994). Strategic compliance might be expected since careers are entailed in the acceptance of aspects of managerialism. Some teachers seem positive about some recent policies. However the overall pattern is of ambiguity marked by variable uncertainty, dilemmas and confusion.

Of the many ambiguities revealed in the work of Helsby and of Osborn *et al*, just two can be noted. One is the ambiguity inherent in the role of the headteacher, exemplified by the fact that Osborn and her colleagues report that the great majority of headteachers regard themselves as 'democratic' but the proportion of headteachers who report themselves as 'taking the final decision' increased considerably between 1990 and 1995. It can be argued that their positions are not incompatible but it is likely that they represent an ambiguity between authority and collegiality. Another source of ambiguity is revealed in the notion of collaboration. Teachers welcome their increased opportunities for collaboration but there is also evidence of what Little (1990) termed 'the persistence of privacy'. Teachers are resistant to collaboration in the form of 'contrived collegiality' (Hargreaves, 1994) which stems from the demands of management rather than the imperatives of teaching.

One culture or two?

We finally return to the question posed in the title of this chapter. Our answer is: one culture. Not an integrated managerial culture. Nor a conflicted political culture. But a culture of which one of the central characteristics is ambiguity. Uncertainty is a characteristic of professional work. Although much of the daily work of professionals is routine it is also characterised by situations of uncertainty in which judgements have to be made. Although the professional claim to autonomy has been criticised as a strategy to avoid accountability, the case for a degree of professional autonomy remains valid. There are limits to the extent to which professional work can be controlled either through management procedures or within the shared values of managerialist culture.

The reform movement has attempted to reduce ambiguity in schools by tightening structures and strengthening cultures. Given the prevalence of autonomy in schools in the 1960s and 1970s, there was a case for greater accountability. However, because of the diffuse and diverse nature of educational goals and the inherent difficulty in demonstrating the determinants of the outcomes of schooling – unless goals and outcomes are prescribed to a degree which would be acceptable neither to parents nor teachers – ambiguity will remain endemic in schools (Berlak and Berlak, 1981; Ogawa et al., 1999). This suggests that there are limits to the culture of managerialism in relation to its absorption of the culture of teaching.

The 'heroic' leadership which the cultural turn in managerialism presents is limited and contingent. Many of the companies which were presented as highly successful in the 1980s have been seen as becoming less successful, to say the least, now. And many of the heroic leaders who the literature portrayed have been displaced. We have no doubts that there have been highly successful educational leaders who have 'turned schools round' but by and large cultures will remain fragmentary, leadership transactional and management pragmatic. This is the nature of professional work. To push an integrationist model too hard is likely to reduce teacher satisfaction and lead to 'exit' (Hirschman, 1970) or non-entry.

References

Berlak, A. and Berlak, H. (1981) *The Dilemmas of Schooling*. London: Methuen

Broadfoot, P., Osborn, M., Gilly, M., and Bucher, A. (1993) *Perceptions of Teaching: Primary Schools in England and France*. London: Cassell

Burns, J. (1978) *Leadership*. New York: Harper and Row

Caldwell, B. J. and Spinks, J. M. (1992) *Leading the Self-Managing School*. London: Falmer Press

Caldwell, B. J. and Spinks, J. M. (1998) *Beyond the Self-Managing School*. London: Falmer Press

Deal, T. E. and Kennedy, A. A. (1982) *Corporate Cultures: the Rites and Rituals of Corporate Life*. Reading, M.A.: Addison-Wesley

Department Of Education and Science (1978) *Primary Education in England*. London: HMSO

Firestone, W. A. and Louis, K. S. (1999) Schools as cultures, in: Murphy, J. and Louis, K. S. (eds) *Handbook of Research on Educational Administration* (2nd ed.) San Francisco: Jossey Bass, p297-322

Grace, G. (1987) Teachers and the State in Britain: a changing relation, in: Lawn, M. and Grace, G. (eds) *Teachers: the Culture and Politics of Work*. London: Falmer, p193-228

Halpin, A. (1966) *Theory and Research in Educational Administration*. New York: Macmillan

Hargreaves, A. (1994) *Changing Teachers, Changing Times*. London: Cassell

Helsby, G. (1999) *Changing Teachers' Work*. Buckingham: Open University Press

Hirschman, A. (1970) *Exit, Voice and Loyalty*. Cambridge, M.A.: Harvard University Press

Hoyle, E. And John, P. (1998) Teacher education: the prime suspect, *Oxford Review of Education* 24 (1), p69-82

Lawn, M. (1987) *Servants of the State: The Contested Control of Teaching*. London: Falmer Press

Little, J. W. (1990) The persistence of privacy: autonomy and initiative in teachers' professional relations, *Teachers' College Record* 91 (4), p509-536

Lortie, D. (1975) *Schoolteacher: a Sociological Study*. Chicago: Chicago University Press

Manzer, R. A. (1970) *Teachers and Politics*. Manchester: Manchester University Press

Martin, J. and Frost, P. (1996) The organisational culture war games: a struggle for intellectual dominance, in: Clegg, S. R., Handy, C. and Nord, W. (eds) *Handbook of Organisational Studies.* Sage: London, 598-621

Nias, J. (1987) *Primary Teachers Talking.* London: Routledge

Nias, J., Southworth, G. and Yeomans, R. (1989) *Staff Relationships in a Primary School.* London: Cassell

Northouse, P. (1997) *Leadership: Theory and Practice.* London: Sage

Ogawa, R. T., Crowson, R. L. And Goldring, E. B. (1999) Enduring dilemmas of school organisation, in: Murphy, J. and Louis, K. S. (eds) *Handbook of Research on Educational Administration* (2nd ed.) San Franciso: Jossey Bass, 277-293

Osborn, M., Mcness, E. and Broadfoot, P. with Pollard, A. and Triggs, P. (2000) *What Teachers Do: Changing Policy and Practice in Primary Education.* London: Continuum

Ouchi, W. (1981) *Theory Z.* Reading, M.A.: Addison-Wesley

Ozga, J. and Lawn, M. (1981) *Teachers, Professionalism and Class.* London: Falmer Press

Perkin, H. (1959) *The Rise of Professional Society.* London: Routledge

Peters, T. J. And Waterman, R. H. (1982) *In Search of Excellence.* New York: Harper and Row

Pollard, A., Broadfoot, P., Croll, P., Osborn, M. And Abbott, D. (1994) *Changing English Primary Schools? The Impact of the Education Reform Act at Key Stage One.* London: Cassell

Rutter, M., Maugham, B., Mortimore, P. And Ouston, J. With Smith, A. (1979) *Fifteen Thousand Hours: Secondary Schools and their Effect on Children.* London: Paul Chapman

Schein, E. (1985) *Organisational Culture and Leadership: a Dynamic View.* San Francisco: Jossey Bass

Wallace, M. (1986) The rise of scale posts as a management hierarchy in schools, *Educational Management and Administration* 14 (3), p203-212

Wallace, M. (1998) A counter-policy to subvert education reform? Collaboration among schools and colleges in a competitive climate, *British Educational Research Journal* 24 (2), p195-215

Wallace, M. and Huckman, L. (1999) *Senior Management Teams in Primary Schools: The Quest for Synergy.* London: Routledge

Waller, W. (1932) *The Sociology of Teaching.* New York: Wiley

7

Crossing an ethical divide: the construction of professional ethics for counsellors and educators

Tim Bond

What is good, is something that comes through innovation. The good does not exist, like that, in an atemporal sky, with people who would be like the Astrologers of the Good, whose job is to determine what is the favourable nature of the stars. The good is defined by us, it is practised, it is invented. And this is a collective work. (Foucault, 1988)

The notion that ethics are not derived from God, or divined by Reason but are the product of social collaboration is a relatively recent one in western thought. If we accept the validity of exploring this line of thinking, however provisionally; there is much to be learned from how networks of people approach the task of constructing their collective ethic and the interaction between different approaches to ethics. This chapter examines the way that two professions have constructed their officially sanctioned ethical discourses in significantly different ways and the implications of this for the people who live and work across that professional interface.

This study is ultimately concerned with a wider social and cultural question. How can professions meet the challenge of their implied claim to 'a disposition to act morally' (Little, 2000:7) in a cultural context where there is no agreement about the meaning of morality and different constructions of morality exist alongside each other? It will be argued that the challenge faced by professionals of all types is not that they work in an anarchic world of moral relativism and

amorality, but that they are besieged by and contribute to the generation of morally laden argument. Professionals cannot step aside or
ignore this without debasing what is usually both a personal and
occupational commitment to being moral. When approached from
this perspective, professional ethics provide intriguing examples of
how people attempt to navigate the late modern, or post-modern,
challenges of moral pluralism in contemporary society.

The two professional groups considered in this study are counsellors
and educators. I have chosen these because the introduction of counselling into education in the 1960s was sudden and controversial. Its
closest rival in terms of suddenness was the school medical service
in 1907 (Daws, 1976: 3). Teachers and lecturers in the mid-1960s
were not generally committed to adopting counselling as a potential
solution to problems within their own institutions. The motivation
for introducing counselling came largely from outside education as
a response to a period of major cultural changes in post war Britain.
Young people in particular were challenging a culture of conformity
and duty that had been reinforced by the way the country mobilised
to meet the challenges of two periods of major military conflict. A
new youth culture was emerging that was more questioning of social
norms and valued respect for and celebration of individual difference. This represented a major challenge to the prevailing
approaches to organisation and discipline in the school. Most importantly, the person-centred thinking that characterised most counselling in Britain of that period (Rogers, 1951, Rogers, 1942)
resonated with innovative approaches to teaching and learning that
questioned existing assumptions about the balance of power between
learner and teacher. These student-centred approaches encouraged
facilitative rather than directive styles of teaching and learning
(Rogers, 1969). Counselling also imported into education awareness
of mental health and emotion. This interest in mental health and
emotional well-being may explain why counsellors have tended to
model their approach to professional ethics on medicine rather than
education. In this respect counselling challenged the prevailing
ethos and culture of education.

Signs of cultural and ethical discontinuity are still evident in the
contemporary life of educators and counsellors. I start my explora-

tion of the nature of these discontinuities by comparing and analysing documents published by bodies that claim responsibility for the construction of professional ethics for substantial proportions of educators and counsellors. This is followed by reflections on the lived experience of those who are currently working in both roles and are therefore well placed to comment on their sense of the ethical culture of each role. The picture that emerged is intriguing. It raises significant questions about the relationship between the collective ethical discourse and the sense of moral purpose of groups and individuals that combine to form that profession. In particular, it raises questions about the way that the language and terminology used to construct an ethical discourse privileges or excludes aspects of professional ethics that are significant considerations for practitioners.

Comparison of written sources of professional ethics

This section examines two documentary sources. These are examples of the type of discourse favoured by the professional bodies that claim significant responsibility for developing and focusing the ethical dimension of the work undertaken by counsellors and educators. I use the terms 'moral' and 'ethical' in closely related but different ways. Moral is the generic term for all types of moral commitment and includes cultural norms and taken for granted assumptions about what is good or bad, that are often closely associated with personal background and life stories. Morals in this sense permeate social life. In contrast, the term ethics is reserved for moral commitments that are the outcome of reflection about what is good or bad and have either been reaffirmed or reconstructed as a discourse to convey the moral commitments of a profession, or subgroup within a profession. It is the discourse by which a profession chooses to communicate its sense of moral commitment to society or particular audiences within society. This degree of deliberation and active involvement in the construction of the discourse adds to the significance of what emerges from the comparisons that follow. For the purpose of comparison I have chosen documents that are contemporaneous, intended to be widely applicable to the profession concerned, and that provide an overview of the applicable ethics. In order to increase the comparative possibilities I have selected passages about the same topic concerning respect for individual privacy and have selected sufficient text to convey the perspective from which this issue is approached.

The first document is the 'Code of ethics and practice for counsellors' issued by the British Association for Counselling (since September 2000 BAC, the British Association for Counselling and Psychotherapy (BACP)). This Code is currently binding on the 20,000 members of this Association, of whom a significant number will have some role in one or more levels of education from pre-school to adult education. The 'Code of ethics and practice' is divided into two parts. The 'Code of ethics' states:

Counsellors offer the highest possible levels of confidentiality in order to respect the client's privacy and create the trust necessary for counselling.

The 'Code of practice' elaborates:

B.3.1 Confidentiality is a means of providing the client with safety and privacy and thus protects client autonomy. For this reason any limitation on the degree of confidentiality is likely to diminish the effectiveness of counselling.

B.3.2 The counselling contract will include an agreement about the level and limits of confidentiality offered. The agreement can be reviewed and changed by negotiation between the counsellor and client. Agreements about confidentiality continue after the client's death unless there are overriding legal or ethical considerations.

... [The obligation to inform the client about limitations to confidentiality is elaborated in the next two sections]

B.3.4 Exceptional circumstances

B.3.4.1 Exceptional circumstances may arise which give the counsellor good grounds for believing that serious harm may occur to the client or to other people. In such circumstances the client's consent to a change in the agreement about confidentiality should be sought whenever possible unless there is also good grounds for believing that the client is no longer willing or able to responsibility for his/her actions.

... [Detailed instructions on how to respond in these circumstances are provided.]

B.3.4.3 Counsellors hold different views about the grounds for breaking confidentiality, such as potential self-harm, suicide, and harm to others. Counsellors must consider their own views, as they will affect their practice and communicate them to clients and significant others e. g. supervisor, agency. (BAC, 1997)

The second text stands in sharp contrast to the first. So far as I can tell there are no codes currently in force for educators working on their professional front line. (A revised code for the educators of teachers (UCET, 1997) and a draft code issued by the General Teaching Council for England (GTC, 2000) will be considered later.) In the absence of comparable codes I have selected a document that carries considerable professional authority and has been written to set out the moral responsibilities of the majority of educators. The National Forum for Values in Education and the Community produced their statement of values in May 1997, after widespread consultation. Condensed versions of this 'Statement of values' are included in documents setting out the National Curriculum issued by the Department of Education and Employment. The full version is available on the National Curriculum web pages and in the Appendices of many of its publications. The document is about one third of the length and is correspondingly less detailed than the code for counsellors. The statement is divided into four sections on self, relationships, society and the environment. Below is the section on 'Relationships' in full.

We value others for themselves, not only for what they have or what they can do for us. We value relationships as fundamental to the development and fulfilment of ourselves and others, and to the good of the community.

On the basis of these values, we should:

• respect others, including children
• care for others and exercise goodwill in our dealings with them
• show others they are valued
• earn loyalty, trust and confidence
• work co-operatively with others
• respect the privacy and property of others
• resolve disputes peacefully.

(National Forum for Values in Education, 1997)

These two statements of ethical commitment are strikingly different in character. The code for counsellors is authoritative, prescriptive and narrow in its focus on responsibilities to the client, with any wider social responsibilities introduced as limitations or exceptions to this focus. Confidentiality is of primary ethical concern. In contrast, the statement of values for teachers is mainly aspirational, exhortatory, and wide in its vision of social responsibility of which respect for privacy is an issue on a level with many others.

The language used in expressing the respective ethical statements is significantly different in terminology. The codes for counsellors are expressed in terms of principles, which are action-orientated statements of moral disposition that can be readily used for ethical justification. The responsibilities concerning confidentiality are based on a principle of the client's right to having his or her autonomy respected. This is characteristic of much of the rest of the code, in which a systematic setting out of the application of the principle of respect for client autonomy is dominant. The statement for teachers is set out in terms of values which present ethical disposition in more general and abstract terms that convey a commitment to a particular ethos. This way of expressing ethical commitment focuses attention away from the working out of tensions between different dispositions and how these should be expressed in behavioural terms in favour of conveying a vision of the ethical aims as social outcomes. In one, the practitioner is foregrounded as the ethical agent responsible for implementing the ethical principles. In the other, the practitioner recedes into being one of a profession that views itself as part of a wider social commitment to moral aims that ought to be shared by the whole of society in pursuit of social good.

One of the characteristics of these examples of ethical statements is that both convey a strong sense of ethical uniformity across the profession to which the ethics apply. Even if the published ethic is universally supported, which need not be so, I would expect to find that practitioners would hold a variety of views on their application For this reason I have discussed the ethical culture of teaching and counselling with practitioners who have experience of both roles. I anticipated that these discussions might confound the suggestion of ethical uniformity within each profession and hoped that the differences that emerged would produce a richer sense of the way ethics are experienced and constructed in routine practice.

Ethical diversity at the interface between counselling and education

I have been greatly helped in the preparation of this section by discussions with eight colleagues involved in different aspects of teaching or researching about counselling and learning at the University of Bristol (see acknowledgement below). By different routes, we have all arrived at a point in our work where we have experience as both educators and counsellors and work across the interface of these professions. I particularly wanted people who stand in both worlds and who are well respected in both as competent and committed practitioners. Between us we encompass the full range from primary to adult education in terms of teaching experience and have provided counselling in primary and secondary schools, colleges of further and higher education, and universities. Some of us have held management positions, for example as Deputy Head of a comprehensive, a HMI or managers of large professional training programmes in counselling. We are all in our forties or older and therefore some of us have direct experience of counselling being introduced into education for the first time in the late 1960s and 1970s or have been responsible for pioneering new services. One of us specialises in the application of counselling skills in personal, social and health education rather than the delivery of counselling services directly. I have drawn upon our collective experience and opinions as a creative force in the writing in the constructivist and narrative traditions of research design rather than conducting an empirical study. We mostly agree that there are differences in ethical practice that correspond to differences in role. We are in less agreement about what these differences in practice signify. These areas of disagreement provided leverage in our discussions for prising open our assumptions about professional culture and ethics.

Our discussions have gone far beyond issues of privacy and confidentiality but it is these issues that proved particularly illuminating in trying to understand the ethical divergences between us and in particular the different degrees of discontinuity we experienced between the professional ethics of counselling and teaching. One of the things that all nine of us share in common is a professional history that includes a commitment to humanistic approaches to counselling and learning informed to varying degrees by person-centred thinking. In this context 'humanistic' implies an emphasis on human potential rather than psychological determinism of classical psychodynamic theory and practice. This shared history in the approach to counselling and learning brought into focus differences between us. I have created two composite depictions of the two positions with regard to counselling ethics within the person-centred tradition. Creating composites from different discussions and sources assisted in protecting the confidentiality of the individuals concerned and the identity of different educational institutions. Presenting them here in the first person is intended to convey the sense of personal commitment rather than conformity to some external authority that the section comparing the ethical statements of professional bodies might have suggested. The two positions are distinguished by whether they take an individualised or communitarian approach to their interpretation of person-centredness.

The individualised approach is expressed in the following way:

> *I see my major challenge in delivering counselling in college as building sufficient trust in me as a professional person, that no-one considers it necessary to try and intrude on my client's privacy or respect for confidentiality. Privacy and confidentiality are essential rights for my clients and the foundation of the trust that I am able to create if I am to work effectively with people who are feeling vulnerable to the negative opinions of others. I see it as of fundamental importance that the counselling service is protected by clear boundaries, is discrete and clearly separated from any disciplinary or administrative functions.*

The alternative communitarian view is presented in very different terms:

> *My vision of any counselling service is that it should be clearly visible and part of a lively student support services. My own service was located in a central position close to the administration. This gave our clients the anonymity of the crowd and avoided conveying inappropriate messages by having them*

sneak into a concealed service on the margins of the campus or tucked into a dark corner. Counselling is not about mental or emotional illness but about living more healthily in many different aspects of life, but especially emotionally. I consider that emotions are an important part of education and that counselling has an important contribution to make to the emotional health of an educational institution in many different ways.

The difference in the physical objects and environments often provide the clue to which approach is dominant. One approach encourages the development of a service on the margins of the institution, tucked away in order to protect privacy and professional boundaries. This might not only be typical of an individualised approach to person-centred counselling, but would be shared by other individualised approaches to counselling and therapy. This is the type of service that is likely to operate out of 'a commodious broom cupboard' (Diggle and Poulter, 1974: 7). There is typically greater concern over negotiating a perceived discontinuity between counselling and educational ethics from this position. This discontinuity is barely sensed in the communitarian approach that has higher physical visibility and makes a more wide-ranging contribution to the life of the institution.

The combined experience of all the contributors to the discussions suggested a much more diverse range of cultural compatibility or discontinuity according to the moral dispositions of different educational institutions. These differences would typically be presented in terms of the aims and values of the institution concerning its contribution to society. The type of institution committed to cultural transmission might have a strong religious culture in contemporary Britain, for example Evangelical Christian, Roman Catholic or Muslim, and view the relationship between morality and education as passing the values of one generation to the next. The moral purpose is viewed as independent of the learner. In contrast, the person-centred approach to learning places the learner as the focus of the moral purpose of education although, as in counselling, there are differences between whether the learner is conceived exclusively in individualised terms or as a contributor to an emotionally aware and democratic community. The latter position potentially overlaps with a commitment to preparing learners for citizenship, which has become an increasingly important part of the curriculum for all schools and colleges and may become the primary goal of some. The fourth moral purpose that may guide some educational institutions views education as committed to advancing national economic competitiveness by enhancing the human resources available for work and re-educating the workforce to adapt to changing trade patterns in the global market. Within any institution there may be differences between sections and between groups or individuals over the chosen moral purpose(s).

By plotting the ethical dispositions of different counselling services against the corresponding ethical dispositions in education, it is possible to identify services that have achieved high levels of shared moral purpose with their institution. Others are positioned as counter-cultural or serving different ethical dispositions. The ranges of potential positions are represented in table 1.

An appreciation of the potential compatibility or incompatibility represented in this table could have significant implications for understanding why some counselling services in education thrive and benefit from the shared sense of ethical commitment with the institution and why others remain marginal and fail to thrive. There are obvious implications for the professional induction of both educators and counsellors. For example, there may be considerable resonance between a communitarian approach to person-centred ethics in counselling and education, with little or no dissonance in an institution dedicated to promoting citizenship. The same ethical disposition may result in much greater dissonance in approaches intended to transmit culture or promote national economic competitiveness, depending on how these are interpreted. The individualised approach to person-centredness is always vulnerable to cultural isolation that may be less problematic in the comparable educational ethos but which could contribute to chasms of misunderstanding in any other ethos. A professional code written solely in terms of a single ethical principle acts as an ethical straightjacket that conceals significant ethical diversity within the profession.

This analysis is of wider significance in professional ethics. It provides one of the clearest examples I am aware of concerning the

Table 1: Educational values and variations in roles

Educational values	Role of pupil/student	Role of teacher	Role of counsellor
Cultural transmission	Passive recipient, one of many to be graded	Guardian, transmitter of appropriate values	Authoritative guide, facilitator of adaptive skills
Person centred	Active, involved, unique constructor of own reality	Facilitator, constructor of beneficial situations for child	Personal facilitator of client's own resourcefulness. *Individualised*: Respect for client privacy and confidentiality emphasised. Counsellor keeps low profile outside working with clients. *Communitarian*: Views counselling as integral to healthy community living. Counsellor active participant in institution
Preparation for citizenship	Active, critical identity gained through interaction in social groups, each seen as contributor	Facilitator, constructor, selector of relevant materials/problems/issues; critical guide, guardian of values from past	Provider of personal support and encouragement for person attempting social change and therapy for the consequences of social hurt
National economic advancement	Someone to be trained into economic machine. Initiative and activity encouraged only as far as it fits with national economic goals or economic destination	Trainer, constructor, transmitter, low-order member of hierarchy	Tutor/facilitator in problem management and social skills training. Vocational guidance prominent

potential range of ethical positions within a single institution. Few institutions exclusively pursue one ethical aim but work towards combinations of different aims in various permutations. The juxtaposition of different values in the Statement of values, considered above, would support this approach. Discussions about ethical aims can be difficult enough where there is a shared ethical discourse. Where the discourses are constructed in significantly different ways, dialogue becomes so difficult that it can be completely frustrated. The analysis of the published ethics for counsellors and educators suggests this may be the position with regard to dialogue between these two professional roles. The absence of commensurate professional ethical discourses is potentially disabling for experienced and competent practitioners who undertake a combination of both roles and who might be thought to be better placed to bridge any ethical divide than specialists working exclusively in either role.

The relationship between ethical expression and professional culture

This chapter opened with a quotation from Michel Foucault, made late in his working life when he was approaching the challenges of constructing moral discourse from a recognition of its potential benefits and the dangers of attributing such discourse to impersonal sources. The analysis of the current state of moral and ethical discourse at the interface of counselling and education draws attention to the danger of any profession constructing its discourse without attention to the extent to which that discourse enhances dialogue within and outside the professional concerned. The apparent coherence of discourses conveyed almost exclusively as either principles or values not only incorporates any intrinsic limitations of each discourse but disables dialogue with others who have constructed their ethics on a different basis. At a time when contemporary uncertainty about the appropriate mores for society is prevalent (Tomlinson, 2000), professional ethics take on a new significance as an arena for working out moral tensions and dilemmas. When moral and applied philosophy points to the limitations of relying too heavily on any single approach to ethics (Beauchamp and Childress, 1994; Almond, 1998; Katz et al, 1999; Bond, 2000), it seems incomprehensible that any profession should choose to construct its ethics on this basis.

Developments within counselling and education suggest recognition of precisely this point. In counselling, a major revision is underway that not only widens the professional ethic beyond a single principle of autonomy to incorporate other ethical principles but also sets out parallel constructions of ethics in terms of values and personal qualities (BACP, 2001). A draft 'Professional code for teachers' issued by the General Teaching Council for Teachers for England sets out 'the beliefs, values and attitudes that underlie teacher professionalism'. The attention to attitudes represents a move towards principles in ways that can accommodate the simultaneous multiple accountability of teachers to different constituencies inside and outside their institution. An explicit emphasis on professionalism is particularly significant for a role that has in the past often been considered as a vocation. One of the characteristics of vocations, such as the priesthood, is such total compatibility between personal morals and professional ethics that there is no point to constructing a professional ethic. The sense of fulfilling the vocation is reward enough without either the status of a profession or its financial rewards (Carr, 2000, p10). The public policy of establishing teaching as a profession is in part an attempt to boost morale and to ensure improved recruitment and retention of teachers. I do not know whether there are any personal or conceptual links with the Universities Council for the Education for Teachers, but this sets out principles in general abstract terms that are then compressed into the shorthand that implies a professional value. It represents an innovatory way of combining different modes of ethical discourse.

These publications by both professions demonstrate that both are aware of the inescapable moral pluralism of contemporary society. This chapter supports the view that there is no 'good life' but only 'good lives'. The challenge of responding to the construction of professional ethics in a personal context requires the full panoply of ethical discourses within each profession adequately to inform the development of its own ethical positions and to ensure a means of communication for encounters on the dividing line between professions.

References

Almond, B. (1998) *Exploring Ethics: a traveller's tale*. Blackwells, Oxford

BAC (1997) *Code of Ethics and Practice for Counsellors*. British Association for Counselling, Rugby

BACP (2001) *Statement of fundamental Ethics for Eounselling and Psychotherapy*. British Association for Counselling and Psychotherapy, Rugby

Beauchamp, T. L. and Childress, J. F. (1994) *Principles of Biomedical Ethics*. Oxford University Press, New York

Bond, T. (2000) *Standards and Ethics for Counselling in Action*. London, Sage

Carr, D. (2000) *Professionalism and Ethics in Teaching*. Routledge, London

Daws, P. P. (1976) *Early Days: a personal review of the beginnings of counselling in English education during the decade 1964-74*. CRAC/Hobsons Press, Cambridge

Diggle, E. and Poulter, M. (1974) *Counselling, Bosworth Papers 4*. Bosworth College, Leicester

Foucault, M. (1988). Power, moral values and the intellectual: an interview with Michel Foucault, conducted by Michael Bess, 3 November 1980. *History in the present*, vol 4, Issue 1, p13

GTC (2000) *Professional Code for Teachers: draft statement of values and practice*. General Teaching Council for England, London

Katz, M. S., Noddings, N. and Strike, K. A. (Eds.) (1999) *Justice and Caring: the search for common ground in education*, Teachers College Press, New York

Little, V. (2000). A code of ethics – does it, should it, help professional practice? In *Ethical Principles for the Teaching Profession – Report of UCET working party. Occasional paper No 7* (Second edition). Vol. (Ed, Tomlinson, J.) Universities Council for the Education of Teachers, London, p7-8

National Forum for Values in Education (1997) *Statement of Values*. Department of Education and Employment and National Curriculum Authority, London

Rogers, C. R. (1942) *Counseling and Psychotherapy*. Houghton Mifflin, Boston, MA.

Rogers, C. R. (1951) *Client-centred Therapy*. Constable, London

Rogers, C. R. (1969) *Freedom to Learn*. Merrill, Columbus, Ohio

Tomlinson, J. (2000). Ethical principles underlying teaching as a profession: context and discussion. In *Ethical Principles for the Teaching Profession – Report of UCET working party. op. cit.*

Tomlinson, J. and Little, V. (2000). A code of ethical principles for the teaching profession. In *Ethical Principles for the Teaching Profession – Report of UCET working party. op. cit.*

UCET (1997) Ethical Principles for the Teaching Profession – Report of UCET Working Party. UCET occasional paper no. 7. Universities Council for the Education of Teachers, London

Acknowledgement

I am very grateful to friends and colleagues who agreed to be interviewed and to discuss the ideas contained in this chapter. They are: Ann Beynon, Carol Graham, Hazel Johns, Sylvia Tate, Jane Speedy, Anne Stokes, Marilyn Tew and Sheila Trahar.

8

The development of a profession: reframing the role of educational psychologists within the context of organisational culture

Alec Webster, Rodney Maliphant, Anthony Feiler,
Eric Hoyle and John Franey

Introduction: claims on the territory known as 'educational psychology'

This chapter starts from the premise that professional groups are shaped in their cultures and evolution by the prevailing ideologies, politics and policies of the societies and institutions of which they are a part. Claims on a professional group made by stakeholders, clients and service providers may be in conflict. How professionals themselves would prefer to work may also differ from what clients and employers request or benefit from. These tensions between competing interests create particular challenges in the initial training and continuing professional development of educational psychologists. Beginning with a review of the emergence and current context of educational psychology, the chapter explores the 'crisis of confidence' in professional expertise and asks how it is possible to construct an identity for psychologists which moves way from its traditional focus on clinical skills and into a more strategic, systemic and preventative role, capable of impacting on broader organisational contexts.

The future role and training of educational psychologists stands at a watershed and has recently been subject to close scrutiny by a government-convened Working Party (DfEE, 2000a). At the beginning of the twentieth century, in the infancy of the profession, educational psychologists adopted roles as psychometricians and clinicians, and were encouraged to do so in order to help an administration increasingly aware of the problem of identifying the nature and size of special educational needs, and how to make appropriate provision within the limited resources available. Descriptors of the currently desired professional persona are much more likely to include psychologists as champions of human rights and equal opportunity, working proactively to facilitate quality learning environments through organisational change (Leyden, 1999). Indeed, the introductory sections of the Working Party Report cited above signal the Government's vision of harnessing the energies of psychologists as 'key agents of change' in implementing its policy agenda of raising the achievement of all children, of social inclusion and parental partnership. This is in marked contrast to much professional practice up to the 1950s with the relatively few educational psychologists employed constrained to operate largely as psychometric athletes with an emphasis on 'test and run' (Maliphant, 1974).

Expectations of what educational psychologists do or should do have long been accompanied by confusion, contention and criticism, even amongst members of the profession itself (Lunt and Majors, 2000). To qualify as an educational psychologist one requires a psychology degree, teacher training and classroom experience, plus a Masters postgraduate qualification. Whilst they may be better qualified academically and have a longer training than many of their education colleagues, questions have frequently been raised about whether psychologists are properly equipped by their training, based as it is on a child-oriented curriculum, to work other than at a clinical, individually-focused level. Academically, child psychology has also not been closely allied to developments in social or organizational psychology. Some critics have argued that the difficulties teachers typically face cannot be approached by focusing only on the needs of individual children, since managing classrooms is no longer, if it ever were, a form of applied child psychology (Desforges, 1988). Confusion further arises because the social contexts in which professional psychologists operate are mostly complex, ill-formed and indeterminate, and there are no simple or ready-made protocols for the problems that arise (Webster, Hingley and Franey, 2000).

Some within the profession have surmised that despite the vision of what psychologists could offer at more strategic levels, individual casework is still the highest priority for schools and Local Education Authorities (Dowling and Leibowitz, 1994; Thomson, 1996). One LEA officer argued recently that schools would far prefer psychologists to test more children and spend time in classrooms, rather than providing consultation on wider school issues. Offering nothing which skilled teachers cannot provide, psychologists will become increasingly marginalised (Maliphant, 2000; Wood, 1998). In essence, what we have are competing claims on the territory known as 'educational psychology'. Practitioners themselves do not feel that 'fire-fighting' – responding to crisis referrals – makes any long-term difference to how teachers and schools operate, yet this is what they spend most of their time doing. Preventative work, strategic research, evidence-based practice for resourcing and intervention, are examples of how psychology services might operate as creative innovators and problem-solvers at organisational levels, but is this what society requires and are psychologists suitably trained to perform these functions?

The emergence of educational psychology and the culture of the 'clinician'

Educational psychology is a relatively young profession which does not exist outside of Western educational settings, except in Hong Kong and more recently in Singapore. The territory which it currently occupies lies somewhere between academic psychology (which is concerned to further our understanding of how living things behave, learn or interact) and a range of societal contexts (such as families, schools, Local Education Authorities). The various domains of academic psychology, particularly experimental work in child development, together with cognitive, social and occupational psychology, generate research of *potential* value in raising achievement and enhancing quality of life. It falls to applied social scientists, which is how educational psychologists see themselves, to interpret and utilise the evidence from academic research in trying to solve the problems which are current in, and specific to, the societies which employ them (Maliphant, 1997).

Historically, the emergence of school psychological services in Europe is linked with economic growth, the demand for selection and training for trades and skills, the development of compulsory education for children and the concomitant issue of how to deal with those individuals whose behavioural or curricular needs were deemed to require special or additional arrangements. An often cited landmark is the appointment of Cyril Burt in 1913 as the first psychologist in the London County Council, whose early work on testing, categorising and understanding 'delinquent' or 'defective' individuals, along with the disputed evidence he gathered on the balance of inherited versus environmental influences, has obscured other contributions. It was Burt, to take one example, who first intimated that educational psychologists might operate at a number of levels: diagnostic work with individual children; facilitating others in direct contact with children to work more effectively; or dealing with the meta-issues of administration in large organisations (Burt, 1969). Even now, the questions of whether and how educational psychologists should shift focus from traditional clinical work with individual children, families and teachers, towards a more strategic orientation, impacting on policy, resources and organisational decision-making, have yet to be resolved.

In the post-war period a stream of legislation has shaped the development of psychological services in the United Kingdom. A major consequence of the 1944 Education Act was the obligation of Local Education Authorities to provide appropriate education for children with (in the terminology of the time) 'physical handicaps', 'maladjustment' or 'educational subnormality', providing momentum for the demand for assessments by psychologists. In 1955 a National Committee reported its findings on services for maladjusted children (Underwood Report) and drew attention to the contribution to 'ascertainment' and treatment of the 140 or so educational psychologists then employed. In 1965, when the Summerfield working party was convened to survey the role and training of educational psychologists, numbers employed in England and Wales had grown to 326. The prevailing image of the professional skills and responsibilities defined by Summerfield was 'the identification, diagnosis and treatment of individual children with learning and adjustment problems' (Phillips, 1971).

Later legislation, such as the Education Act of 1981 which followed the publication of the Warnock Report, was championed at the time for broadening our view of how children's special needs should be defined, identified and met. In retrospect, the 1981 Act substantially increased the pressure on psychologists to make formal assessments of children towards 'Statements' (legal specifications of individual needs and the provision to be made to meet them) as this enabled mainstream schools to secure additional LEA funding. This in turn has resulted in a severe curtailment in the range and scope of the practice of educational psychologists, tying up their time in 'legalistic, and often adversarial, statutory procedures' (Williams and Maloney, 1998, p18).

Educational psychologists have never been entirely comfortable with the view that the 'problems' of disability, emotional and be-havioural difficulties, or disaffection can be dealt with by referral to them for assessment, diagnosis and disposal, without reference to the social contexts which generate them and give them meaning. Hence the desire to find alternative models of working which have a more positive influence on the quality of learning environments in families, classrooms and schools. In the late 1970s and 80s a number of 'reconstructing' movements challenged the quasi-medical frame-work within which children's needs were conceived and approached. Dessent (1978), as one of the key proponents of the reconstruction movement, attributed the clinical emphasis of traditional educational psychology to its historical roots and the earlier preoccupation with the detection and treatment of deviance or abnormality.

Furthermore, the emphasis on using psychometric tests (such as intelligence and personality tests) in an attempt to discover the causes of behavioural or learning difficulties had a number of un-avoidable consequences. It located problems (or, more pejoratively, *failure*) within individuals or their families, rather than within class-rooms, schools, local education authorities, government policies or societal attitudes. Adopting such a conceptual framework resulted in psychologists working towards solutions through direct contact with the individual referred case. This perception of the role sustained the expectations of teachers and administrators that psychologists were employed to 'treat' or remove unmotivated, undesirable, unwanted or simply '*different*' individuals from one part of the education system to another. Evidence to support the positive impact of psychologists working within this model was generally hard to find. Regrettably, current emphasis on assessments of all kinds and at all educational levels has reinforced this stereotype, as well as providing an expanding and stultifying bureaucracy.

The current context of educational psychology

Most of the 1800 (full-time equivalent) educational psychologists currently employed in England and Wales (DfEE, 2000b) would claim that they perform an important set of social functions as applied social scientists working in community and school settings, drawing on and contributing to bodies of research knowledge which inform practice. There is a confident assertion that psychologists know a great deal about cognitive, social and emotional development and the different patterns which these may assume according to the interactive dynamics of individuals in contrasting environments. Recently, Lunt and Majors (2000) have argued that educational psychology has achieved a degree of professional recognition and autonomy because of the perceived relevance and complexity of its knowledge base in the eyes of government and society.

The skills and competences of educational psychologists have been set out by the British Psychological Society in an effort to provide a clear account of the range and nature of the work of the profession for those outside it (BPS, 1999). In this document psychologists are described as problem-solvers who use psychological principles to establish details of situations, develop hypotheses and test them out: 'There is a continuous process of generating new knowledge and ideas in relation to individual children's learning and behaviours and also in relation to organisational issues' (*op cit*, p2). Examples are given which depict practitioners in a number of roles: working with a teacher to draw up an intervention programme to increase a pupil's self-esteem; devising strategies to manage an autistic child's poor sleep patterns; action research to reduce reading difficulties in low-achieving secondary school pupils; implementing a 'thinking skills' project for nursery-age children; appraising the 'organisational health' of urban comprehensive schools to tackle truancy; consultation to Youth Offending Teams on preventative strategies; working with carers of children in public care to increase confidence in dealing with challenging behaviour.

In each of these examples it is assumed that psychologists are knowledgeable about recent research, local and national policy guidelines, and can collaborate with clients and other professionals to find 'best practice' solutions. As sensitive and responsible professionals, psychologists work within ethical guidelines and are publicly accountable for their behaviour, judged according to 'quality standards'. Given the wide range of role demands, this BPS publication concludes with training implications for educational psychologists, recognising the urgent need for an extended and practice-based curriculum 'to ensure the future delivery of effective and high quality applied psychology services', but providing no indication of how this might be achieved or on what theoretical foundations it might be grounded.

Most educational psychologists are employed by local education authorities (LEAs) and work within the Code of Practice for the identification and assessment of children with special educational needs, as prescribed by the Department for Education and Employment (DfEE, 1994). The basic principles of the Code and its recent revisions (DfEE, 2000c) are a staged systematic approach to the gathering of information about pupils for whom there are concerns, with increasing involvement of outside agencies to create and monitor individualised learning or behaviour plans. The Code was intended to promote early intervention, parental involvement, interagency collaboration, and the development of school-based strategies for differentiating the curriculum in order to widen access for more children, including those with significant learning obstacles, to a broad and balanced learning experience.

In reality the Code has often been seen by schools in its narrowest terms as a set of hurdles to be leapt over as quickly and effortlessly as possible, in order to access additional funding for individual pupils. In some, but not all, LEAs educational psychologists are responsible for managing the statutory assessment phases of the Code when statements are prepared. Even where this gatekeeping role has been relinquished, psychologists spend a high proportion of time contributing evidence towards statutory assessments and defending actions taken by parents against decisions they are unhappy with in tribunals (Webster, Hingley and Franey, 2000).

The post-Education Reform Act era is characterised by National Curriculum Programmes of Study, assessment and testing arrangements, publication of league tables, benchmarking, Local Financial Management, OFSTED inspection and monitoring of standards. The current context of market forces, consumer choice, parental rights, centralised control, accountability measures based on performance indicators and 'value-added', has not left psychology services unscathed. The balance of activities undertaken by educational psychologists reflects the shift in priorities imposed upon schools, such that schools are wary about using their own resources to support children who have complex needs or who bring down its league table position. The push to involve psychologists at individual case level for resource-driven purposes continues unabated and remains a key pressure point for the profession (Wagner, 2000).

The government working party set up to examine the future role and training of educational psychologists in England and Wales reported its findings in what has been heralded as the 'first major study of the current work and future direction of educational psychology' since the Summerfield Report (DfEE, 2000a, b). The brief of this working party was not *apolitical* and the backdrop of the Labour government's education agenda to improve school and LEA effectiveness is openly acknowledged. The findings of the working group are prefaced by an intention to change the balance of psychologists' activities towards earlier intervention, improving services and provision, and taking 'crucial' supportive roles in initiatives such as Education Development Plans, Early Years Development and Childcare Plans, behaviour support, literacy and numeracy strategies, the new SEN Code of Practice, and policies to promote inclusion. Interestingly, the need to move psychologists away from statutory assessment is recognised, but this is ostensibly so that they can take more creative roles and '*so that their expertise is used more effectively*'. The confluence of interests here is a powerful formula for change: government urging new roles and a shift in priorities; psychologists shedding their clinical persona to become more strategically-minded, capable of operating within and having an influence upon organisational contexts.

The working party's research distils to a handful of conclusions which set the agenda for the profession into the foreseeable future. First, that psychologists' knowledge and skills are 'highly regarded' by user groups, but there is a need for greater clarity and transparency about the range of services they offer and what users can expect. Second, psychologists are 'key agents for change' but may not have the necessary skills or training to adopt broader proactive roles or to specialise in a particular area. Third, that a re-orientation to preventative problem-solving is partly in the hands of psychologists to empower other education colleagues to work more effectively and to promulgate 'where and how they can add value'. Fourth, that parents and schools require direct and regular access to psychologists, whilst early intervention and 'joined-up' planning with other agencies will in the long term offset the demand for reactive interventions. Barriers to change include conflicting expectations of psychologists, demands of time in relation to statutory work and individual referrals, and a lack of safeguards for ensuring consistency, equity and transparency in services. Overcoming these barriers provides the rationale for a radical overhaul of the necessary skills, competences and training, but also betrays how Government will seek to reform the ways in which professional practice will be managed and held to account.

The crisis of confidence in professional knowledge and training

Eraut defined professional conduct as 'wise judgement under conditions of uncertainty' (Eraut, 1994, p17). Defining what constitutes a profession and how professional behaviour may be characterised, has proved elusive. Attention has typically been drawn to the perceived features of the most powerful professions (medicine, law, engineering, architecture) which others seek to emulate (Hoyle and John, 1995; Webster and Hoyle, 2000). These ideal characteristics include the exercise of important social functions in situations which are not wholly routine, hence requiring long periods of higher education and training in order to acquire and apply a body of systematic knowledge. In order to exercise skilled judgement, practitioners also lay claim to a high degree of autonomy with relative freedom from state interference. The proper exercise of professional responsibilities is guaranteed by a set of client-oriented values, typically acquired through supervision by senior colleagues and enshrined in a code of ethics. Professional bodies steer, monitor and regulate their members and have an influential voice in the shaping of policy in their domain of activity.

These criterial attributes of knowledge, autonomy and responsibility have each been subject to criticism in relation to their validity, whose best interests they serve, and whether or not they have been instrumental in determining which professions achieve full recognition. In relation to *knowledge*, critics of professionalism have argued that much of the academic content practitioners are required to accrue through ever-increasing periods of higher education and the inflation of credentials, has had very little influence on professional practice, based as it often is on common-sense, intuition and experience. In relation to *autonomy*, critics see the relative freedom of practitioners as serving the self-interest of professionals themselves, a defence against public accountability and the challenge that clients may know better than providers how their needs should be served. In relation to *responsibility* or professional ethics, critics have taken the stance that codes of practice typically protect the interests of practitioners rather than clients, and even though professional bodies apply sanctions in cases of extreme negligence, they do very little to enhance good practice.

The crisis of confidence in relation to the professions has been expressed in a number of ways. The central issue which summarises policy towards the professions from the 1970s until today is accountability in various forms: greater degree of central control by government; increase in consumer choice and rights, for example, as defined by 'service charters'; strengthening of management structures and surveillance of professional activities (Day, 1999). In some occupations, such as teaching, there has been a movement back along the continua which mark high status professions in terms of their eliteness, scope and skill: loss of autonomy; erosion of boundaries so that people with lower qualifications take on aspects of the work which was previously restricted to the professional group; reduced influence on government policy by professional bodies; transfer of decision-making to managers.

Professional training has also been scrutinised. To become a professional in the current context, is arguably to acquire a set of skills through competence-based training which enables one to deliver, according to contract, a client-led service in compliance with accountability procedures collaboratively implemented and managerially assured (Webster and Hoyle, 2000). This hypothetical projecting forward from current trends paints what to some might seem a nightmare scenario of objectification and managerialism, the pursuit of efficiency at the expense of effectiveness (counting patients on waiting lists as opposed to appraising quality of care).

The image of competence-based training stands in stark contrast to the view that professional education must equip practitioners with the ability to deal with situations of uncertainty, uniqueness and conflict, and that 'wise judgement' is as much about developing intuition and artistry. Good professional practice is by its nature diffuse, holistic and subtle and is not fully captured by skill criteria and performance indicators, couched in contractual terms and evaluated by 'throughputs'. Schon (1987, 1996) has brought a number of metaphors to bear on professional education. He suggests that issues in real-world practice seldom present themselves as well-formed. Most problems occupy the 'swampy lowlands' characterised by mess and conflict and which defy technical solution. Professional education, however, occupies the 'high ground' of theory and technique. The irony is that high ground problems are usually relatively unimportant to the people involved while issues of greatest concern lie in the 'swamp'.

Civil engineers, for example, know technically how to build roads suited to particular sites and specifications. However, when they decide what road to build, their problem is not solvable by the application of technical knowledge of soil conditions, building materials, dimensions or surface grades. Instead they face a complex and ill-defined set of political, environmental and economic factors. In order to prepare professionals for dealing with value-conflicts, uncertainty and the lack of protocol, Schon advocates a form of professional education which inculcates patterns of reflective practice and an emphasis on the coaching of learning by doing: 'Students learn by practising the making or performing at which they seek to become adept, and they are helped to do so by senior practitioners who... initiate them in to the traditions of practice' (Schon, 1986, pp16-17). Out of the dialogues between coach and novice (referred to as the 'reflective practicum'), new professionals acquire the skills to function in situations where there are no right answers or standard procedures.

Proposals are currently under consideration to restructure professional training in educational psychology from one to three years leading to a doctoral qualification. Whilst this issue has been debated for a number of years and the exact content of a three-year curriculum has yet to be finalised, the DfEE Working Party has added momentum to the push for reform. As we have seen, competing claims have also been made on the professional curriculum, its content and structure. Undoubtedly, there are areas of poor fit between existing training and the demands of practice. New role demands require a restructuring of professional qualifying routes. But in realigning priorities for psychologists, the DfEE also has to steer a precarious course. Enhancing job training, status and scope must be balanced against the downside of increased autonomy, lowered accessibility to clients and reduced compliance to work on political agendas with which the profession is out of sympathy.

The future landscape of educational psychology

Despite the plethora of reforms the education system has been subjected to in recent years, it is still unclear what kind of system the DfEE is aiming for. An emphasis on consumerism may take us a step forward, but this is not synonymous with clear leadership or vision. Despite this policy vacuum, increasing central involvement in the role and training of educational psychologists will inevitably lead to psychology services being more closely tied to national agendas and priorities such as the Programme of Action for meeting special educational needs (DfEE, 1998), inclusion, raising achievement and school improvement, Excellence in Cities, literacy and numeracy strategies, behaviour support plans, together with initiatives to promote the effectiveness of LEAs through early years and childcare provision, support for failing schools, and Education Development Plans. The problem here is how to sustain a professional culture which has values, norms and beliefs shared by psychologists with very different roles, for example, as creative innovators and organisational strategists (what we might term 'complexity professionals') and those practitioners who will seek to preserve traditional ways of working as clinicians and psychometricians (what we might term 'constrained professionals').

If psychology services are retained within the public sector, we can expect them to be subjected to accountability measures directly monitored by OFSTED-style inspection. Terms such as 'best-value', 'benchmarking' and 'outsourcing' will be part of the professional lexicon. As educational psychologists take longer to train and their skills become more specialised, the market place will determine who carries out certain tasks. It will be cost effective for other education staff to undertake some of the work currently done by fully-qualified educational psychologists. Specialist teachers, for example, now provide advice to examining boards on special arrangements for candidates and a wider range of tasks may be similarly taken over by non-psychologists, such as 'consultants' in autism, behaviour, literacy. Psychology services are likely to become structured like the 'firms' which characterise legal or medical practices, with the majority of tasks, such as routine individual casework, statutory reporting and reviews, carried out by trainees, assistants, newly- or part-qualified staff under supervision. The problem here will be how to handle the professional boundary with teachers, social workers and other colleagues, and where conflicts of culture and role ambiguities may be exacerbated by the changing professional cultures of psychologists.

It is inevitable that there will be moves to define the core competences expected of educational psychologists, school entitlements and minimum quality standards from services, together with performance indicators for service efficiency. It is unlikely that there will be a sudden escalation in the amount of funding available to train educational psychologists and, in order to maintain supply, a three-year mandatory qualification must depend on widening access to training, for example, by dropping the requirement for teacher training, and accrediting prior experience in related fields such as speech therapy or social work. There must also be much greater collaboration between LEA services and higher education, with closer integration of fieldwork and training. Supervision of part-qualified and new entrants will have to be taken far more seriously, since the shaping of 'people resources' within the profession will be increasingly refined, extended and shared. As psychologists become subject to greater management and accountability measures, such as regular outside surveillance of their professional behaviour and performance, ethical codes will be strengthened to protect both clients and professionals. Chartership of professional bodies and central registration will be axiomatic for licensed practice. The problem here is how to sustain a professional culture of educational psychology without – particularly senior staff – drifting into a culture of managerialism, or management to excess.

An extended professional training will be ineffective in bridging the gap between theory and practice if it simply requires more of the same. In this chapter we have posed the central question in terms of how it might be possible to reshape a professional persona which is traditionally focused on clinical skills, into a preventative, systemic, research-orientated role. In this model of professionality, knowing how to intervene in authentic organizational contexts, such as the family, school or workplace, is at least as important as intervention at individual case level.

For example, a secondary school refers a series of children to a Psychology Service because they present challenging behaviour in science lessons. A traditional starting point would be for a psychologist to spend time with the individual pupils, drawing up profiles of ability and achievement, and discussing appropriate teaching and learning styles with the teachers concerned. The school's expectation is that the problem lies with the pupil, requiring an outside 'expert' to fix it, or to give advice on how the teacher might individualise teaching. Should improvement fail to materialise, this is typically ascribed to the pupil's inability to change, leading the school to argue the case for enhanced resourcing in the form of additional classroom assistance, or for removing the pupil elsewhere. Approached contextually, a psychologist would start by affirming a role in which ownership of the problem remained with the teachers and any intervention would be to enable staff to work more effectively on their concerns. The precise nature of the problem would also be defined in relation to the learning context, perhaps by direct observation of how lessons are conducted and what prompts the problematic behaviour. This form of consultative approach inevitably highlights issues such as school policy on discipline, how staff are encouraged to develop skills in pupil management or differentiation, and the flexibility of systems to adapt to the learning needs of individuals. The culture clash here resides in the fact that schools continue to focus on individual pupil 'misfits', when solutions must be found within the curriculum and organisation of the school, while psychologists traditionally seek to provide answers from the perspective of individual learning, when any significant impact must involve the learning context and their managers.

Arguably, the most compelling theoretical basis for professional training is one which draws upon socio-cultural psychology in order to foreground elements in social settings which determine how well adults and children develop and acquire competence, and how they may be facilitated. We can illustrate this using some examples from our own research. Social contructivists argue that individual thinking, learning or professional practice is bound to specific contexts in ways that are reflected in forms of professional dialogue or other communication means. In order to study the learning of literacy, for example, it is important to examine the social and linguistic practices which organise them in the classroom. A teacher in a primary school introducing topics in history is developing children's ability to organise information, sift and prioritise data, reflect on the status of evidence, speculate and draw conclusions, through the medium of literacy. The literacy of design technology serves a different purpose to the literacy of science or geography and is thus represented differently in the procedures for reading texts, for recording and in the kind of dialogues which arise in the classroom.

Interestingly, whenever literacy becomes a concern, such as might be discussed with a psychologist in school, the teacher inevitably formulates the problem in terms of the pupils' competence. Our study of literacy across the curriculum of an urban school cluster revealed a general 'teacher perspective' on reading and writing as the acquisition of a hierarchy of mechanical skills to be mastered outside of most subject areas of the curriculum, and hence *someone else's* responsibility. We sought to capture how literacy is harnessed, within each school subject domain, to the practices of listening, categorising, thinking and concept-formation, information-seeking, problem-solving, recording, analysing, communicating, reflecting and planning, and thus *every* teacher's responsibility (Webster, Beveridge and Reed, 1996). The culture clash here arises because psychologists are expected – because this is what they have traditionally always done – to view literacy through a narrow lens, as the decoding or encoding which takes place in children's heads. The challenge of reframing literacy development in terms of the social and linguistic contexts of the curriculum, requires of psychologists a wide-angle view of literacy learning and the organisational contexts in which it may be more effectively promoted, for example, by subject teachers constructing lesson 'scripts' with pupils in which the scope, function, key words and concepts, text inputs and outputs are made clear.

A fine-grained study of the interactions which take place in nursery or playgroup settings between blind children and fully-sighted adults and children, revealed a deeply held belief that lack of vision is an insurmountable barrier to play (restricting the kind of toys given to blind children), language acquisition (adults talk about what is present, not what is out of reach) and social interaction (adults follow blind children about to ensure they do not hurt themselves). These perceptions are partly sustained by psychologists, whose traditional approach to blind children is to assess delays in language, motor, social and cognitive skills compared with the developmental milestones achieved by sighted children. The culture conflict here arises, as in previous examples, from a reluctance to adopt a wider perspective which acknowledges that children do not learn in isolation from the peers, adults and learning contexts in which they are socially embedded. Intervention to promote inclusion takes the form of bridging between the world as experienced by the child firing on different sensory cylinders and the world beyond, for example, by explaining what other children are doing when they play hide and seek and finding ways of including them in apparently unlikely activities (Webster and Roe, 1999). A socio-cultural perspective typically reframes the problems children have in learning so they are recognised as problems teachers have in teaching, and highlighting strategies for intervention to facilitate inclusion (Webster and Heineman-Gosschalk, 2000).

To achieve the kind of professional shift we propose for educational psychologists requires a training which pays much greater attention to the contexts for learning, to research methodology which unearths the complexities of contexts for human interactions, to the management of innovation and change within institutions. In the newly-developed and accredited professional training programmes for educational psychologists with which the authors are associated, an explicit interface has been designed which involves trainees in 'live' research commissions addressing issues of concern to LEAs. Our vision for the future of educational psychology builds on the clinical role, rather than replacing it, since the market place continues to demand this. Whatever the aims of education, these aims cannot be achieved without the recognition of individual differences and the need for some form of classification or categorisation of need in order to use society's resources equably and appropriately. We see increasing collaboration between local authority services and training providers as the means to achieve the kind of 'reflective practicum' advocated by Schon (1987, 1996) to prepare professionals for dealing with the uncertain and ill-formed. A research-orientation, drawing on some of the tenets and methods of socio-cultural psychology, holds promise for a new kind of educational psychology, which uses its expertise to address issues that matter not just to politicians, but also to teachers, parents and children themselves.

References

British Psychological Society (1999) *The Professional Practice of Educational Psychologists*. Leicester: BPS, Division of Educational and Child Psychology

Burt, C. (1969) Psychologists in the education services. *Bulletin of the British Psychological Society*, 22, p1-11

Day, C. (1999) Linking personal and professional change: responses to reform initiatives. Paper presented at the British Educational Research Association Annual Conference, University of Sussex at Brighton, September 2-5, 1999

DfEE (1994) *Code of Practice on the Identification and Assessment of Special Educational Needs*. London: HMSO

DfEE (1998) *Meeting SEN: A Programme for Action*. London: HMSO

DfEE (2000a) *Educational Psychology Services (England): Current Role, Good Practice and Future Directions: Report of the Working Group*. London: HMSO

DfEE (2000b) *Educational Psychology Services (England): Current Role, Good Practice and Future Directions: The Research Report.* London: HMSO

DfEE (2000c) *Draft SEN Code of Practice on the Identification and Assessment of Pupils with Special Educational Needs.* London: HMSO

Desforges, C. (1988) Psychology and the management of classrooms. In N. Jones and J. Sayer (Eds) *Management and the Psychology of Schooling.* London: Falmer Press, p11-23

Dessent, T. (1978) The historical development of School Psychological Services. In B. Gillham (Ed) *Reconstructing Educational Psychology.* London: Croom Helm, p24-33

Dowling, J. and Leibowitz, D. (1994) Evaluation of educational psychology services: past and present. *Educational Psychology in Practice,* Vol 9, No 4, p241-250

Eraut, M. (1994) *Developing Professional Knowledge and Competence.* London: Falmer Press

Hoyle, E. and John, P. (1995) *Professional Knowledge and Professional Practice.* London: Cassell

Leyden, G. (1999) Time for change: the reformulation of applied psychology for LEAs and schools. *Educational Psychology in Practice,* Vol 14, No 4, p222-228

Lunt, I. and Majors, K. (2000) The professionalization of educational psychology. *Educational Psychology in Practice,* Vol 15, No 4, p237-245

Maliphant, R. (1974) Educational Psychology: testing, testing? (Or will it be fine tomorrow?) *Bulletin of the British Psychological Society,* Vol 24, p441-446

Maliphant, R. (1997) Tomorrow will also be history: A commentary on the past, present and future development of Educational Psychology Services. *Educational Psychology in Practice,* Vol 13, No 2, p101-111

Maliphant, R. (2000) Quality and quantity demands in educational psychology: Strategic objectives for the 21st Century. *Educational and Child Psychology,* Vol 17, No 2, p16-26

Phillips, C. J. (1971) Summerfield and after: the training of educational psychologists. *Bulletin of the British Psychological Society,* Vol 24, p207-212

Schon, D. A. (1987) *Educating the Reflective Practitioner.* London: Jossey-Bass

Schon, D. A. (1996) *The Reflective Practitioner: how professionals think in action.* Hants: Arena

Thomson, L. (1996) Searching for a niche: future directions for educational psychologists. *Educational Psychology in Practice,* Vol 12, No 2, p99-106

Wagner, P. (2000) Consultation: developing a comprehensive approach to service delivery. *Educational Psychology in Practice,* Vol 16, No 1, p9-18

Webster, A, Beveridge, M. and Reed, M. (1996) *Managing the Literacy Curriculum: How schools can become communities of readers and writers.* London: Routledge

Webster, A., Hingley, P. and Franey, J. (2000) Professionalization and the reduction of uncertainty: a study of new entrants to educational psychology. *Educational Psychology in Practice,* Vol 16, No 4, p431-448

Webster, A. and Hoyle, E. (2000) The 'new professionalism' and the future of educational psychology. *Educational and Child Psychology*, Vol 17, No 2, p93-104

Webster, A. and Roe, J. (1998) *Children with Visual Impairments: social interaction, language and learning.* London: Routledge

Webster, A. and Heineman-Gosschalk, R. (2000) Deaf children's encounters with written texts: contrasts between hearing teachers and deaf adults in supporting reading. *Deafness and Education International*, Vol 2, No1, p26-44

Williams, H. and Maloney, S. (1998) Well-meant but failing on almost all counts: the case against Statementing. *British Journal of Special Education*, Vol 25, No 1, p16-21

Wood, A. (1998) Okay, then: what do EPs do? *Special Children*, May, p11-13

9

Same/different: establishing a mathematical classroom culture at the transition from primary to secondary school

Laurinda Brown and Alf Coles

Introduction

Caroline, a year 7 (11-12 years old) student, wrote, one month after starting secondary school, on 'What have I learnt about mathematics?':

> I've learnt that you have to think about the problem and not just do the sum. Also you have to maybe carry on thinking about the problem and see if it carries on. You could also have suggestions on why there are problems and how the problem works. It is a lot different to primary school because at primary school we just had to do the sum, we didn't think about the problem of the sum we had to just do it.

Caroline is talking about how in her sense of the values and purposes of doing mathematics differed in primary and secondary schools. What happened in her secondary mathematics classroom which changed what she did when doing 'sums'? In this chapter we look at how a mathematical classroom culture, a common sense of values and purposes, was established in one secondary year 7 classroom, taught by Alf Coles, and how students like Caroline negotiate the clash with their previous habits and expectations.

Alf Coles and Laurinda Brown have been involved in a research project [see note om p151] looking at the developing algebraic activity in year 7 classrooms. We have been working to give an account of the developing practices of teaching and learning mathematics over one academic year in four classrooms. To support our descriptions we have used lesson observations, videotapes of lessons, interviews with teachers and students, student exercise books and written responses by students to the question 'what have I learnt?'

Background

There are reports that, when students in the UK move at age 11 from their primary schools (Key Stage 2) to the new secondary school (starting Key Stage 3) they mark time in most subjects for a year:

> In general, pupils make too little progress in Key Stage 3. They often start their secondary education enthusiastically, but may become disheartened ... if insufficient account is taken of what they already know and can do. (Ofsted, Commentary, 1999-2000)

> This transition is certainly a significant event in pupils' lives, but inspection and research evidence shows that for too many this 'new start' is all too often a 'start again'. Secondary schools can often repeat unnecessarily work that has already been grasped. (DfEE, 1998, para. 167, p69)

Given such reports, we wanted to explore ways of establishing a mathematical classroom culture in which the students' previous experiences are not only used and valued but also extended. We planned for this extension particularly by encouraging the students to use the cultural symbols of algebra within meaningful (for them) contexts. In previous work (Coles, 2000) students' need for algebra was linked to asking and collaboratively trying to answer their own questions.

We viewed the emerging culture and ethos of the mathematics classroom as a 'community of practice' (Lave and Wenger, 1991), where the practice is mathematical 'inquiry' (Schoenfeld, 1996). Learning algebraic thinking is part of learning mathematics, and algebra becomes a language the students use to express themselves. The students are not entering a community of mathematicians but they and their teacher can become a community of inquirers where asking and answering questions including 'why?' is valued.

Caroline's observation indicates that she has experienced a mathematical culture of engaging in meaningful problems. We recognise that the students come from several primary schools, where they have mostly been taught by one teacher for a number of subjects, and bring with them new expectations of classroom conduct. For instance one new student said: '*I used to be able to walk around at primary school, now I have to put my hand up*'. The new school discipline codes are seldom open to negotiation.

There will inevitably be discontinuities between the ways the primary teachers see mathematics and how comfortable they themselves are with the subject. This will have affected the mathematical culture of each primary classroom. What teaching strategies, in the unfamiliar context of the students' new mathematics classroom, can we use to allow a genuine confluence of all these different mathematical cultures? If we teach a skill in isolation we run the risk of boring some students and losing others; many will simply mark time. If the agenda is always set by the teachers, a single culture is imposed which can be ignored, resisted or adopted, but not negotiated. How can the agenda of mathematical behaviours be negotiated i.e the students be involved in establishing the new classroom culture over time? We call the central teaching strategy we have employed to allow all the students to use and extend their past experiences from the start of the new school year: 'same/different'. This idea is now explored:

How do you learn in unfamiliar contexts?
We take as given that we can only bring to a context what we already know i.e. initially we can only see that which is familiar. Faced with the strange, where worldviews meet, we can ignore, resist, oppose or subvert (Chapter 1, page 10) or allow ourselves to let the strange become familiar. Is there a mechanism to support us in learning where worldviews meet? What can we do when faced with the strange when we don't want to ignore or resist? Before describing how the mathematical classroom culture was developed in one of Alf's year 7 classrooms, we offer an activity to engage you in observing how you learn in a new context. Mathematics as a subject often presents us with the strange, and the reaction of many to learning the subject

is to ignore or resist rather than to engage with what seem to be meaningless symbols. What do you do?

Activity: What is the same? What is different?
Look at the following set of expressions. What do you see? Can you say anything about this set of symbols?:

$$g(x + h) \simeq x + h.g'(x)$$

$$g(x + h) \simeq x + h.g'(x + h/2)$$

$$g(x + h) \simeq x + h.\{g'(x) + g'(x + h)\}/2$$

What happened to you? Did you ignore or resist? There are many responses, but the invitation to say what you see seems to provoke people to talk about what is the same or different about the expressions. In one seminar a non-mathematician made the observation that: 'The expressions on the left are all the same and the ones on the right are all different so whatever that sign is in the middle it's not what I thought an equals sign was.' He had found a need for knowing the name of the 'approximately equals' sign. Being distracted by your feelings and emotional reactions may be an appropriate initial response to years of mathematics being meaningless for you, but you will not learn! If you want to learn, the offer of contrasting examples leaves the way open for you to use what you know now to ask questions about the new.

In the remainder of this chapter we use descriptions from a sequence of lessons with students at the start of year 7 to illustrate how a negotiated mathematical culture was established using same/ different and distilling out two principles that can be used when planning lessons for learning where worldviews meet.

**Lesson part one: Letting go of chickening out –
the story of Stan**
At the start of Year 7 Alf offers a number problem which involves the students in doing a subtraction and probably giving different answers. Alf issues the following instructions, setting out one example on the board:

Pick any three digit number with 1st digit bigger than 3rd

Reverse the number and subtract

Reverse the answer and add

$$
\begin{array}{r}
7\,5\,2 \\
-\,2\,5\,7 \\
\hline
4\,9\,5 \\
+\,5\,9\,4 \\
\hline
1\,0\,8\,9
\end{array}
$$

Alf made clear that the students could use any method they had previously found useful.

Students who have previously experienced feelings of failure in the subject find this hard. But they can all write down a three digit number, reverse it, and attempt the subtraction. Several comments were made by students that they also got 1089 and the challenge to the class was: *Can you find a number that does not end up as 1089?*

In the first lesson there is evidence that Stan could not do a subtraction.

<u>Classwork</u>   4/9/98

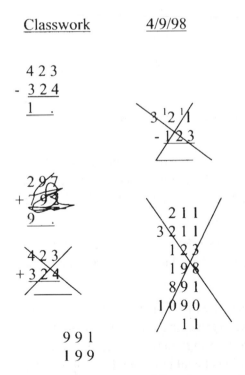

Fig 1a: First page of Stan's exercise book

His work after the next lesson, however, illustrates a move from initially not being able to achieve anything to a developing confidence.

Fig 1b: The following lesson

Homework   6/9/98

```
  402        632        312        514
- 204      - 236      - 213      - 415
  198        396        099        099
+ 891      + 693      + 990      + 990
 1089       1089       1089       1089
    1          1          1          1


  462        803        921        430
- 264      - 308      - 129      - 034
  198        495        792        396
+ 891      + 594      + 297      + 693
 1089       1089       1089       1089
    1          1          1          1
```

A further 8 calculations were similarly presented pn the page along with a written comment: 'Not one of my sumes came up to any diferent than 1089'.

Other students extended themselves through asking the question: 'Why does this always work?' Alf showed them their first algebraic proof in response to this question. The students had discovered a need for algebra.

At the end of a sequence of lessons related to the same activity Alf invites students to write about 'what have I learnt?'. At the end of the 1089 problem Stan wrote:

> I have learnt how to (do sums with) bigger numbers in five or four digits. I have been able to think like a mathematician. I have been able to say the five or four digit numbers without chickening out. I can understand things I couldn't when I was at primary school. I have enjoyed doing maths.

Learning in this environment has given Stan a new voice and a new pattern of behaviours that allow him not to chicken out! For homework he chooses numbers to try in response to the challenge and writes: 'Not one of my sums come up to any different than 1089.' When he goes on to 4 and 5 digit starting numbers there are, in fact, different answers (see Figure 2) and the students share their results and look for patterns.

It seems that it was through the acts of seeing, comparing and contrasting, that Stan took the opportunity to be present in his perceptions and felt the energy of making connections for himself that led to his enjoying mathematics and feeling that he was learning. He could have remained with the negative emotions of his past chickening out, and this would then have inhibited his forming new patterns of acting.

We believe that learning in unfamiliar contexts takes place through the use of our powers of discrimination, seeing difference and similarity. What seems important is that, as we enter a new culture, we are present in our perceptions and are able to say what we see. If we experience an emotional resistance, we need to let go of previous habitual behaviours (c.f. Guy Claxton's dismissal of much of contemporary art (Chapter 1, page 1), Stan's chickening out) to see anew. How then do we plan for our students' learning at the start of their secondary education in mathematics?

The story of Stan illustrates our first principle in planning for students' learning:

First Principle for planning: Begin each lesson with something that all the students can do.

Examples of this principle could be having the students describe what they see or discuss homework with each other in groups or share questions they are working on. The focus on the students describing their experience helps to root them in their present perceptions and avoid the debilitating emotions of fear of failure. The teacher can then decide how to structure the lesson contingently upon what the students bring with them.

Establishing the secondary classroom culture

In the first lesson with a year 7 group, Alf offers the class the notion that, as well as learning a lot of new mathematics, this year is about them becoming mathematicians and learning about thinking mathematically. Alf then states a few things he means by thinking mathematically, including: looking for patterns, thinking about what you are doing at the same time as doing it, writing down what you are doing, asking questions – particularly, why?

In each lesson, using his own powers of discrimination, Alf describes to the whole class the behaviours he observes which seem to him to be mathematical, e.g. 'This group had an idea which they tested and found didn't work, so they changed their idea and are trying something else. That's a great example of what it means to think and work mathematically'. Evidence from observation notes and video recordings of lessons show that these comments are especially frequent early in the year, as ways of working and patterns of behaviour are becoming established. What gets commented upon depends upon what the students do. Some behaviours, such as asking 'why?', are used increasingly by the students themselves in establishing their particular mathematical classroom culture. The students also comment on their behaviours. Both teacher and students seem to be using such comments as 'objects of perception, thought and action' when commenting on their practices as mathematicians and inquirers. At the start of their secondary schooling, they are not so much changing their previous outlook on the world as relativising it. The culture here is emergently created in action at the confluence of the multiple primary and secondary classroom norms.

At the end of each extended piece of work on an activity the students were invited to write about 'what have I learnt', both about the mathematics itself and about becoming a mathematician. Within a few lessons students are writing comments in their books such as: 'I'm going to be organised by putting my results in a table'. In two responses to 'what have I learnt?' we see one student commenting on a behaviour 'write why' originally described by the teacher, and the second making a comment on the culture of the classroom – 'I have learnt it's OK to make mistakes' became part of the on-going communications of the group, informing future actions.

I've learnt mathematicians have to think quickly and solve a lot of problems. You've got to jot little theories down. On a lot of theories you have to write why. You've got to correct your mistakes. You've got to confirm things ... You got to explain your findings.

I have learnt it's OK to make mistakes ... maths is more exciting in secondary school than in primary because in primary school we copied from textbooks and that is so boring. I hated maths but I like it here because you can write on the board and make suggestions and talk about the work and write in our books.

There is evidence of some of the students being able to let go of behavioural habits from their classroom experiences in their previous primary cultures. In some of these cultures, presumably, it was not OK to make mistakes. In this secondary culture making a mistake is seen as a precursor to learning, conjectures can be modified, calculations can be checked. Mathematics is not something that is always right first time, a perception held by many students and adults that can be inhibiting.

Lesson part two: Classifying and questioning, the use of common boards

Students were invited to try out their own starting numbers and see what happened. Any students who got answers that did not come to 1089 were invited to write their starting number on the board with their initials next to it (whenever a structure is in place to allow students a public space such as whiteboards or posters or flip charts for recording questions or results, we call the space a 'common board'). Alf encouraged other students to check these numbers and, if they disagreed, to find and talk to the student who first wrote it. There followed much practice of basic skills and students sorting out problems with technique when they realised that they had not got the same answer as many of their peers. The majority of students consistently got one of two answers, 198 and 1089. Some groups allowed both answers whilst others argued for there being only one answer, 1089 (try the problem for yourself if you want to know where two answers might come from). There was some whole class discussion about the reasons for the two. The students were encouraged to ask questions as they worked and these were collected on the whiteboard. Some students wanted to try to ascertain why there are nines in the centre column of the calculations, others wanted to try the process for a larger number of digits. Students worked together in later lessons on classifying the possible answers for 4-digits:

Figure 2: Common board in lesson 21/9/99

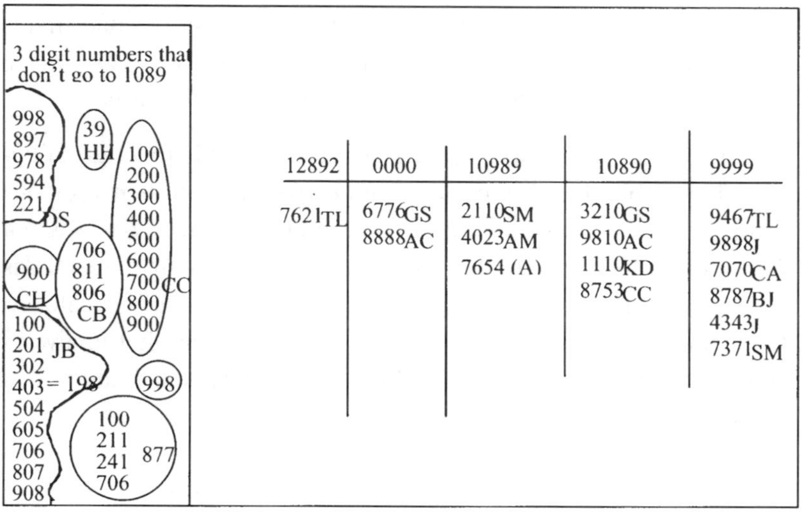

A similar mechanism (to that of the three digit case) of students writing their initials and checking each others' answers was used. One effect of this was that everyone in the class had access to an accurate set of results.

What seems important when faced with the strange is that we allow patterns to emerge. Discussions within a community can help in this process. The teacher here, having previously worked with students at the start of secondary school on this problem, has greater experience and awarenesses than his students of where the problem can go. However, they are all fishing in the fog – needing to create meaning from what the other says and finding supportive communal patterns of behaviour to support their work together. They need to develop skills of listening and hearing and of asking for support or questioning others if they do not understand. These are the skills that are important in this classroom and the teacher cedes the control of the content to the students, commenting on the mathematical behaviours he observes as the culture emerges.

Second Principle for planning: Work with mathematical activities that lead to classification.

By being organised and collecting together exemplars on common boards, students can exercise their use of same/different and when they discuss where they have different perceptions they raise many questions. These questions are often recorded on common boards too, so that students have a choice about which questions to address or which results to verify.

Illustrating the use of same/different by teacher and students

Alf's motivation for working at becoming mathematicians with his year 7 students was to allow a classroom culture to develop in which the students found a need for using algebra. For us algebraic activity underpins the whole of the doing of mathematics as we describe and structure our world. In expressing the patterns and structures they observe, the students will be exploring and using algebra, the language of mathematics, with meaning. They develop a need for using algebra to express their ideas and find out what they could not know without it.

Figure 3 illustrates the classroom discussion later on in the same sequence of lessons. The transcript is annotated to show evidence of students and teachers using the questions 'what is the same? what is different?' from their different perspectives. Classification by the students and teacher comments on behaviours and conjecturing are also part of the classroom practices.

The class works on a problem that is complex enough for the students to have individual or small group choice over the questions they will engage in over a sustained period of time – anything up to three weeks. During this time they will often take part in whole class discussions where they will find out what each classmate is working on and connections can be made across different ideas. The common boards are crucial in offering public access to otherwise private spaces.

Fig. 3: Student use of same/different highlighted and teacher use of same/different underlined with comments surrounding the transcript:

Classifying numerically collected results for five digits from which these more general statements are emerging.

Student L: If the first number is the same as the middle and the last it will go to zero, zero, zero because when you reverse it, it will be in the same order. It will equal zero.

Teacher D: So, in terms of a, b, c, d and e, what can you say? (Pause.) Can someone else say Student L's conjecture in terms of a, b, c, d and e? (Pause.) Can you say it again in words? What did you say?

Student L: If the first number's the same as the middle and the last and the first and the ... (Pause.)

Student J: Third.

Student L: ... third number are the same ...

Teacher D: Second and ...

Student L: It will go to ...

Teacher D: Student N, can you say that in terms of the letters?

Student N: If $a = c$ and e and $b = d$ it will come to (unclear).

Student D: Sir.

Teacher D: OK, I will write that down. I can see that you're wanting to speak Student D, I'll ask you in a second. Student L's conjecture: For 00000 in the starting number. I use that 'no.' as a little abbreviation for number sometimes. In the starting number ... Can you say it now Student L? Now Student N's said it? Can you say it in letters as well this time?

Student L: Um, if b ... No. If $a = c$ and $c = e$ ...

Teacher D: So, we can write that in one line, If $a = c = e$ and, Student N added a second thing which I think was what you were trying to say as well.

Student L: ... and $b = d$ ...

Teacher D: And $b = d$. Fantastic. Brilliant. So, For 0000 in the starting number $a = c = e$ and $b = d$. Wonderful. OK, we'll write this down here, because we're going to probably write other things. Anything more? Oh, sorry, Student D had a question, a point about this.

Student D: Because we said that we were not allowed to use the first number is the same as the last number, so that conjecture is not right.

Teacher D: OK.

Student D: It is right but it's not like what we was discussing.

Teacher D: Brilliant. OK. So, in terms of what we're doing on the table here we're agreeing with the conjecture but we're saying we're not going to include it on the table. Fantastic, and that's what mathematicians do all the time, we're making conjectures and we're thinking 'OK, well I'm not going to look at that one now, I'm going to focus on the rule like this' and we can maybe come back to that another time. Brilliant, very nice point, Student D.

Stressing the importance of conjecturing (seeing what's the same or different) as what mathematicians do.

Throughout the transcript

Students classify and conjecture in relation to the mathematics.

Asking students to say the same thing in different ways.

Return to the original speaker to invite a different attempt.

It would seem to be a simple conclusion that the students use same/difference only within the mathematics, while the teacher uses it across a wider spectrum of awareness. But as the year progressed, we saw some evidence of students commenting about mathematics to support the work of the wider community.

Final comments

In her final 'what have I learnt?', our student Caroline illustrates the sense of the culture becoming established throughout the year. The communications and expectations of what it means to be a learner of mathematics in this classroom emerge through the interactions of the students with their teacher and each other. Crucial to this process are the students' explorations of what mathematics is and what it means to them to do mathematics so that what emerges is a genuine confluence of the cultures of each participant. The use of same/different, through supporting the voices of the students discussing what they see and the related teaching strategies, allows this emergence from the first lesson of the year. It is as if the teacher needs to place their attention away from the mathematical content itself. It is the students' responsibility to understand the mathematics and the teacher's to understand the students, commenting to them on their actions and the processes of learning the subject. In this way the teacher is making it possible for some of the students to be aware of *how* they are learning mathematics at the same time as they are doing so. This is Caroline's observation at the end of Year 7:

> I have learnt how to do long division and also algebra so now I can do algebra in sums. I have also got better on my times tables and sums.

> Thinking mathematically: I have learnt about thinking mathematically ... that you have to share your problems with other people and also share your finding outs. Also try to help other people with their problems so you have to work together. Also you can never find out an answer to a problem because there are always other questions you can ask yourself. Or you can call them extensions. I think our class has worked mathematically all of this year.

Note

'Developing algebraic activity in a 'community of inquirers'' Economic and Social Research Council (ESRC) project reference R000223044, Laurinda Brown, Rosamund Sutherland, Jan Winter, Alf Coles. Contact: Laurinda.Brown@bris.ac.uk or Laurinda Brown, University of Bristol, Graduate School of Education, 35 Berkeley Square, Bristol BS8 1JA, UK. For more information browse: http://www.regard.ac.uk/

Thank you to the headteacher, governors and staff of Kingsfield School, South Gloucestershire, UK for their unfailing support and encouragement of this research.

References

Coles, A. (2000) 'Developing a need for algebra', in: *The Teacher Research Grant Scheme, Summaries of findings 1998-1999*. London: Teacher Training Agency, Publication Number 150/8-00

DfEE (1998) *The Implementation of the National Numeracy Strategy*. Sudbury, Suffolk

Lave, J. and Wenger, E. (1991), *Situated Learning: legitimate peripheral participation*, Cambridge University Press, Cambridge

Ofsted (1999-2000) *Standards and Quality in Education, the Annual Report of Her Majesty's Chief Inspector of Schools* (http://www.official-documents.co.uk/document/ofsted/hc102/102-03c.htm)

Schoenfeld, A.H. (1996) 'In fostering communities of inquiry, must it matter that the teacher knows 'the answer'?' *Journal For the Learning of Mathematics*, 16-3, p11-16

10

The textbook as cultural artefact: reproducing the culture of science

Susan Molyneux-Hodgson and Keri Facer

Introduction

Scientific developments and scientific opinion today play roles central to many aspects of our everyday lives. Through innovations in the fields of biotechnology or developments in our understandings of climate change, for example, 'science' is playing an increasingly visible role in determining policy and practice in fields such as public health, human development and global environmental safety, impacting on the food we eat, the children we raise and the cars we drive. With this raised profile come calls for the scientific community both to communicate more effectively with a lay public and to render itself accountable as representative not only of specific sectors of the population but of the concerns, interests and passions of the wider national and global communities. At precisely this time, however, trust in the scientific enterprise amongst the public is low. Within an educational context, the scientific community is witnessing difficulties in recruiting students to science courses at school and university levels, in sustaining student involvement in scientific research after graduation and, despite thirty years of feminist politics, continues to fail to attract representative levels of female participation.

These educational concerns are not new. Repeated attempts over the years to identify why scientific practice appeals preferentially to particular sectors of the population have been made (for example, in relation to gender, Kelly, 1987; Thomas, 1990; Byrne, 1993). These attempts, however, seem to have made little if any inroads into widening participation in scientific activities. Why should the culture of science hold so little appeal to large swathes of society? We believe that the time has come to reassess the approaches being taken towards increasing participation and to ask not, 'what is it about particular groups?' but instead 'what is it about the culture of science?' Our contention is that the images the scientific community projects of itself may lead to self-exclusion of certain groups and that no attempt to increase participation that does not address these normalised constructions of science is likely to succeed. Now, more than ever, as 'scientific advisors' become a resource to politicians requiring a justification for national and global policy, we need to examine what it may be that shapes patterns of participation in science. We need to ask what it means for individuals to decide to become part of a scientific community and, centrally, to explore how that scientific community itself represents the idea of 'being a scientist' to students and would-be practitioners in the field. To explore these questions we have drawn on literature, which frames our own backgrounds – and disparate disciplinary cultures – of science, science education and cultural studies, to analyse representations of scientific community within UK undergraduate education.

What is 'scientific community'?

Unlike national cultures, in which community is frequently delineated by physical boundaries – whether natural or manmade – the idea of scientific community extends across nations and cultures. Benedikt Anderson's analysis of the production of religious communities in the 'pre-scientific' era (which, he argues, was supplanted by the development of scientific community) focuses on the role of language and ritual in the construction of non-geographically bounded communities. These religious communities, he argues, were '*imaginable largely through the medium of a sacred language and written script*' (Anderson, 1991, p54) and functioned across continents and cultures specifically because the acquisition of this language was considered a means of fundamentally altering the characteristics of the individual – a 'heathen' could become Christian, for example, by acquiring an understanding of Latin. The acquisition of the sacred language and written script was seen as both an indication of and injunction to hold a specific worldview.

In the field of social studies of science, numerous studies of scientific workplaces have been conducted which give insights into the day-to-day workings of 'scientists' and the ways in which the idea of a scientific community is promoted through structures such as conferences, peer review, international collaborations and the world wide web, as well as shared practices such as particular interpretations of instrument signatures and the use of representations (e.g. Lynch and Woolgar, 1990; Latour and Woolgar, 1979). In her analysis of enculturation practices for novice scientists, Traweek (1988, px-xi) notes that

> Novices must learn what sorts of things they need to know to be taken seriously; they must become .. practitioners of the culture, .. thinking about the world in a characteristic way.

In the case of scientific community this characteristic world view, it could be argued, is acquired through the understanding and use of not a sacred but a secular scientific language, that functions both as organisational and hierarchical mechanism and as the basis for the establishment of authority and accepted practice within a community.

Central to any understanding of the ways in which 'community' is produced amongst a group of geographically and culturally disparate people, however, must be an engagement with the processes by which the core knowledge and social practices expected of novices also include tacit demands on them to behave in particular ways and to identify themselves as part of a community, rather than simply as individuals 'using a language' – it is possible, for example, to speak French without considering oneself French, or to use a computer without considering oneself part of an identifiable community of computer users. We therefore need to explore the ways in which the learning of, for example, mathematics, is rendered constitutive of the development of self-identification within a community of scientists.

Bourdieu (1984) argues that hierarchies and classifications (that tend to be constructed and embedded in language, for example, words such as 'professor' or 'doctor') produce behaviours in individuals that reproduce the cultural expectations of the significations of these words. In other words, a 'scientist', being so named, is under a tacit demand to fulfil the 'role' of scientist, to reproduce the cultural perception of what it means to 'be' a scientist, perceptions that extend far beyond the production of papers and running of academic departments and which may include such disparate elements as appropriate dress, leisure interests and taste in music and conversation.

> *The official differences produced by academic classifications tend to produce (or reinforce) real differences by inducing in the classified individuals a collectively recognised and supported belief in the differences, thus producing behaviours that are intended to bring real being into line with official being. Activities as alien to the explicit demands of the institution as keeping a diary, wearing heavy make-up, theatre going or going dancing [...] can thus find themselves inscribed in the position allotted within the institution as a tacit demand constantly underlined by various mediations.* (Bourdieu, 1984 p25)

In this statement Bourdieu suggests that community is constructed not only along the lines of the 'explicit demands of the institution' such as the acquisition of specific subject knowledge and practices but that, through the 'tacit demand constantly underlined by various mediations' (such as the textbook, graduation ceremony or peer interaction) specific types of behaviour are required to indicate participation within a specific community. Psychoanalytic analyses of the function of language in constructing community indicate, further, that not only does the language that describes the individual as 'scientist' place demands upon the individual to engage in practices common to community perceptions of what is meant by this term, but that this process of naming also sets in place the concept of borders to a community. Namely, that the name 'scientist' precludes other activities, in the same way that 'red' introduces the concept of 'not blue' or 'not white' (Lacan, 1991). The use of naming as a delineation of boundaries brings into the concept of scientific community a signification of what it means to 'not be' a scientist.

These practices, or the cultural connotations that sustain the tacit demand upon the individual to reproduce specific behaviours, however, require constant processes of justification the language spoken within and about that community must be constantly reproduced as 'authoritative' discourse in order to sustain such behaviours. As Foucault (1990) argues, the function of the 'myth of origin' of community serves to sustain the representation of such language as 'authoritative' by embedding the evolution of such language, and its tacit demands, within a historical tradition that naturalises such behaviour, bringing it into the domain of common sense and rendering it safe from critique. To explore the ways in which scientific community is constructed, therefore, we need to explore the ways in which this community is constituted as a historical phenomenon (see later).

The function of the textbook in constructing scientific community

While the image of the scientist is constructed in diverse ways for the general population, not least through the mediation of popular culture – the dressing of scientists in white coats for news reports, the sustaining Frankenstein myth when describing scientific developments through film and television – the ways in which students are apprenticed (Lave and Wenger, 1991) into an understanding of what it means to be part of a 'scientific community' over the course of their educational experience takes distinct and identifiable forms. These educational experiences, for example, include periods of study in institutions such as universities, where students are inducted into community practices through participation in subject-specific activities (e.g. lectures; laboratory work) and related social practices (e.g. interaction with professors and peers, attendance at conferences). Learners' subject-related experiences at university are primarily via formal instructional situations such as lecture, tutorial, laboratory and examples classes. Within these instructional situations, students experience what is represented within the community as *authoritative discourse* (Bakhtin, 1981): 'the authoritative word demands that we acknowledge it, that we make it our own; ... we encounter it with its authority fused to it'.

Central to the production of authoritative discourse within these situations is the set textbook which is given legitimacy by its position as a pedagogical tool, recognised by existing members of the scientific community and proposed for purchase and use as an important artefact in the completion of a given programme of study. These textbooks are generally seen as simply presenting information, canonically-accepted by the professional community, in ways that relate to the authors' – and publishers' – views of the information. We argue, however, that these texts also function as a way of offering a general view of the community, of what it means to 'be a scientist', in contrast to a more specific view offered by individual members of the existing community (such as course lecturers).

To illustrate how these authoritative texts serve not only to present information but to reproduce the existing dominant construction of what it means to participate in scientific community, this chapter reports on a detailed analysis of one textbook: *Introduction to Electric Circuits* (Dorf, 1993; 1996). The book is the recommended text for the first year undergraduate module on 'Linear Circuits and Electronics', delivered to around 60 students studying the Electrical and Electronic Engineering; Electronic Engineering, and Electronic and Communications Engineering programmes at a University in the south-west of England. The subject matter coverage at this level would be accepted as 'standard fare' for any programme in the physical sciences, from pure physics to applied engineering and we do not propose to delimit sub-cultures (of say, electronic engineering) within the construction of 'scientific community'. Indeed, the textbook elides the notions of science and engineering and describes scientists and engineers as engaged in the same activities (Dorf, p2). Although the research setting is England, the textbook has a US author and publisher, a point to which we return later.

Drawing from existing research into the production of community (e.g. Anderson, 1991; Bourdieu, 1984; Cohen, 1985; Lacan,1981), we explore the function of the scientific textbook in re-producing scientific community through the following questions:

- How is the authority to speak within and on behalf of the community established within the textbook?

- How are the languages and practices of the community represented and proscribed within the textbook?

- How is the community distinguished from other sectors of society?

Further, by drawing on the work of Hall (1977) we will begin to explore how the constructions of community evident within the textbook may be read by differing constituencies.

A central aim of this chapter is to make the familiar strange, to approach the genre of textbook publishing with an eye to exploring how the rules, traditions and customs of this genre serve to construct a specific disciplinary identity for both the would-be student and for the community which it represents. Although offering only one example of such texts, we seek to explore how the characteristics of such texts serve a purpose much wider than the simple presentation of information, central to the production of disciplinary community.

Framing discourse – the historical production of authoritative discourse

Although, as we have already outlined, the scientific textbook is constructed as authorised artefact within the educational institution, a significant effort is made *within the text itself* to establish the textbook as authorised discourse. The first encounter between reader and text, for example, underlines the authority of the author to speak as a member of and on behalf of the scientific community. In the preface to this edition, and in the cover notes on the reverse of the textbook, Professor Dorf's right to speak is signified by his title and by a detailed description of his extensive experience as researcher and industrial practitioner around the world (Dorf, pv).

> Richard C. Dorf, professor of electrical and computer engineering at the University of California, Davis, teaches graduate and undergraduate courses in electrical engineering in the fields of circuits and control systems. He earned a PhD [...] an M.Sc [...[and a B.Sc [...] he has written and lectured internationally on the contributions and advances in electrical engineering. Professor Dorf has extensive experience with education and industry and is professionally active in the fields of robotics, automation, electric circuits and communications. (Dorf, pv)

The function of this preface establishes the right of the author to speak but it also functions to produce specific constructions of what is meant (within this text) by the idea of 'scientific community': first, it identifies scientific community as international (it is written in the USA and used in the UK); second, it instructs the reader that the languages and practices learned in the text have international applicability within this community; third, it underlines that authorised scientific discourse is located within the wider field of academic discourse; and finally, it suggests that this language is a means of describing and acting upon the 'real world' through the 'fields of robotics, automation, electric circuits and communications'. While this is recognisable 'marketing' discourse within the field of academic publishing, this preface also contains key elements necessary to the construction of community as outlined above: as a community of practice, entrance to which is gained by the adoption of a universal language and membership of which holds tacit demands on the individual to engage in particular types of activities – in this case, commercial as well as academic practice.

The authority of the textbook as artefact having been established both by the context within which it is presented to the reader and through the credentials of the author, the text functions to construct the languages and practices of scientific community as, in themselves, authorised and desirable practices. In this particular textbook a specific characteristic of the production of authoritative discourse is the use of historical vignettes included at the beginning of each chapter. These vignettes are included, according to the author, to 'enable the reader to witness the past and current motivation for the development of modern engineering devices and methods as well as to grasp the excitement of engineering in the 1990s'. (Dorf, px)

Given the injunction to widen participation in the scientific community, this reference to 'real life' experiences and practices can be read as an attempt to locate scientific practice as a relevant activity in the modern world. If we consider the first of these vignettes, however, it is apparent that their function is also to underline the authority of scientific discourse and to inform specific constructs of scientific community:

> From the beginning of recorded time, *humans have explored* the electrical phenomena they have experienced in everyday life. *As scientists developed the knowledge* of electrical charge, *they formulated* the laws of electricity as we know them today. (Dorf, p2)

This opening statement from 'the beginning of recorded time' to 'today' constructs scientific practice as coterminous with natural human evolution, a construction that is repeated in the following section of the textbook ('The early history of electrical science'), which traces the development of electrical science from 'prehistoric people' to James Clark Maxwell in 1873. These historical vignettes, however, locate scientific practice as at once analogous with and distinct from human development. In the paragraph above we can see the shift in language from 'humans' 'exploring' to 'scientists' developing 'knowledge' and 'formulating laws'. Where humans merely experience, the authorised work of the scientist is to add to the body of knowledge (thereby implying the need to record results) and to develop laws (thereby implying the need to ensure re-peatability of findings). As we outlined above, this type of narrative functions to define communities, by implying reasons for their exis-tence (the idea that this is a natural and necessary activity) and by distinguishing the borders of the community (the idea that not all people are scientists). Even in this opening chapter, the rules of entry to scientific community are being made explicit. The language and practices that are the result of this evolutionary endeavour are those that will be presented within the text that the student is reading.

Dorf further links the historical development of the scientific com-munity to the language now used by that community by citing the examples of previous scientists who have been instrumental in con-structing that language. He lists Volta and Ampere amongst others as great scientists who have contributed to science by 'developing prac-tices' and 'identifying models' that have then been named after them. Dorf recounts that Volta 'was remembered 54 years after his death when the electromotive force was officially named the volt' and that Ampere 'was honored by having the unit of electric current, the ampere, named after him in 1881'. Inscribed in the language of science, Dorf therefore implies, is both practice and precedent. The use of this language functions as tacit demand upon the individuals who use it to reproduce the types of activities and practices exem-plified by those instrumental in its development.

The use of the scientific language presented in this text is therefore both justified by historical precedent and, because of that historical precedent, places tacit demands upon those who use it to reproduce the types of activities and practices exemplified by those instrumental in its development. This historical introduction to scientific community places scientific language at the heart of membership of that community, a language, however, that is far from neutral but represents and embodies specific types and motivations for human endeavour. Just as the 'heathens' were considered to be christianised by learning Latin (Anderson, 1991), so ordinary humans can be made scientists by learning this language – in both cases, however, the language functions as a medium for delineating particular ways of understanding and acting within the world. This process of delineation functions, we would argue, as a framing discourse within which acquisition of the core discourse of scientific language should be understood.

Core discourse – scientific language and scientific practice
Even within the bounded world of the textbook, however, access to scientific language and practice is not open to all, as the text constructs specific subject positions for its readers. The introduction underlines, for example, that 'the presentation is geared to readers who are being exposed to the basic concepts .. for the first time' (pvii). The students reading this text should in effect be novices needing apprenticeship into the community, and if they are not, they will still be required by the linear structure of the text and the 'unfolding' of gradual levels of information within the text, to read 'as if' occupying the position of novice. Importantly, the text also delineates boundaries even for entry into this preliminary stage, underlining that 'Students should come to the course with a basic knowledge of differential and integral calculus' (pvii). Although the students are constructed as novices to the scientific community, an acceptance of the authority and validity of mathematical language is constructed as a prerequisite for entry into the next stage of scientific apprenticeship.

Scientific language
In this textbook the language of the scientific community is constructed as authorising specific ways of representing and conceptualising information: for example, written text; symbolic notations; graphs; photographs; and diagrams.

Central to the text is the encoding of physical phenomena in the symbolic representation of mathematical-scientific notation, an encoding offered as essential to professional practice, which we have labelled the 'core discourse'. For example, the notation required to represent the relationship between voltage and current is agreed within the scientific community to be $v=Ri$. This discourse delineates the areas of knowledge recognised as essential in the enculturation process. Learners are assisted in their endeavour through textual strategies of naming, for example,

> Resistance is the physical property of an element ...
> The unit of resistance R was named the ohm ...

and representation , for example,

> ... it is represented by the symbol R.
> A resistor is represented by the two-terminal symbol ...

The parameters within which to operate are also explicitly delineated, for example, by the explication of assumptions or limitations,

> Ohm's law ... requires that the I versus v relationship be linear.
> We will assume that a resistor is linear ...
> .. we will use a linear model ...

This information constitutes the canon with which learners are expected to become familiar. Not only must they acquire the components of scientific language (e.g. resistance) but they must also learn the authorised ways in which this language is used to communicate, the constraints, limitations and applications (Cohen, 1985). Learners must be able to replicate the canon if required, but they must also, like Volta, Ampere and the other figures listed throughout the text, be innovative with it, for example, solving problems that are different to those the learner initially faced. That is, as well as learning the canon, students must learn ways to work with the information which would enable them to operate in new situations, evidenced by the large numbers of 'problems' for the learners to solve at the end of each chapter. For example, at the end of the chapter which includes resistance,

> An electric heater is connected to a constant 250-V source and absorbs 1000W. Subsequently, this heater is connected to a 210-V source. What power does it absorb from the 210-V source? What is the resistance of the heater?

Scientific language, therefore, must be constructed within the text as widely applicable, as a meta-language that can be used in a variety of given situations. (For example, 'Norton's theorem', is formally stated on p160, algorithmised on p161 and is the subject of eight 'problems' at the end of the chapter, each requiring different uses of the original theorem). This construct of applicability justifies the use of US textbooks in UK lecture halls, and constructs scientific language as universal. Within this construct of scientific language, and within the production of reader positions for students as novices, there is no space for 'local' or 'specific' languages, or for an understanding of everyday phenomena that draws on lived experience; rather, the authorised language disqualifies all others. In this way the language functions as a marker of scientific community by establishing its authority over other languages.

Scientific practice

The preface (pvii) states that 'The analysis and design of electric circuits is a critical skill for all engineers', implying that the enculturation process and engagement with the book will lead to learners becoming skilful practitioners as well as knowledgeable scientists.

The process of solving problems is emphasised throughout the text as a central practice in which novices must become skilful. For example, the numerous example and exercise problems all provide answers immediately following the question, implying that the process of getting to the answer is considered more important than testing whether the correct answer was achieved. At certain junctures in the text the author explicitly states his view of the problem-solving process, giving multi-step outlines as a guide to a general methodology. For example, the following step-by-step method to solving design problems is offered:

> (1) state the problem, (2) define the situation, (3) state the goal, (4) generate a plan to solve the problem, and (5) take action using the plan. (Dorf, 1993, px)

The author offers explicit statements of exemplary practice, in the form of an heuristic rather than context-specific practice. This way of presenting scientific practice has resonance with Dorf's earlier description of 'true' 'scientists' as those who 'formulate', rather than humans who 'explore' (Dorf, p2). Membership of the scientific community is thus constructed as a way of acting as evidence of thinking about the world in a characteristic way (Traweek, 1988).

A further key element in this way of 'thinking about the world' lies in Dorf's emphasis on models. A definition is introduced in Chapter 2 of the book: 'Engineers use models to represent the elements of an electric circuit', and continues 'a model is an object or pattern of objects or an equation that represents an element or circuit' (Dorf, p34).

That is, a model is a representation of a physical system which 'we generate ... in order to manipulate parameters'. The statement 'we will construct models ... to predict and explain' signals to readers the purpose of this characteristic practice. Models, like the universal language, are widely applicable and flexible, a framework within which the world can be analysed. Once again, the concept of the 'local' and the 'specific', or the space of the individual within the scientific community, is subordinated to the idea of universally applicable constructs.

The social nature of core discourse

While the models and representations of scientific language and practice are to some extent acknowledged by Dorf to be culturally and historically constructed – as we have already discussed in his description of the historical creation of scientific names and symbols – the ways in which this practice and language gains its authority within the community is not given the same degree of attention. For example, Volta's 'discovery' of the volt is constructed within the text as historically contingent practice. How this discovery was validated or given authority within the community by the process of naming, however, is not considered to be historically contingent but is represented as an inevitable recognition of scientific endeavour. The Volt 'was named' and Ampere 'was honoured'. The subject of this sentence (the 'thing/person/community' that names and honours) is absent, yet it is this subject which provides authority and validity to scientific language and practice both within the text and in the wider scientific community. In this passive sentence construction, the subject remains invisible, and the processes by which scientific language and practice are given authority remain outside scrutiny. The absence within scientific discourse of the social practices surrounding the construction of scientific 'fact' is the subject of a substantial literature (e.g. Latour and Woolgar, 1979; Collins, 1985; Knorr-Cetina, 1981) but these social aspects of science do not yet appear to be reflected within educational practice. Thus, while Dorf may concede the historical and social contingency of scientific language and practice, the framework for its development and promulgation remains unscrutinised. This framework of references to the social world of author, text and community – the 'framing discourse' of border definition – provides the focus for the final section of our discussion.

Framing discourse – who counts as 'scientist'?

We use the concept of borders to explore some of the ways in which the idea of the scientist, as both practitioner and individual, is constructed in the text. We suggest that this construction relies on a complex process of including and apprenticing novice learners to the scientific community while simultaneously constructing that community as a bounded entity to which not all may have access.

Borders – problematic exclusions?

People have always watched but few have analysed that great display of power present in the electrical discharge in the sky called lightning [...] In the late 1740s, *Benjamin Franklin developed the theory* that there are two kinds of charge, positive and negative[...] Franklin [...] *was the first great American electrical scientist.* (Dorf, p3-5)

Just as we do not know who 'authorised' the recognition of Volta and Ampere, so the justification for Dorf's assessment of Franklin as 'the first great American electrical scientist' is not explicit within this statement but must be inferred in the delineation of borders between scientists and humans. Just as Dorf's introduction of a historical survey of the evolution of science served to delineate between 'humans' and 'scientists' as a distinction between those who 'explore' and those who 'develop knowledge', so this trope is repeated here, distinguishing between people who 'watch' and Franklin, the great scientist who 'analyses' and 'develops theory'. As suggested earlier, the injunction to university students to develop models with universal applicability is underlined in this comparison between members of the scientific community who analyse and 'humans' or 'people' who 'watch'. The author of this distinction, however, is again absent. Dorf simply makes the statement and, as authorised voice of the scientific community, represents history as fact, rather than deduction, opinion or impression. Rather than making explicit the value-laden assumptions about the nature of scientific community, Dorf rewrites history from a perspective that excludes other practices from entitlement to scientific authority. The exclusion, for example, of 'common sense' or the daily lived and localised experience of science renders the reader a novice, a 'human' rather than a scientist in the face of this historical text. The reader must then desire to learn the scientific practice in order to identify with and accept the authority of the scientific practices as represented within the text by figures such as Franklin. There is consequently no space in this history, and by inference in current practice, for alternative methodologies or explanations or even for alternative identities – such as female.

We must return to Dorf's argument for including historical vignettes in the textbook. He argued that a vignette, 'enables the reader to witness the past and current motivation for the development of modern engineering devices and methods as well as to grasp the excitement of engineering in the 1990s' (Dorf, px).

The reader is positioned by this statement as a subject who should identify with the history as it is thus presented, an identification that will crucially enable them to participate not only practically but emotionally ('grasp the excitement') in current scientific communities. This text relies for its efficacy in encouraging enthusiasm and emotional engagement with the subject matter on readers 'witnessing' the historical development of science from a point of identification with the position of the author; they must view the history of scientific practice through the eyes of the already established scientist. The introduction of 'history' and the 'real world' into the text is not neutral, but may be interpreted differently by readers from different backgrounds and with different attitudes and opinions of the history of white, male, western scientific practice as represented in the text. The extent to which readers can identify with the role models established by the text may be limited by how closely they align themselves with this identity in their lives as individuals who may, or may not, also be considering entrance into the scientific community. Finally, the reader may be female. When the history as it is represented in this textbook excludes all reference to women scientists (see Ogilvy, 1988 and Alic, 1986 for criticism of this approach) and includes only one picture of a female – and that is as a user of the new domestic technology of the vacuum cleaner – we can begin to generate oppositional readings of this text among particular constituencies of readers (Fish, 1981; Hall, 1977). Given the perceived shortage of female science practitioners, this analysis of the function of historical referents within the textbook is worth consideration.

These observations are made specifically in response to Dorf's stated desire that a historical understanding of scientific practice should lead to an emotional and interested engagement with current practice. Our analysis suggests that just as scientists may be aware of the historically contingent production of scientific language, they should also develop a sensitivity to the socio-cultural construction of scientific community, particularly when they make forays into the field of historical and cultural representations.

Defining borders – problematic inclusions

Alongside these historical vignettes functions another, syntactical, means of constructing community: the 'We' structure of the text. The following example highlights this structure:

> Engineers use models to represent the elements of an electric circuit. We generate models for manufactured elements and devices in order to manipulate parameters and establish bounds on the devices' operating characteristics... In our work we will construct models of elements and then interconnect them to form a circuit model. (Dorf, p34)

This process in which the community is defined – 'Engineers use' – followed by an inclusion of the author and possibly the students within that community – 'We generate' – is concluded with a link between practices within the engineering community and the practices required within the textbook. 'In our work we will...'. The 'we' of the community is elided with the 'we' of the textbook and the lecture hall; 'we' the readers, it therefore follows, are engineers. Although this model of reading, in which students are encouraged to locate themselves within the engineering community, seems unproblematic, the incursion of an alternative syntactic construction provides a possible site for conflict within the construction of student as engineer.

Throughout the text students are faced with the imperative '*determine* I and v for the circuit shown', for example or '*Find*', or '*show*' requiring the performance of certain acts. They are not the independent, brave, analytic figures presented by Franklin and Edison. Rather they are subject to the discourses of the educational institution in which they are constructed as apprentice not practitioner. Thus learners are presented with *inclusive* narratives and *exclusive* injunctions. In contrast to these historical figures, it is unlikely, within the educational institutions in which students are working, that the problems presented to them are truly novel. They are more likely to be contrived by the existing engineering community as problems require students to demonstrate their grasp of key aspects of the canon.

The point of identification with the 'we' of the scientific community is essential if students are to participate within that community (Cohen, 1985), yet this process of shifting from an individual interest in subject matter to a collective identification with a group embodied within subject language and practices is rendered problematic by Dorf's constructions of scientific community. Within any didactical text the moment of transition from apprenticeship to participant in the community will always be complex – 'we' can be read as 'us' the current practitioners and authorised voices and, by implication, 'not you' the learner. When the 'we' of the scientific community is constructed within the textbook as white, male and western, the textual structure and the sensitive and complex relationship embodied within it begins to raise questions about the likelihood of particular groups of students making the transition from 'you' the scientific community to 'we' the scientific community.

Reading strategies: dominant, negotiated, oppositional

How might the construction of scientific community be read by different constituencies? We do not believe it possible to generate a textual analysis that will predict exactly how which different groups of readers will respond to a text, particularly since students will experience possibly competing definitions of scientific community in their interactions with other authorised members of that community, such as lecturers, older students etc. Drawing on substantial work within the fields of literary and media analysis, we suggest three models that may function to characterise different interactions with a textbook such as Dorf's. Let us apply these models to the text in conjunction with our analysis of core and framing discourses. Rather than 'misunderstanding' the language and practices of scientific community represented in these texts, it might be more accurate to consider the process of using textbooks (and, indeed, the enculturation process as a whole) as one of 'systematically distorted communication' in which there is 'no necessary correspondence' between the intentions of the author and the ways in which a given text will be read by its audience (Hall, 1977).

Hall suggests that in a 'dominant' reading of a text, the codes within it are understood in the same way by both producers and readers of the text – transmission of the information is therefore unproblematic. In terms of our analysis, then, this would suggest a reader position in which both framing and core discourses are accepted – all the language, practices and context for these practices are taken as comprehensible, sensible and practicable. Within this group of readers we might position the lecturer who suggests the text, who reads the historical vignettes as exhaustive and exemplary representations of the development of scientific practice and who takes the results of this development – the core discourse of scientific language and practice – as central to acceptance into the scientific community. Centrally, the gendered, socially constructed nature of the communication will be read as value-free because the values embedded in the representation correspond to the values held by the reader of the text.

Hall suggests a second type of reading is – a negotiated reading, in which certain elements of the code are understood and accepted by readers while others are rejected. So readers might accept the validity of the 'core' discourses while reading the 'framing' discourses as problematic. Within this group of readers we might position, for example, a female science student who, although aware of the absence of women within the historical vignettes, accepts the practices that have arisen from this particular tradition as having authority to be applied universally and which can be used by members of the scientific community. She may then desire to change the framing discourses by interpolating herself as a 'great scientist', by seeking out other histories about the role of women in science or by stressing the gendered representation of science as it currently presents itself. At the same time, she accepts the language and practices required to participate in the community.

Hall also suggests, finally, an oppositional reading, in which all elements of the code are rejected by readers. In our analysis, then, readers would reject the universalising claims both of the evolutionary history of science and of the validity of the core discourse's practices and language. Within this group of readers are students who read every mention of great electronic scientists as 'not me' and reject the viability of scientific models for universal application. This rejection might lead to students changing course or career, or to the development of alternative scientific practices.

Summary and implications

Our analysis of this one text is necessarily coarse and simplistic. The intention is to raise questions about the ways in which the framing discourses that construct scientific community are mobilised within scientific textbooks, and to problematise the prevalent assumption that an introduction of the 'real world' into textbooks will necessarily engender greater acceptance of the core discourse of practices and languages of the scientific community. Just as scientific language is socio-culturally constructed, so, it is important to underline, is the construct of scientific community proffered by the textbook. Crucially, the introduction of the 'real' or 'historical' worlds into scientific textbooks also introduces greater possibilities for 'systematically distorted communication', possibilities which must be acknowledged and reflected upon by authors.

We would contend that much science education research has focused on what we have termed the core discourse, leading to research agendas which ignore the framing discourse of education. A potential outcome of this approach is that even when innovative approaches to the 'core' are developed and evaluated, the non-accounting for the framing discourse means that over time little changes. For example, the numbers of students who study physical science post-16 in the UK remains static and the numbers of females entering higher education to follow science and engineering programmes is unchanged over decades.

In addition, our analysis questions the status of textbooks as offering an unambiguous transmission of information and highlights the difficulties students may encounter in engaging with the discourse, when that discourse is mapped onto their pre-existing frameworks of knowledge.

A critical implication of this study relates to research methodology. This chapter arose from a collaboration between researchers with backgrounds in science education and cultural studies. As an exercise in multi-disciplinary research, the task has been both challenging and productive, and underlines the importance of stepping outside a discipline to take alternative views, and to question what might be meant by the 'we' of scientific community, a process that may in some ways replicate the delicate and complex moment of transition from the 'I' of the individual student/learner to the 'we' of membership of a community.

The analysis in this chapter highlights that the production of scientific community is constructed on the establishment of an opposition between a 'scientific community' privy to the meanings and practices of the secular language of science, and a 'lay community' who are unable to operate as engineers or scientists through lack of access to these languages and practices. If we are to foster a future scientific community which meets the needs of the wider population, the fundamental establishment of such oppositions between 'scientists' and 'humans' as a bedrock assumption central to the process of 'becoming a scientist' needs to be critiqued and questioned, not only because it sets up an opposition between the scientists advising on behalf of the wider population, but because it may continue to limit the degree of participation in scientific community of a wider cross-section of the population, which may be interested in being part of humanity rather than distinct from it.

Acknowledgements

We want to thank the Economic and Social Research Council, UK for funding the projects 'Mathematical Experiences and Mathematical Practices in HE Science Settings' (Award No. R000222571) and 'ScreenPlay: a study of techno-popular culture' (Award No. R000 237298) which supported the writing of this chapter.

References

Alic, M. (1986) *Hypatia's Heritage: a history of women in science from antiquity to the late nineteenth century,* London: The Women's Press

Anderson B. (1991) *Imagined Communities: reflections on the origin and spread of nationalism,* London and New York: Verso

Bakhtin, M.M. (1981) *The dialogic imagination: four essays by M.M. Bakhtin,* M. Holquist (ed.) Austin: University of Texas Press

Bourdieu, P. (1984) *Distinction: a social critique of the judgement of taste,* London: Routledge and Kegan Paul Ltd

Byrne E.M. (1993) *Women and Science: the Snark Syndrome,* London: Falmer Press

Cohen A.P. (1985) *The Symbolic Construction of Community,* London: Routledge

Collins H. (1985) *Changing Order: replication and induction in scientific practice,* Sage:London

Dorf, R.C. (1993, Second Edition; 1996 Third Edition – with J.A. Svoboda) *Introduction to Electric Circuits,* New York: J. Wiley and Sons

Fish, S. (1980) *Is there a Text in this Class? The authority of interpretive communities,* Cambridge, USA: Harvard University Press

Foucault M. (1990) *The History of Sexuality: Volume 1,* trans. by Robert Hurley. London: Penguin

Hall, S. (1977) *Encoding and Decoding in Television Discourse,* CCCS Stencilled Chapter, no.7

Kelly, A. (ed.) (1987) *Science for Girls?,* Milton Keynes: Open University Press

Knorr-Cetina, K. (1981) *The Manufacture of Knowledge,* Oxford: Pergamon Press

Lacan, J. (1981) *The language of the self, the function of language in psychoanalysis* Wilden, A (trans.) Baltimore, London: Johns Hopkins University Press

Latour, B. and Woolgar, S. (1979) *Laboratory Life: the social construction of scientific facts.* Beverley Hills, CA: Sage

Lave, J. and Wenger E. (1991) *Situated Learning: legitimate peripheral participation,* Cambridge: Cambridge University Press

Lynch, M. and Woolgar, S. (eds.) (1990) *Representation in Scientific Practice.* Cambridge, USA: MIT Press

Ogilvy, M.B. (1988) *Women in Science: a biographical dictionary* Cambridge, USA: MIT Press

Thomas, K. (1990) Gender and Subject in Higher Education, Buckingham: Open University Press

Traweek, S. (1988) Beamtimes and Lifetimes: the world of high energy physics, Cambridge, USA: Harvard University Press

Part III:
Formal and Informal Cultures

Editors' introduction

Across the world, the aims, organisation, institutions and processes of schooling reflect many differences – but they also face many of the same challenges. Amongst the most significant is how to manage the interface of the formal education that takes place in schools and the informal learning that occurs as part of diverse other activities in life. Of course, educationalists configure curriculum, pedagogy and assessment systems on behalf of their societies – to teach knowledge, engender understanding and skills, to draw children and young people into value systems and appropriate forms of social identification, and, at best, to attempt to maximise the potential of each individual. In such ways they act, as Jerome Bruner once put it, 'to do society's serious business'. But the tragedy of such formalised efforts to inculcate, educate and improve, is that they can be premised on a narrow and uni-directional vision of what is needed and how it should be provided.

But what if, instead of conceptualising schooling as some form of transmission, we tried to draw more fully on the cultural resources and opportunities that are associated with informal learning? After all, such processes of learning powered human development for millions of years before the introduction of formal education. What if we could draw more fully on the experiences and learning that occur daily in homes, playgrounds, streets and workplaces – and on the expertise of parents, siblings, peers, mentors and others? In principle, it might be possible to harness the energy and high motivation that is often apparent in such settings, and offer levels of support for new learning that would be impossible within schools. Can we, in other words, maximise educational opportunities at the interface of such cultures and practices?

Sadly, this challenge has proved extremely difficult. The world-view of those in schools and other educational institutions tends to be quite specific, and is reinforced by many constraints and requirements. Conversely, the lived realities of actors in informal settings press in other diverse ways, producing a wide range of circumstances, life-styles and perspectives with which those in school often find it hard to engage. There may be a confluence where such cultures are brought together – but collision or indifference seems to occur more frequently than cooperation.

The chapters in this section illustrate the tensions that surround this opportunity. Chapter 11, by Martin Hughes and Pamela Greenhough, focuses on homework as a vehicle of interchange between the cultures of home and school. Could it enable constructive synergy between formal and informal cultures and thus enhance learning? Reviewing recent perspectives and practices of parents, students and teachers, Hughes and Greenhough conclude that there are significant difficulties – in the tasks set, the settings in which homework is carried out, and the feelings that participants have about it. Andrew Pollard and Ann Filer continue this theme in Chapter 12 through his focus on the strategies adopted by parents in their interaction with schools. A common medium for direct interaction between parents and teachers in primary school concerns the annual reporting of pupil progress. How do parents receive, interpret and mediate this? Pollard and Filer suggest that parents adopt a range of strategies to make sense of reports and to support their children in their own terms. Such school assessments are classic one-way inter-cultural statements which do little to harness the informal knowledge of parents and the home.

In Chapter 13, Keri Facer, John Furlong, Ruth Furlong and Rosamund Sutherland explore information technology as a site for formal-informal cultural exchange. Focusing on 'edutainment' software, they demonstrate the penetration of new media into the informal cultures and practices of children and young people and consider its immense educational potential. In particular, they emphasise the structured support for playfulness embedded in many games – but deemed by many to be increasingly driven out of formal educational experiences in schools, despite what is known about its contribution to learning. Once again, the potential offered by this confluence of cultures is immense.

This section thus highlights a challenge. It appears that learners have a great deal to gain from the development of constructive forms of interaction between formal and informal cultures and practices. But it also seems that we are a long way from evolving the understanding and forms of social organisation that could make this possible.

11

Homework: Learning at the interface between home and school cultures

Martin Hughes and Pamela Greenhough

Introduction

Most children move on a daily basis between the two cultures of home and school. In doing so, they participate in two quite different learning environments. In terms of the familiar distinction between *formal* and *informal* learning (Coffield, 2000), schools can be seen as embodying the former, and homes the latter. School learning is characterised by a prescribed curriculum, the presence of trained instructors, timetabled lessons, and the regular assessment of learning outcomes. Home learning, in contrast, arises out of the spontaneous interactions of family members as they carry out the business of everyday life (Tizard and Hughes, 1984).

As well as embodying different learning environments, there often appears to be a strong boundary between the cultures of home and school. Whereas children may move freely across this boundary, parents and teachers generally do not. Parents often report that they do not know enough about what is happening to their children in school, while teachers may make judgements about parents – and about home cultures more generally – on the basis of little or no direct experience of what actually goes on in homes (Hughes, Wikeley and Nash, 1994; Desforges, Holden and Hughes, 1994). Moreover, attempts to weaken this boundary by bringing parents and teachers closer together are often constrained by disparities in power and status between the two groups (Vincent, 1996).

There are important differences between the cultures of different homes (Solomon, 1994), just as there are important differences between the cultures of different schools. Differences in home background are widely acknowledged to be a major factor in accounting for differences in school attainment (Wang, Haertel and Walberg, 1993; Marjoribanks, 1994). Moreover, detailed investigations of different home cultures and their relationship to school cultures point both to the complexities of this relationship, and to its vital importance for children's learning (Brice Heath, 1983; Lareau, 1989: Gregory, 1996; Pollard and Filer, this volume).

In this chapter, we explore the complex relationship between home and school cultures by studying homework – the work is set by teachers to be done outside the classroom, usually at home. We are explicitly following Jean Lave's suggestion that one might obtain insights into the boundaries between home and school by looking at something which regularly crosses those boundaries: 'homework... moves back and forth between home and school, and actually to the bowling alley, burger bar and so on' (Lave, 1996).

In terms of the watery metaphor which underpins many of the contributions to this book, homework can be compared to the daily ebb and flow of the tide washing against the shore. But the process is by no means simple. Just as the tide may influence – and be influenced by – the nature of the shoreline, so the cultures of home and school may influence each other through the daily movement back and forth of homework.

Taking this perspective raises a number of questions. For example, how far does homework resemble the formal learning of school or the informal learning of home? To what extent does it manage to bring together, or make connections between, these different kinds of learning? How much does homework weaken – or strengthen – the boundary between home and school? What does homework tell us about the nature of this boundary, and about the relationship between the two cultures?

Drawing on some recent research on homework, we look in particular at the nature of homework assignments, the social context in which homework takes place, and the way in which homework is perceived by parents, teachers and students. First, though, we describe the nature of the research and the wider national and international context in which it took place.

The homework research project

Our research on homework took place in the UK from 1999 to 2001. During this period educational policy and practice was strongly influenced by the New Labour government's desire to raise educational standards, particularly those of literacy and numeracy in primary schools. Homework was seen as a key part in this process, and in 1998 the Department for Education and Employment published guidelines which set out how much time was to be spent on homework at different ages (DfEE, 1998). A particular feature of these guidelines was the clear expectation that homework should be set throughout the primary school years

The homework guidelines were supported by regular statements from ministers and other educational-policy makers that homework is essentially a good thing. For example, within weeks of taking office, the Secretary of State for Education wrote in a popular newspaper that 'Homework is not a punishment and it is not a chore. It is an essential part of a good education' (Blunkett, 1997). In addition, ministers were quick to round on researchers who appeared to be critical of their policies. For example, when a study was published which showed no correlation between the frequency of homework and academic progress at primary level (Farrow, Tymms and Henderson, 1999), the Secretary of State commented that:

> Some researchers are so obsessed with 'critique' and out of touch with reality that they churn out findings that no-one with the slightest common-sense could take seriously ... They believe it is right to read a bed-time story to their own child, but think homework for other children is damaging. (Blunkett, 1999)

In fact, previous research on homework in the USA has suggested that there is little evidence to support a connection, at primary level, between homework and educational attainment (eg Cowan and Hallam, 1999). However, it is also the case that relatively little research on homework has been carried out in the UK.

The overall aim of our research was to explore the contribution homework makes to student learning. We adopted a broad socio-cultural approach to learning, influenced by theorists such as Wertsch (1991), and Pollard and Filer (1996). In particular, we took the view that we needed to look at homework within the social and cultural contexts in which it is set and carried out, paying particular attention to the purposes and intentions of the participants in those contexts, the interaction which takes place between them, the value placed on the activities being undertaken, and the material, cultural and linguistic resources available for them to draw on. This meant that we needed to make an in-depth study of homework in a relatively small number of locations.

Our research was based around four secondary and four primary schools in the South West of England. The secondary schools served contrasting catchment areas. Two had a high proportion of students eligible for free school meals, with many students in one of them being from ethnic minority groups. A third was a city-based church school, which drew students from all over the city, while the fourth served a large rural area. The catchment areas for the primary schools were similar, as each was a feeder school for one of the secondary schools. In each secondary school we focused on Year 8, and selected six students (three boys, three girls; two high attainers, two medium and two low) for intensive study. In the primary schools we adopted a similar procedure, taking six students in Year 5. In each school we interviewed teachers on a wide range of subjects, and headteachers, parents and students, and observed homework being set in class. We also focused on particular homework assignments, attempting to track them as they moved from school to home and back again.

The nature of homework assignments

The vast majority of assignments observed in our study were closely related to the school curriculum and required few, if any, connections to be made with life outside school. A typical mathematics homework would consist of problems similar to those worked on in class, for example

On the same graph, draw the lines $y = 2x - 3$,
$$y = \frac{1}{2}x,$$
$$x + y = 9.$$

Take values of x from 0 to 8. Write down the coordinates of the three vertices of the triangle formed. (Year 8)

English homeworks were varied and ranged from producing a front page for a newspaper reporting the death of Caesar to rewriting the conclusion to Pilgrim's Progress in modern English.

There were some exceptions to this general pattern. One class of Year 8 students was set an assignment which required them to find a number of items, such as cosmetics which were still in their original packaging. The students were asked to draw up a chart showing the overall volume of the goods purchased as a percentage of the overall volume of the packaging. The students found this task quite engaging, and commented afterwards on how revealing it had been.

> If I'm going to buy something then I would know how much I'm actually spending on packaging and how much I'm actually spending on what I want. (Year 8 girl)

Students also enjoyed a German homework where they had to write about a day in the life of a famous person, as this offered an opportunity to write about their favourite celebrities, and even make jokes, as in 'An evening with David Beckham':

12:30	Ich gehe ins Bett mit meiner Frau Victoria.
	I go to bed with my wife Victoria
03:00	Ich stehe auf und ich trinke eine Flasche Wasser
	I get up and drink a bottle of water
03:05	Ich gehe ins Bett.
	I go to bed
09:00	Ich stehe auf – schon weider morgen und ich bin sehr müde.
	I get up – tomorrow already and I am very tired.
	(Year 8 boy)

Our observations on the nature of the homework assignments were supported by the students' comments. Some of the students were asked whether there was anything in their life outside school which had helped them with particular homework assignments. The vast majority said that they couldn't think of anything. We asked the same group whether they could see ways in which their homework might help them with or be relevant to, life outside school, to which most replied 'no' or answered in a rather general and hypothetical fashion (e.g. that their science homework might help them if they were later to become a scientist). There were some exceptions, as in the case of the volume calculations above, or the Year 8 boy who observed that if he decided to bet on sport, an exercise on probability would help him calculate his chances.

The social context of homework

Perhaps not surprisingly, we found that the great majority of homework was done at home. Some students tried to get as much as possible done while they were still at school – for example, at lunchtime, in the breaks between lessons or even during the lessons themselves.

> Student: I did it before the lesson in between, with my friend, which was.. it took about 5 minutes, it wasn't that difficult.
> *Interviewer: Right so is that sort of in a lesson, or.. ?*
> Student: No, just when.. we were waiting for the teacher to come back from going off to collect something I think
> *Interviewer: And how much effort did you put into that one?*
> Student: Well I had to work hard to actually get it done, because you know I was trying to get it done there and then, and finish it, so I didn't need to worry about it (Year 8 boy, French)

Homework done at home was usually a solitary task. Some students would work in their bedrooms; others in the public rooms of the house, often with other activities going on around them. Some students managed to combine their homework with watching TV, as one student aired:

> I like to do my homework in front of the TV, as it helps take your mind off it. (Year 5 girl)

Some of the students sought help with their homework from parents or siblings, who usually tried to comply. (Later in the chapter we provide an example of the difficulties that this could pose for parents.) On the whole, the Year 8 students completed their homework on their own with little outside assistance, although Year 5 students received more help.

TV soap operas such as Neighbours often portray homework as a collaborative activity in which students meet up at each other's houses to work on it together. But we did not find this in our research. Students told us that they would occasionally phone their friends to check on what the homework was, and on whether they had done it correctly, but as a rule they did not work on homework assignments together. There was a tendency among the students to keep their homework and their social lives separate. A parent who had tried unsuccessfully to set up a homework club at her home told us:

> *Interviewer: But the homework club was the bit that got abandoned...?*
> Mother: It was a bit.. cos I keep saying to him, why don't you bring your mates home, you know, you could all do the same homework together, and.. he likes to keep it separately, you know, if he's going to play with his mates, he'd rather go off and play with them rather than continue the school thing through the house. (*Parent of Year 8 boy*)

Parents' perceptions of homework

Most parents were positive about homework, especially in the secondary school. They saw it as serving two main purposes – which were somewhat in conflict. The first was that homework was essentially an extension of school: it could provide extra time to get schoolwork done and/or reflect on lessons. The second was that homework offered something essentially different from school: in particular, an opportunity for students to develop study skills and work independently.

> I think they need it really because sometimes there's not enough time I suppose within a subject to finish a piece, ...so sometimes it might not be long enough to complete it type of thing so if they haven't finished it during the lesson then yes I think they should bring it home. (Parent of Year 8 girl)

> *Father:* (If it were abolished) *I think that would be really a tragedy to some extent.*
> Mother: It would give them no self discipline and no ability to research their own work and work things out for themselves. It

would just take away all initiative, I think. (Parents of Year 8 boy)

Where parents were opposed to homework it was because they saw it as encroaching on students' out-of-school lives. This perception was much more frequent among the parents of primary age children.

> The starting assumption is... there's more to life than school for god's sake and I find the intrusion of school into the rest of life, if you've got a rich and full life outside school, yeh the tendency is still to resent it really. (Parent of Year 8 girl)

> I'm not happy really about homework at their age. I don't really think the pressure should be on them at all, I think they should just be encouraged to enjoy it, the learning and I don't.. I don't think it's the right space for them to be doing it actually, at the end of the day when they're tired, and they need some leisure time really, they do. It's not a great amount of work that they have to do, but it's the principle of it really, (my son) feels that that's his time. (Parent of Year 5 boy)

One of these parents described their role in relation to homework as defending the child against it.

> Well I think they (parents) should protect them from it a bit really [laughs] you know... it should be in partnership with the school but it's difficult to be in partnership if you feel there is far too much of it. And particularly when sometimes you know it's just sort of meaningless twaddle that we're being told to do, like colour in your new cover or something [laughs], you know for a new project or something like that.

Defensive or protective actions taken by these parents included writing letters excusing their children from their homework, or limiting the demands of the homework, sometimes by offering to help or by redefining the task. But some parents had difficulties when they tried to help, irrespective of the stance they took towards homework. As we saw, homework tasks are located in a school-oriented curriculum which often seemed to be discontinuous with the perspectives and practices of the world outside school. Parents, as well as children, sometimes struggled to make sense of the tasks.

Father: They wanted to know... they set them one thing.. they wanted to know the three dimensions like, 3D.

Mother: 3D that's right, yes.

Father: Of things in the house.

Mother: Oh that's it, yeh.

Father: It was 3D. It wasn't explained what they meant and (our daughter) didn't understand exactly what they were on about. I actually thought 3 dimensional, you know, as you are looking at an object but they meant height, width and depth. But it wasn't explained as height, width and depth. So we didn't know what she was on.. what she had to do and she didn't know exactly what she had to do. So we couldn't do it ... we've got no objects here which I [believe is/would read as] 3D. (Parents of Year 8 girl)

As this example shows, homework could founder in the gulf between the everyday understandings of the home and the more technical language of the classroom.

Teachers' perceptions of homework

The teachers were much more ambivalent about homework than the parents, and mixed feelings were common. On the positive side, many teachers felt homework added something to class work. It allowed them to extend their teaching beyond the classroom, and provided an opportunity for students to practice procedures learnt in class, to consolidate or build on classwork. Some said they simply couldn't get through the curriculum without it.

> I think particularly for Year 8 it's essential.. we have very little, comparatively very little time with Year 8s to cover the amount of work that they're expected to have done by the end of the year, and homework is essential in ensuring that work is covered. For the most part.. I know in my teaching studies, we've focused quite a lot on how it's important to continually re-visit, to re-inforce ideas, and I really do see that as the way to ensure that these things get sunk in. (Maths teacher)

The teachers also expressed a number of reservations about homework. Some were concerned about homework being imposed on home life, displacing other valued activities:

My personal feelings are that I prefer it to be more informal than formal and that I think to try and set them too much at this age group is kind of.. not counter productive but I.. I would like children to have their.. their childhood if you like and have time for playing, because we do.. the pace that we're working at the moment, is with literacy and numeracy hours, that the mornings are quite intense, the afternoons are quite long but we're expecting quite a lot from the children... (Year 5 teacher)

The perception of homework as an imposition did not only come from parents. Many teachers felt that they were under pressure to set homework, whether because of government policy, school policy or parents:

I do not think that homework is incredibly valuable myself, but I go along with it because the school policy is to, and parental pressure is to, see homework as important. I think if you're going to do something like that you have to pretend that it's important and try and get pupils to engage with it. It does actually serve as important, because when they go away and do research on their own it does actually have academic value. But what I don't like is punishing children who haven't managed it, especially if they come from homes where it's a little bit disorganised or the pressure is for them not to get on with their work, because that puts them... it means they're being punished at school because of the disorganisation of the home. (Humanities teacher)

A common perception amongst the teachers was that they felt locked into a school homework timetable that meant they had to set homework at certain times in the week, whether or not they considered it appropriate. Several teachers summed this up with the phrase: 'I don't like homework for homework's sake'.

Students' perceptions of homework

We expected that the students would be virtually unanimous in their dislike of homework. But this was far from the case. At both primary and secondary levels the students fell into three roughly equal groups – those who were positive about homework, those who were negative and those who had mixed feelings.

Students who were positive about homework tended to emphasise two things. First, they felt that homework in some way helped their learning, and that this was usually a good thing. Secondly, they felt that homework gave them something to do at home, and if it were abolished they would be bored:

> I think it (abolishing homework) would be like a very big mistake, cos every person needs to have a homework, or every child needs to have a homework when they goes to school or college, something to do when they get home, so that they make sure they know and get it into the brain, how to do it. (Year 8 boy)

> Well I would feel upset (if it were abolished) because when I have homework I will know a lot more and if I don't, I probably won't know that much and the work might be harder. (Year 5 boy)

Students who were negative about homework tended to emphasise the way in which homework encroached on what they saw as their own time:

> I would say it (the amount of homework) was too much because we spend our whole day at school doing work and then they expect us to come home and spend more time doing work. (Year 8 girl)

Other students were less explicit about their reasons for disliking homework. When asked how they would feel if homework were abolished, they simply said 'happy', 'really happy', 'over the moon', or even 'over the moon, there would be a god!'.

A third group of students were more ambivalent about homework. On the one hand they could see its value for their education, or as a safeguard against boredom, but on the other hand they resented its capacity to encroach into their lives:

> I think we should have it because it gives you more education, you can understand it more, it's like another lesson really, but sometimes I think they give you a bit too much but then that's just me. I don't really like homework but it's all right sometimes. (Year 8 girl)

(If homework were abolished) the children would probably.. at first they would think 'hooray', but then they would get... sometimes you might get a bit bored at the weekend... because normally homework does take up quite a lot of time and they might think 'I'm getting really bored, what shall I do' and the adults would have said 'go and do your homework' but then they can't say that because it's been taken away. (Year 5 girl)

Discussion

We can now revisit the questions and issues raised in the introduction in the light of the above findings. First, to what extent does homework create links between home and school cultures? Clearly, homework has considerable potential in this respect. Yet our research suggests that – in our admittedly small sample – this potential is not being fulfilled. There seem to be two main reasons for this.

The first lies in the nature of the assignments. As we have seen, most homework assignments resemble the formal learning of school far more than they resemble the informal learning of home. Homework tasks are typically elements of the school curriculum, which are generated and assessed by teachers and seen by students as having little relationship to their lives outside school. In the words of one Year 5 student, homework is essentially 'a little bit of extra school except that it's not at school'.

The second lies in the social context in which homework takes place. Homework is primarily an individual activity which takes place in isolation from other people. As a rule, students do not involve family and friends in their homework unless they are stuck, and even then help is not always forthcoming or particularly helpful. Indeed, our overall impression was that students saw homework as a necessary chore to be disposed of with minimal effort and engagement, rather than an opportunity to engage in collaborative learning.

We can also ask what homework tells us about the interface between home and school cultures. Our research suggests that there are strong – and at times conflicting – undercurrents in the waters. On the one hand, there is a perception, shared by a number of students, teachers and parents, that homework represents an unwelcome encroachment by school on home and family life – what Edwards and

Warin (1999) have referred to as 'the long arm of the school reaching into the home' (p332). On the other hand, we must recognise that homework is seen as a good thing by the majority of parents, and by many students: thus the encroachment is in many cases a welcome one. Indeed, some of the teachers reported feeling under pressure from parents to set homework when they felt it was not appropriate – what might be termed 'the long arm of the home reaching into the school'.

In summary, we have tried in this chapter to throw light on the practice of homework and its position at the interface between home and school cultures. We are tempted to conclude that homework has obtained some kind of symbolic value, in which layers of meaning and expectation have been placed upon what is essentially a straightforward, if rather mundane, practice. The participants in this practice – students, teachers and parents – may consequently have become locked in to something which is playing only a limited role in enhancing student learning. If the potential of homework is really to be fulfilled, a process of deconstruction may well be needed before a more positive reconstruction can take place.

Acknowledgement

The research on which this chapter is based was supported by ESRC grant no R000 237857 on 'Homework and its contribution to learning'.

References

Blunkett, D. (1997) Turn your children off TV and on to learning, *The Mail on Sunday*, 22 June

Blunkett, D. (1999) *The Independent*, July

Coffield, F. (ed) (2000) *The Necessity of Informal Learning*. Bristol: The Policy Press

Cowan, R. and Hallam, S. (1999) What do we know about homework? *Viewpoint*, 9, Institute of Education, University of London

Department for Education and Employment (DfEE) (1998) *Homework: Guidelines for Primary and Secondary Schools*. London: DfEE

Desforges, C., Holden, C. and Hughes, M. (1994) Assessment at Key Stage One: its effects on parents, teachers and classroom practice. *Research Papers in Education*, 9, p133-158.

Edwards, A. and Warin, J. (1999) Parental involvement in raising the achievement of primary school pupils: why bother?, *Oxford Review of Education*, 25, 325-341

Farrow, S., Tymms, P. and Henderson, B. (1999) Homework and attainment in primary schools, *British Educational Research Journal*, 25 232-341

Heath, S. B. (1983) *Ways with Words: language, life and work in communities and classrooms*. Cambridge: Cambridge University Press

Hughes, M., Wikeley, F. and Nash, T. (1994) *Parents and their Children's Schools*, Oxford: Basil Blackwell

Lareau, A. (1989) *Home Advantage: social class and parental intervention in elementary school*, London: Falmer Press

Lave, J. (1996) Transcript of first Oxford Seminar on Situated Learning in Mathematics Education

Pollard, A. and Filer, A. (this volume)

Pollard, A. and Filer, A. (1996) *The Social World of Children's Learning*. London: Cassell

Solomon, J. (1994) Towards a notion of home culture: science education in the home *British Educational Research Journal*, 20, p565-577

Tizard, B. and Hughes. M. (1984) *Young Children Learning: talking and thinking at home and at school*, London: Fontana

Vincent, C. (1996) *Parents and Teachers: power and participation*, London: Falmer Press

Wang, M., Haertel, G. and Walberg, H. (1993) Towards a knowledge base for school learning, *Review of Educational Research*, 63, p249-294

Wertsch, J. (1991) *Voices of the Mind: a socio-cultural approach to mediated action* London: Harvester

12

Parental strategies at the intersection of home and school cultures: the mediation of formal assessment

Andrew Pollard and Ann Filer

Introduction

In this chapter we consider the interface between the formal cultures of primary schools and the informal cultures of pupils' homes. We focus on parents' strategies in mediating between these cultures on behalf of their children, and concentrate on formal assessment activity and reports, seeing these as a powerful form of communication between the two cultural settings. In particular, we offer an analytic framework for mapping both parents' strategic responses and the ways in which these change over time as they learn how to mediate and interpret school-derived assessments in terms of family life, existing identities and relationships.

In recent years, the work of teachers in English primary schools has become highly codified. National structures, requirements, inspections, forms of training and performance management have dramatically impacted on their cultures, affecting language, social practices, assumptions and expectations. Whilst there was an ideological struggle with previous 'child-centred' ideas, a gradual transformation in the values of teachers has been recorded (Osborn *et al* 2000). The introduction of a national system of assessment reflected and extended such changes. Children are now regularly tested and annual reports on their progress are provided for parents.

However, data gathered through the *Identity and Learning Programme* (Pollard and Filer, 1996, 1999, Filer and Pollard 2000) on which this chapter is based, intriguingly suggested that parents made little direct use of the formal information such reports contained. Rather, they re-interpreted it in the context of many other factors such as their knowledge of particular teachers, of their child, his/her identity, previous experiences and trajectory, dynamics and relationships within the family. What was going on? On what basis did parents mediate and interpret these potentially high stakes, categoric assessments? How did they make sense of such data, and weigh it in relation to their views on the school and teachers, the performance of other children, and circumstances within their own families? How, in other words, did they manage this powerful interjection and judgement about their children, handed down at at the interface of school and family cultures?

The families in the *Identity and Learning Programme* were drawn from two distinct parts of a city in the south of England, and faced very different socio-economic conditions. Ten pupils from each of two schools, Greenside and Albert Park, were tracked through seven years of their primary schooling. The main focus of these longitudinal ethnographies concerned the ways in which the pupils progressively shaped their school identities and careers in the context of judgements made by teachers, families, friends and peers. We can also consider the same data-set in relation to parents.

Teacher perceptions

Teachers in the two schools viewed the parents of their pupils and their involvements in their children's education in quite different ways. At Albert Park, the predominantly skilled working class parents were generally viewed, *en masse*, as active in their children's schooling but in entirely the 'wrong' way. Many staff were critical of parents as being too confident, vociferous and challenging to school in relation to their 'rights' with regard to such issues as school uniform and selection for sports teams. On the other hand they saw most parents as lacking concern and as being unlikely to raise issues about academic decisions or outcomes that might affect their children's attainment. But: 'if their son doesn't get selected for the football team, fathers that you never see will be up here like a flash'

(Teacher at Albert Park). Further, some staff commented that, though poverty and unemployment was not a great problem for most families, many exhibited a kind of 'shallow consumerism', a lack of 'culture' in their recreational pursuits. One teacher remarked that many families had: 'plenty of money but not much couth – if that's not being unkind' (Teacher at Albert Park). However, we found parents at Albert Park often to be *apparently* more accepting of teacher assessments and perceptions of their children than those at Greenside School, but as this chapter reveals, the picture was not that simple.

The parents at Greenside School were often criticised for being *too* active. Though the ethos and the school intake changed somewhat over the time of the study (see Pollard and Filer, 1999) many parents in the community were perceived by school staff (and indeed among themselves) as 'pushy', having unrealistic expectations and putting undue pressure on their children. One parent was denounced for questioning the reading level attributed to her child and described as: 'one who would take over her child's education if she could' (Teacher at Greenside School). Greenside parents often perceived teachers as defensive, even in one case as 'unprofessional' when parents questioned their children's levels of achievements. Parental intervention in their children's education in Greenside School often led to a deterioration, at least temporarily, in home-school relationships.

In both schools, we might interpret such teacher perspectives as reflecting the staff cultures. In working together to provide educational services, teachers also developed particular ways of characterising their client groups – a common response, first documented by Becker (1953). National assessment processes then placed them in posession of supposedly objective evidence on pupil performance. This is a powerful evaluative position.

Analysing the parental response

Parents are in an interestingly anomolous position at this interface. On the one hand, they are the clients, the consumers, the customers, who have a right to expect high quality services and whose rights have been strongly reinforced by recent political rhetoric and legislation. On the other hand, they are vulnerable supplicants, with less knowledge than teachers on educational issues and curriculum requirements, daily sending their children into the crowded classroom, yet being absent themselves from the school setting. This structural reality embodies inherent tensions and there is considerable scope for diverse responses by parents. Because of its power and intrusiveness, we have focused on assessment issues as a device to illuminate such responses.

How then, did parents respond to the assessment messages and reports about their children that were formally delivered to them? And how could this be understood over time? To address these questions, we adapted a model of strategic action which we had in fact developed to analyse pupil biogragraphies (Pollard and Filer, 1999) (see Figure 1 below).

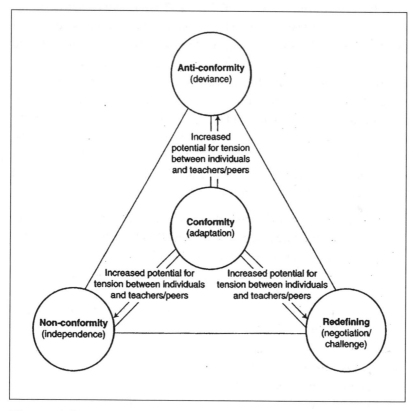

Figure 1 A model for plotting the dynamics of strategic action

This model represents four 'dimensions' of strategic action – conformity, non-conformity, anti-conformity and redefining. Such strategies resonate with the discussion of responses to culture-clash which were rehearsed in the introduction of this book. However, it is important to see how such strategies evolve over time and in new circumstances and how parental strategies change. So we also developed a way of thinking about the 'dynamics' of strategic action, seeing movement across and within the triadic model in response to new learning or new circumstances over time.

When characterising the strategic action of parents as interpreters and mediators of their children's assessment and school experience, we found that the model also provided a useful analytic framework. Indeed, by showing parents (as with pupils) in dynamic interaction with teachers, it could be set against simplistic assumptions and one-dimensional caricatures of parents as 'lacking interest' or 'pushy'; 'supportive' or 'non-supportive'.

This analysis is illustrated below: first, through illustration of each of the four 'dimensions' and second, through discussion of the 'dynamics' of parents' strategic mediation and action.

Dimensions of parents' strategic action

Let us start with the most accepting and adaptive responses, which we have termed 'conformity'.

Conformity: characterised at 'reification' and adaptation to procedures and curricular expectations, and low risk strategies in conformity to the agenda of school

Many parents, particularly in Albert Park School, appeared generally to support school assessments and trust teachers to assess and report their child's achievements objectively. For instance:

AF: So, reflecting on those results, and the sorts of teachers' assessments that you've had over the years generally, have you always felt that they are a reflection of Chris's achievements, or of Chris's abilities?

Father: I think, I suppose I'd have to say that the teachers who dealt with him at the time know him best for what he achieves in class. And we can't comment on that, but we've – you know,

it's our place to listen to their opinion. At (his brother's) secondary school, I questioned one particular teacher about the way
things were done when we visited the school, but not at Albert
Park. (Albert Park School, parent interview, July 1995, Y6)

This is the norm, the most frequent and expected response, reflecting an acceptance of teacher authority and judgement. However,
without seeking to challenge the system, some parents were more
independent and backed their own judgement, a stance that we
called 'non-conformity'.

Non-conformity: characterised as a measure of 'indifference' and
'independence', parents holding their own agenda

Some parents expressed a measure of indifference to school agendas
for success and attainment outcomes, and this was sometimes an expression of dissatisfaction with the evaluations of school as
irrelevant to the cultural norms or educational ideologies of the
family. Such families often recognised the disjunction of cultures
and values, and simply opted to accept it whilst retaining their views.
Robert's mother, attracted to some elements of the Steiner school of
educational philosophy, provides a good example of non-conformity:

> Though pleased with Robert's early school reports and evidence
> of his fast developing reading skills, Mrs Osborne expressed
> doubts about early formal education, either institutionalised or
> in the home:

> I would say he has got on very well, because I think it is very
> young to be bothered with that. I think it is very young. I mean,
> I am not a teacher, I know nothing really about education in that
> sense, but you know, you hear about people teaching them at
> play-school how to read and mothers teaching children to read
> before they go to school, and what is the rush really? (Greenside
> School, parent interview, March 1988, Reception)

Sometimes non-conformity represented an adaptation to a lack of
responsiveness on the part of the school to pupil or family concerns.
For instance, Alison's parents felt that school assessment of her
attainment was not in accordance with her ability. Indeed, they felt
that she was frustrated by the pace of study and by teacher expecta-

tions for her. They were asked how they interpreted that situation for their daughter and how it was managed.

Mother: Well, what we used to do was, we used to say that she'd have to do what the teacher told her but then what she wanted to do we did at home.

AF: Ah, right.

Mother: The next stage we did at home, so that way she was doing both and she was still getting what she wanted.

AF: One step ahead of school and doing what she wanted. And does it continue in that way?

Mother: Yeah, and now she's ready to go to senior school – now. (Senior school begins in Year 7 – over a year away for Alison).

Father: She was ready last year really. I feel she was. She finds some things still menial at school and she helps others, as you're probably aware. But while she's helping others she's not getting ahead herself is she? And we feel that you shouldn't hold anyone back who's got the ability. I know it's difficult in a class of thirty children for a teacher to cater for every individual child, she's got to go with the majority and clever children are a minority in most classes. (Albert Park School, parent interview, July 1994, Y5)

Quite often however, parents took a proactive stance, and attempted to influence the judgements of the school, to cross the cultural divide in bid to 're-define' the situation.

Re-defining: characterised by 'identification', high-risk strategies for influencing a shared agenda, negotiation and challenge

Some parents, whilst they identified with and supported school assessment procedures and curricular expectations generally, often disputed the school's, or a particular teacher's interpretation of satisfactory levels of achievement, either for pupils generally or for their own child in particular. This was particularly common in Greenside School, especially in the context of anticipating entrance exams for independent schools. Parents were involved in negotiating higher achievement outcomes and school expectations, for instance through requests for extra homework, a focus on one of the areas their child finds difficult or to help them to progress faster through maths or reading schemes.

The following are examples of re-defining strategies:

> *Mother*: One thing I have noticed (different) from last year – some of David's spellings – I've noticed they've been quite easy, whereas Ms Luke used to grade them a bit more. I think in that way he needs to be pushed a little bit more (..) (Albert Park School, parent interview, Nov 1994, Y6)

> *Mother*: I went in to see Mrs Hutton to ask her if he could have some more difficult spellings to do, because he was finding them too easy. And so I did go and mention it at open evening, that if he could have some more difficult.. (Albert Park School, parent interview July 1995, Y6)

> *Mother*: I was disappointed with Mary's progress after she had been back at school for a few weeks. This is because I had been told (and also thought) that she was bright, interested and her attitude was just right and she should take off with her reading at any time and it just hadn't happened. I went to see [the teacher] to talk about this. Anyway, her progress has been a lot better recently and she seems to be more interested again. (Greenside School, parent diary, October 1988, Year 1)

> The researchers' notes record this meeting as quite charged. There was a somewhat stormy encounter between Mrs Inman and Miss Scott with Miss Scott believing that Mrs Inman was making Mary over-anxious. Nevertheless, following their discussion, Mary received a steady stream of books to take home and more attention at school. (Pollard with Filer, 1996 p59)

These accounts exemplify how re-defining could be a relatively high-risk strategy for parents. However, managed carefully, and in the context of mutually respectful parent-teacher relationships, this approach can influence outcomes and achievement levels for their children. Where there were many such parents, as in Greenside School, it was also likely to have been highly influential in raising levels of school expectations for pupils generally. Managed poorly, however, it was interpreted as criticism, viewed by teachers as 'deviant' and could lead to re-defining home-school relations. Which brings us to anti-conformity:

Anti-conformity: characterised by 'rejection', high-risk strategies associated with oppositional agendas and actions perceived as 'deviant'

Some parents' alternative views or expectations regarding their child's achievements challenged school assessments. Anti-conformity largely represented a failed interventionist strategy to redefine; parental attempts to negotiate for change were interpreted by the school as 'deviant'.

The case of Harriet provides an example. After a year of schooling, Harriet's reading achievement in relation to the graded reading scheme did not accord with her mother's estimation of her potential. Her wry assessment of the situation was: 'She is nearly up to the standard she was when she left playgroup last year'. There was a gulf between what Harriet's mother thought she should be reading and school reading level expectations. The level of graded reading books being selected by mother and daughter for home reading lead to accusations that she was 'pushing' Harriet, contributing to strained relations with teachers generally.

Her mother took into school a newspaper article suggesting that 'children respond to more of a structured approach'. She sought Harriet's teacher's opinion on the issue:

> *Mother*: That went down terribly. Harriet's teacher interpreted it as I was finding fault with Mrs Long (teacher of Harriet's sister). I never mentioned Mrs Long but there is so much tittle-tattle in that school. I was called in by Mrs Long – did I have any complaints about her teaching? It was awful. So unprofessional! (Greenside School, interview with Harriet's parents, July 1988, Reception. (Pollard and Filer 1999, p235)

Such patterns of interaction occurred more often in our affluent middle class Greenside sample than in Albert Park. This was also reflected in the schools' perceptions of the communities they served. Some of the teachers in Greenside School saw parents as 'pushy' or as 'taking over' their child's education, holding educational ideologies and expectations for outcomes that pressurised the children but also themselves, the teachers.

However, there was nothing fixed or inevitable about parental patterns of response. Neither indeed did surface appearances of conformity or 'good' and 'supportive' home-school relationships always reflect parents' underlying, more complex feelings about teachers' evaluations and expectation of their children and of them as parents. We discuss some of this complexity and its implications for ways in which school assessments could be interpreted and mediated within families in the next section.

Dynamics of parents' mediation and strategic action

We found no inevitability in parental patterns of response. Indeed, the model of dimensions and dynamics does not describe the parents but the types of available response. Additionally, the model highlights the gap between conformity and other strategies as potential sites of tension across which home-school relationships are played out over time.

Assessment is a multi-dimensional process, and, parents also made assessments of teachers. The degree of trust and respect in the teacher's professionalism and judgement was crucial. Where this was high, assessments were likely to be accepted, the parents would 'conform', and tensions across the home-school interface would be minimal. Where there was doubt about the teacher or where irreconcilably different values existed between home and school, nonconformist or anti-conformist strategies would be developed. Use of redefining strategies also reflected how much confidence parents felt in a particular teacher's approach and their perception of the appropriateness of formal measures of attainment. Over the school career of their child, parents would adapt their responses to unfolding circumstances and their opinions about successive teachers. Patterns of response would be varied and adapted as judgements on how they could best support their children were made.

Parents often attempted redefining, especially in the early years of their child's education – though this strategy was not without risk. If things went wrong, parents might be labelled as trouble-makers by the school and antagonistic relations could develop. However, failures of the redefining strategy could also reflect the school's unresponsiveness to parental attempts to influence outcomes for their child. Something of the dynamics of one parent's strategies during her daughter's career at Greenside primary school is illustrated below.

Earlier we described the attempts of Harriet's mother to redefine teachers' expectations for her daughter. These were actually realised as strategies of 'anti-conformity' as they became increasingly interpreted by the teachers as 'deviant'. From those early antagonistic relations with school, she began in Year 1 (age 6) a gradual withdrawal from involvement in her daughter's schooling which culminated by Year 6 (age 11) in an almost complete separation of home and school concerns and experience for both mother and child.

> *AP*: Tell me a little bit more about how you see her self-confidence with maths
>
> *Mother*: Well really, not being in the classroom, I can't say, and I always find it very difficult to find out exactly what is going on because if you ask too many questions you're labelled anxious. So I can't tell you.
>
> (........)
>
> At one time I was helping her to chose the (reading) books but that went out of my control completely. And I didn't find the books very good that she was bringing home. It makes it sound as if I am very pushy and anxious but in the end I thought, I can't. I won't do anything at all. Just let it slip.
>
> *AP*: So really, your policy over the year was to keep your head down, in a sense?
>
> *Mother*: Yes. I mean, I wish that teachers would appreciate parents who are anxious to find out what their children do. Why don't they? Tell me. (Parent interview, July 1989, Year 1)

Over time Harriet's mother moved to a position of 'non-conformity', adopting a measure of indifference to school agenda and assessments. For instance, she was not convinced that Harriet was doing as well in maths as teachers reported. She explained:

> Well, you know, they always write really nice reports but I imagine they probably do for most people and I honestly don't think Harriet's got much of a clue in her maths and yet they all

say she's got a good grasp. But delve below the surface and she knows very little. (parent interview, July 1993, Year 5)

Some of Harriet's maths improvement in school her mother believed was due to the extra tutoring they now were paying for, but which Harriet was resisting. Although concerned about Harriet's maths, her mother now expressed a more philosophical perspective on the children's education. She thought that, with a busy family life that did not leave a lot of time for over-close supervision of learning, they were, as parents, probably not 'pushy' enough to see high academic success coming from their children. For the same reason she felt relatively relaxed that (all three children) did less homework than they should have done and she understood their perspective if they wanted a less 'chasing around' and demanding life than they saw their father lead. (Pollard and Filer, 1999, p224 – 279)

At Albert Park the apparent conformity of parents was often strategic in relation to interaction with teachers, and was regularly contradicted by the parents' mediation and re-interpretation of assessments in later discussions with their children. Their sincere concerns for their children's progress were often mixed with a desire to hold off pressure, on teachers as well as their children, and for good relations at school and home. This meant that evaluations of poor achievement made by teachers, or underachievement generally, might be interpreted as 'not important so long as you're trying' or mediated, for instance, 'just like my report when I was a kid'.

Apparent conformity also usually hid ambivalent, antagonistic feelings, and oppositional agendas (anti-conformity) which ran beneath what were, on the surface, supportive home-school relations. The case of Adrian illustrates this.

Throughout his primary career, Adrian's failure to apply himself to tasks meant his attainment was well below what his teachers and parents knew he was capable of. His parents had frequent contacts and relaxed, supportive relations with teachers. However his father explained:

(I get told) he's been fighting in the playground, or he hasn't done his work, he should have sent some homework in. And sometimes you think I shouldn't be put in that position. And I never feel hostile to teachers or anything, because I'm a professional myself, I deal with children and I know how difficult it is. So I'm not going to go round there saying 'Why haven't you flipping *made* him do his work?' But you do wonder sometimes. You think, 'Well, why should I? I'm a parent and I'm supposed to love him and protect him and care for him and develop him. Why have I suddenly been given this task of actually meting out some discipline? (You think), 'Don't tell me. Just deal with it. Nine to four. School. Deal with it'. I find that a bit disturbing (that) automatically I feel compelled – I must do something about it. Ultimately it makes me an antagonist (and) I'm not comfortable with that. (Albert Park School, parent interview, July 1994, Y5)

...and I think we've got enough on our plate without every minute of the day thinking, Oh he's got to improve. I mean, you can end up putting him under so much pressure.

...and it's not (just) a case of I'm trying to sit him down saying 'do your homework'. (The trouble is) he doesn't know about study skills. He doesn't know anything about setting out conclusions, what do you want to say? what do you want to show? It's no good you just writing a few pages if you mean absolutely nothing by it. I don't think he's been taught that. They haven't been prepared for study. But I'm not going to... I shouldn't be too critical because, you know, they're good teachers, but I look after children with *learning* difficulties and I expect far more from them! (Albert Park School, parent interview, November 1994, Y6)

Conclusion

In this chapter, we have shown how the formal assessment of pupils in primary schools has a powerful inter-cultural message. School assessments can be seen as a judgement made within the formal, standardised and professionalised cultural milieux of schools and delivered to multiple informal contexts of families, each with their own micro-cultural practices, understandings, values and relationships. We have documented the ways in which families variously act upon, contest, challenge, support or ignore the official and un-official voices of both teacher and standardised assessment emphasising the significance of the families' interpretation of the assessment outcomes.

The longitudinal nature of the *Identity and Learning Programme* enabled us to trace the *dynamic* development of families' charac-teristic repertoires of strategic involvement and influence in both shaping school assessment outcomes and mediating and interpreting them with their children. It provides an analysis over time, going beyond a simple comparison of the two schools or the social class background of the communities they served. In so doing, it extends a structural analysis of class-based differences to show how variations both exist and develop. In particular, we would argue that the dynamics of home-school relationships cut across the structural analysis of power inequalities of working and middle classes (Vincent and Tomlinson, 1997). Our analysis thus problematises simple dichotomies of 'supportive' or 'problem' families which pre-vail in public and political discourse and among practitioners. For parents, sustaining children's identities and making sense of family life at the confluence of home-school cultures is a complex and skilled activity – a form of 'fishing in the fog' which calls for sophisticated strategies of mediation and interpretation.

Note: A fuller version of the analysis presented in this chapter is available in Filer and Pollard (2000).

References

Becker, H. S. (ed.) (1953) 'The teacher in the authority system of the public school', *Journal of Educational Sociology* 27 pp128-41

Filer, A. and Pollard, A. (2000) *The Social World of Pupil Assessment: Process and Contexts of Primary Schooling.* Continuum: London

Osborn, M., McNess, E. and Broadfoot, P. with Pollard, A. and Triggs, P. (2000) *Policy, Practice and Teacher Experience: Changing English Primary Education.* London: Continuum

Pollard, A. with Filer, A. (1996) *The Social World of Children's Learning.* London: Cassell

Pollard, A. and Filer, A. (1999) *The Social World of Pupil Career.* London: Cassell

Pollard, A. and Filer, A. (2000) 'Assessment and parents' strategic actions', in A. Filer (ed.) *Assessment: Social Practice and Social Product.* London: Falmer Press

Vincent, C. and Tomlinson, S. (1997) 'Home-school relationships: 'the swarming of disciplinary mechanisms'?' *British Educational Research Journal* 23: 3 pp361-77

13

'Edutainment' software: a site for cultures in conflict?

Keri Facer, John Furlong, Ruth Furlong and Rosamund Sutherland

Calvin and Hobbes (a five year old and his tiger) are on holiday, it's the summer vacation and they're running around getting into trouble as usual when they come across a snake 'Is it dangerous? What does it eat?' Calvin asks. Hobbes' blank look in response leads them both to bemoan their lack of knowledge about reptiles – a solution is offered: Hobbes will find a book on snakes and then they'll 'know everything there is to know about them'.

Five minutes later they are lying on the ground in the sun reading said book when suddenly Calvin jumps up 'hey, we're not supposed to be learning anything, it's summer'.

Hobbes responds with a tone of finality: 'if no one makes you do it, it counts as fun'. (with thanks to Watterson, 1997)

While it would be difficult to argue on principle that 'learning' and 'fun' are mutually exclusive experiences, they are frequently constructed in popular discourse as distinctly different. Learning is frequently equated with formal and involuntary educational experiences, while fun is often constructed as any voluntary activity that does not involve coercion. Within this potentially problematic construction, fun and learning are set up in opposition to one another. As questions are being raised about the extent to which formal educational experiences attract young people's interest and attention, and as lifelong learning is considered an essential aspect of an economically competitive society, the question of when learning might count as fun is of increasing concern to today's educators.

Drawing on a two and a half year project[1] *Screen Play: an exploratory study of children's techno popular culture* this chapter explores how the emerging genre of edutainment software, which aims to combine games technology with educational objectives to bring together fun and learning, is being received and used by young people in their day to day lives. This chapter does not focus on what young people might be learning when engaging with such software but rather examines the clash of cultures between children's leisured and schooled identities as highlighted by the introduction of edutainment software into the domestic environment.

Background

Over the past five years we have witnessed growing concern over the ability of traditional formal education to retain the interest and engagement of young people who are growing up in what is seen to be a fast moving, multi-media, multi-channel world outside the classroom walls (Smith, 1995; Green and Bigum, 1992). One strategy to reignite young people's interest in traditional schooling is the emerging genre of edutainment software which aims to appropriate features of computer games technology in order to achieve formal educational outcomes. This strategy is premised on the assumption that formal educational experiences are rarely constructed by young people as fun and that the attributes of experiences that would be counted as fun by young people may be found in the artefacts of their techno-popular cultures, the games, videos, films and multi-media environments seen as 'the proper space of youth' today (Green and Bigum, 1993). As Nixon (1998) argues *'Learning with computers is promoted as being 'fun' and 'exciting', the antithesis of the supposedly 'boring' education associated with the old technologies of chalk and talk, or pen and paper'* (p36).

While schools are being challenged to appropriate these qualities of young people's extra-curricular entertainment experiences, young people's techno-popular culture outside school has long been targetted as itself fertile ground for formal learning objectives. *'Learn-*

ing has never been more effective or more fun [than with an Atari computer]' summarises the message of the marketing campaigns (Atari, 1983, quoted in Selwyn, 2001). Parents purchasing home computers are offered the possibility of children willingly and happily learning at home through fun activities, improving literacy and numeracy, accessing a wealth of useful information for school and improving examination results all through the mediation of a technology that can be bought off the shelf in the local PC store. Edutainment software is marketed as the choice of young people, only better, in that this software offers the added benefit of transferable skills and knowledge:

> Unlike your average video game, they require lots of reading, note taking or research outside of the game in order to play properly. They encourage students to use their problem-solving skills and communicate as part of a group, teaching them to try different strategies and examine the consequences of their actions. (Computer Living, February 1995:44 quoted in Nixon, 1990)

Edutainment software, then, is designed and sold as a half-way house between fun and learning – just fun enough to capture young people's imaginations and sufficiently educational to justify to parents the time spent playing these games. Importantly, however, edutainment needs to compete for attention against mainstream games which, unlike edutainment, are designed solely and purely for fun (Johnson, 1999; Choi, Kim and Kim, 1999). However, it has been argued that the experience of fun is not necessarily a property of a given activity but rather *'a relationship between that activity and the individual's goals at the moment'* (Draper, 1999, p118). What might happen then when software designed to provide both fun and learning meets the potentially divergent goals of young people's out of school cultures? Will this experiment to capture the features of out of school entertainment for educational purposes count as learning or as fun in bedrooms and sitting rooms around the country?

Edutainment software: (re)configuring learning as fun

As a result of the marketing strategies of computer companies, which offered bundles of free educational software with the purchase of a new computer in the 1990s, and the computer publishing industry, which cover mounted CD-ROMs on popular titles such as PC Magazine, young people with a home computer are likely to have access to a wide range of software which could broadly be categorised as educational. The following example from one of our case studies indicates the breadth of this software that ranges from reference works through games to encyclopedias and simulations:

> *Karen's Dad is an avid Computer magazine reader, buying a wide range on a regular basis for their features and for the free cover mounted software. An inventory of the 'educational' CD-Roms available to her at home highlighted the rich resources she had at her disposal, amongst which were: Comic Zone, David Bellamy's endangered wildlife, Echo the Dolphin, Kids Print Machine, How Animals Move, Design Works, Press Works, Solar System Explorer, Interactive World Atlas, Learning French, Learning German, Encarta, Mind Maze, Cartoon Maker, Recipes, Asterisk, My First Encyclopedia, The Human Body, Microsoft Oceans, The Louvre, Student Reference Library, Mario is Missing, World War One, Chronicle of the Twenty First Century, ...the list goes on as CDs are found scattered around the room or in drawers long untouched...* (Karen Simons, aged 10, Visit 2)

Despite the prevalence of such software environments, however, figures from the survey[2] suggest that the use of educational software remains low compared with other digital entertainment activities such as mainstream games play. In response to the question, 'have you done any of these things on the computer in the last three weeks (either in school or at home)?' educational software as a whole compared poorly with games play:

	Whole Survey Sample (n = 855)	Computer Owners in Survey Sample (n = 740)
Mainstream computer games	75%	81%
Educational Software	26%	31%

Similarly, if we examine the prevalence of use of educational software amongst the case study sample, the huge gap between mainstream games play and edutainment 'playful learning' is apparent. All eighteen case study young people were observed to participate frequently in some form of games play during the period of the study, as against only seven who participated in any form of edutainment play. Examining both the software itself and young people's techno-popular leisure cultures outside school may help us understand some possible reasons for this difference in usage.

While most, if not all, the educational software titles in homes attempt to incorporate elements of entertainment into an educational agenda, such as the use of interactive features to animate a reference CD-ROM or cartoons and simulations to provide a narrative about subjects as diverse as the Louvre, Solar System or the history of the 21st century, only a small number would be classified as *edutainment* software in which learning goals are embedded within a software environment modelled on computer games features. Educational software such as interactive reference CD-ROMs, for example, is clearly identified as a learning experience which is made more entertaining through interactive and narrative features:

> *Welcome to Encarta ® 97 Encyclopedia, an interactive mutlimedia encyclopedia that turns your personal computer into a rich resource of information, education and entertainment.(Encarta* introductory booklet – Microsoft – 1997)

Entertainment, in these environments, is a spoonful of sugar to render learning more acceptable or amusing. Interestingly, in many of them learning is predominantly, and mistakenly, categorised primarily as the acquisition of facts and information. It is unsurprising that such a narrow definition of learning should require embellishment to render it more interesting.

In contrast true edutainment software aims to provide the young person primarily with a fun experience in which learning becomes part of a process of playing a game, and through which the flow of the games experience (a theory of 'optimal experience' or happiness experienced in 'periods of positively valued total immersion' argued to be characteristic of the pleasures of games play (Csikszentmihalyi, 1990)) is uninterrupted by the intrusion of an overtly identified learning activity. In other words, the learner is intended to learn by stealth, unaware of the learning involved in the activity.

Edutainment software is designed with the purpose of immersing young people completely in an environment in which learning occurs as part of the process of a playful activity rather than as an intentional and explicit product of that activity. This software, like mainstream computer games, adopts a variety of strategies which draw for their structure on already existing popular games with proven track records of popularity and also adopt techniques from other entertainment industries such as film and television. Edutainment environments embed both game theory and narrative strategies within their design, providing challenges, obstacles, solutions and puzzles from game theory within a framework of visual and aural narrative. While edutainment, like mainstream games, varies widely in the complexity of its design, and in the emergence of a wide range of yet to be fully categorised or theorised genres, in the interfaces which link player with games text, two key voices are discernible which address the player in significantly different ways.

The first broad category of 'instructional' environments, could be considered to embody an affinity with school cultures, relying, as they do, on a question and answer, or quiz structure, often with specifically articulated praise from computer to child built in. These consist of activities such as quizzes where children are explicitly asked questions they need to answer, or puzzles in which they are required to identify the correct solution to a problem and enter it into the computer. This basic question and answer structure is occasionally also embedded within an adventure game format in which the child is required to answer questions in order to progress to the next stage. The structure of these games is heavily reliant upon explicit challenges and rewards and emphasises what Choi et.al (1999) have called 'cognitive fun', that is, that the pleasures of the games experience are predominantly associated with the mechanics of the games, 'the physics of the world which set the constraints on how we conceive our ability to navigate and manipulate the games world'(*ibid*, 1999 p94) rather than the pleasures of the interface. The relation between player and software is usually mediated via a series of explicit instructions, offered either as disembodied text or voices or, in the more visually sophisticated forms, via animated characters on the screen. The objective of the game is *to learn to play the game*, to identify the rules and actions which will generate completion of the game and approval from the games text, often in the form of explicit comments to the player, such as 'brilliant, you're a genius' or 'well done, player one, move to the next screen'.

In the following example, Karen, is playing an 'instructional' French vocabulary game designed to engage the child through a series of questions and answers from an animated character which addresses her directly and steers her through different environments and levels of challenge. The *mise en scene* of the game is predominantly a series of static images of scenes, onto different elements of which the player has to click in order to answer the challenge set by the game.

Karen   *Well to become a genius there's a game where you have to answer a load of questions. I got a genius for that game. The French one.*

PC   *Clique sur le sol. Watch, sol is french for....*

(Karen clicks on the image of the floor on the computer screen)

PC   *Merveilleux!*

Karen   *I've got to think what the thing is*

PC   *Tu as clique sur le plafond, clique sur le mur*

PC   *Mur is French for wall. Clique sur le mur*

(Karen clicks on the wall)

PC   *Tu es super!*

(Karen Simons, aged 10, Visit 2)

In contrast, the second voice evident in edutainment software is what we might call experiential environments. These consist of exploratory environments, often including or consisting entirely of simulations. Whereas instructional texts predominantly address the player as a student, issuing instructions which must be responded to in order to achieve success ('click on the wall') and in which help is offered from the computer in the form of short-cut completion of given tasks ('*Mur* is French for wall') in experiential environments, users are positioned much more powerfully as the creator of a solution or environment. In these environments children are required to experiment, to theorise about possible solutions to problems posed, and to draw on a range of different information resources available to them within the digital texts. These environments also emphasise more strongly what Choi *et al* identify as 'perceptual fun', the 'game interfaces [that] are the input and output mechanisms that connect the gamer to the world [and] affect players' perception, that is, they watch characters or background images and listen to sounds' (Choi *et al*, p94). The objective of the game is not only the successful navigation of the challenges and rules of the games mechanics but the experience of navigating a complex environment.

In the following example, Simon is playing an experiential game *Dinosaur Hunter* which is structured around the simulation of an archaeological dig in which players have to use their knowledge of the dates of the existence and habitats of different dinosaurs to identify and excavate dinosaur bones. When all the bones of an individual dinosaur are successfully collected, the dinosaur is animated into life for the player. The *mise en scene* of the game is a dark subterranean world full of creatures, bones and archeological artefacts; players interact with this world through the mechanism of a cursor in the shape of a hand and a magnifying glass which they use to look more closely at the world and to transport the bones into the archaeological identification case shown on the screen.

Simon	(reading from the computer screen) *'The six skeletons displayed are progressively harder to complete if excavated in the following order, but you can choose to complete them in any order you wish...Triceratops, Heradontosaurus..... the excavation shaft has three tunnels, each at a different depth. You are advised to search all three tunnels to find the missing bones for each dinosaur... to select the skeleton click on any of the six fossilised skeletons displayed in front of you...'* [...] *see I've got to find how old the Tyrannosaurus Rex is [...] 68-65 million years ago.*
Q	*So that's got a picture of him and this is now...*
Simon	*Oh, it tells you all about all the [different periods] and then you go on to...the cross is Don't Excavate*

and the tick is Excavate. So now I'm going to go on that. I want that and then I want to go down to the first level. [...] Say I get this...the little hand, that takes a scan and it gets all these lines round it. And it makes a noise it goes uhuhuh...see that there, look, 85-78 million years ago. Don't need that so I discard.

Q   *Why don't you need that one?*

Simon   *Because it doesn't say...down here I've got to 68-65 million years. But that didn't ....that had 85-78 million years ago.*

[the dates of the bone do not correspond with the dates of the T.Rex he is looking for]

Simon   *I just really want to find all the bones and then make it and then you'll be able to see what it's like when it all makes it and all that.*

(Simon Hodgson, aged 10, Visit 2)

Importantly, however, in both the instructional and experiential genres, the design of the software is intended to ensure that the pleasures of the software are experienced in the process of playing and are not necessarily dependent upon any identifiable acquisition of skills and knowledge to be taken away from the experience afterwards. This software (unlike, say, Encarta) is designed to be 'fun' in Draper's terms:

> Inherent in the notion of fun seems to be that it doesn't matter what the product is [...] i.e. it is an activity carried out for its own sake, the sake of the process. (Draper, 1999, p118)

What constitutes fun for one child, however, may not be the same for his older sister. Indeed, it was noticeable that amongst our case studies the older cohort were more likely to associate instructional edutainment games with younger children. Whether this is because the language and tone of address of these games is more in keeping with the tone of formal education and consequently rejected by older children as too school-like, would require further research to determine. What was clear was that when talking about games they enjoyed, various elements of software design became significant, such as the lack of immediate manipulation barriers to playing the game (how easy was it to control the mouse or controls, for example) and the identification of clear goals (what was the aim of the game they were playing). Where manipulation barriers existed and where the reason for playing (the goals) were not evident, the incentive to give more than cursory attention to the software was diminished. Stephanie, for example, had been trying to play a game that required inserting letters into boxes to make words and had given up playing the game because the skill required to manipulate the mouse was too complex for her at that time and she was little motivated to develop that skill, even though she had reached the final stages of the Lion King game only the day before, after persisting for several weeks:

Q	*Is that because it's difficult you don't like it?*
Steph	*Yeah, it's when you have to try and get it into the right box and it keeps moving off*

(Stephanie Field, 10, Visit 3)

Jones (1998) usefully cites the following technical components as key in creating engagement with edutainment environments:

- Task that we can complete

- Ability to concentrate on task

- Task has clear goals

- Task provides immediate feedback

- Deep but effortless involvement (losing awareness of worry and frustration of everyday activity)

- Exercising a sense of control over our actions

- Concern for self disappears during flow, but sense of self is stronger after flow activity

- Sense of duration of time is altered.

Importantly, however, while these attributes can go some way to reducing barriers to frustration and lack of interest, the extent to which a young person will experience this software as fun will also depend on their present attitude and energy (what sort of challenges do they want), their sense of humour (do they like comedy cartoons inserted into the text), the time of day or week (how much time they have to spend), amongst other things.

Bringing edutainment home

As Draper (1999) has argued, the experience of fun is not necessarily the property of an activity or of any specific aspect of software design but rather '*a relationship between that activity [such as playing an edutainment package] and the individual's goals at that moment*' (p119). As he argues, what one might find fun in the middle of a day on holiday is not necessarily fun when woken in the middle of the night during the working week. So he adds an essential attribute to the criteria outlined above for the successful creation of a fun experience: 'connection to the person's deepest values and goals' (*ibid*). In order to examine how well edutainment software achieves its aim of making learning fun, we would need to consider the ways in which this software rubs up against the motivations, values and interests of young people's digital cultures outside school.

Two inter-related factors mitigate against edutainment software fulfiling Draper's final component of a fun activity for young people out of school. First is the prevalent construction of learning as an activity distinctly in opposition to fun, and second is the construction of edutainment software as a form of approved games play.

Interestingly, the computers on which edutainment software is designed to run have a long history in the home of being identified with fun and leisure activities by young people. As the following example from one case study family indicates, for up to twenty years many of the families in this study had owned and were familiar with using a wide range of computers and consoles for games purposes:

> *The first digital media technology to enter Tim's home was a ZX Spectrum in about 1983, bought specifically in order to play a football games that Tim's Dad had seen at a friend's house, closely followed by an Atari attached to a television, which was won in a raffle. There were immediate and obvious drawbacks to both of these – the Spectrum took 'ages to load' and then malfunctioned and the Atari 'only played Pong'. The Atari is no*

longer in the home, although they're not sure where it went but the Spectrum is still in the attic. Following this early incursion into technology the next purchase was a Sega Master System bought for Tim to play games on. The games console was gradually updated from this original Master System, through a Sega Megadrive, to the current Nintendo 64 that Tim plays in his room. Finally, the family decided to buy a PC. (Summary of Jones' [Brannigan] family digital technology history 1983 – 1999)

For the young people in these case studies growing up in the 1990s, the primary function of a computer was to entertain. Unlike their parents, who generally first encountered computers in the workplace, computers are embedded in out of school cultures of pleasure and play. The introduction of learning as a necessary bedfellow of fun is hardly a welcome intrusion into the digital ecology of the household. Moreover, as the pressures on young people to compete in a test driven school environment increase and as arguments to lengthen the school day become more vocal (through drives to manage parents' support of children's learning at home for example), the extent to which young people actively protect their leisure time from any activities remotely associated with school practices may increase. The long term failure of homework to impact significantly on children's out of school activities underlines how much leisure and fun are actively defended by young people as valuable. The promotion of edutainment software as fun learning rather than as intrinsically exciting and valuable may well encourage sales of the software to parents, but it is unlikely to encourage young people to actually use the software. Indeed, the low levels of use of edutainment games by both case study families and the wider survey sample in comparison with mainstream games indicates that they are failing to compete as pleasurable within children's wider techno-popular culture. That edutainment is predominantly purchased by adults for young people rather than actively sought out by young people themselves is not, then, surprising.

Nor is it surprising that edutainment is evaluated not against other home activities such as homework, but, against the other rich digital media offerings now available to young people:

I had educational software for ages. When I was old enough to realise that there were better games out there I pestered my Mum to get those better games. And she would say 'You're not going to play on these games until you've had half an hour on this game' (Morris Family, Richard aged 15, Visit 2)

Outside school young people have far more choice about how to spend their time than in school – even as their geographical space is constricted and their opportunities to access outdoor space in the UK are increasingly limited, many children are surrounded by a wealth of artefacts with which they can choose to spend their time (Livingstone *et al*, 1998). Television, radio, computer games, computers, board games, family conversations, play with friends, organised out of school activities all compete for attention. It is within this context that edutainment games, if they are to fulfil their promise of 'making learning fun' need to compete, within the context of the unencumbered fun of *MTV*, of *Eastenders*, of *Doom and Tomb Raider*, of riding skateboards and playing with pets.

It is also important to recognise that the familial construction of edutainment games as an approved and valued activity in the home may also mitigate against these being appropriated into young people's out of school cultures in a similar manner to mainstream games. Playing mainstream games on the home computer was characterised in many of the case study families as oppositional to more suitable activities such as homework and was seen as testing the rules of family life, whether in terms of the time spent playing games or in terms of the content of the games. This sort of unauthorised games play often functioned as a subversive and challenging activity to the authorised practices of the home and was centrally important to certain young people in developing and determining their identities within the family and amongst their peers (see McNamee, 1998; Facer *et al*, 2001b). Parental approval of edutainment games, however, means they cannot be used in such an identity and boundary defining manner.

Moreover, one of the pleasures of playing mainstream games is the culture of cheating that surrounds it and which enables young people to trade techniques, such as programming different codes into the computer to allow them to operate as god-like figures, immune to failure. This trade in cheats (or insider knowledge) for games is central to much interaction around games, through magazines, websites and between individuals. Cheating or subverting the games program is embedded within the mainstream games culture as an essential part of playing the game. Thus cheating is an important part of learning to play the game. In edutainment environments, the ability to bypass the challenges, to reach the goal without passing through the requisite tests is problematic, akin to reading the answers to problems at the end of a textbook. In mainstream games environments, in contrast, this cheat facility serves another purpose. As well as allowing the player to explore the different possibilities of the game, to develop strategies for tackling these problems and test out these theories when the cheat facility is removed, the trade in 'cheats' and insider knowledge of games environments serves a fundamentally social purpose, bringing together young people within a digital games culture (McNamee, 1998). That edutainment is not currently supported by this culture of cheats and the paraphernalia (website, magazines, books) that surrounds and supports mainstream games weakens its hold on young people's out of school cultures.

The implicit attempt in edutainment software to provide a games environment that presents no challenge to the stability of the family but reinforces the values and practices of school activities, and in which a culture of cheats and insider knowledge is absent, may render these forms of software, no matter how well designed, incompatible with the goals and values of young people's out of school cultures. Designed to support learning they may be, but, within the out of school context it is unlikely that they will be considered fun.

What these preferences indicate is that what constitutes a good game, a valid entertainment as well as educational experience, depends on a range of factors within the software design itself and also on young people's constructions of fun and learning, constructions that go to the heart of the opposition between school and out of school cultures.

Discussion: where next for 'edutainment' software?
Two strategies for future development emerge from this analysis. Neither suggests the continued expansion of an edutainment sector,

along its current lines, as necessarily desirable for enriching young people's out of school activities.

Valuing playful activities

The results of the *Screen Play* study and other research into young people's out of school digital activities suggest that many forms of digital activity outside school could be recognised and valued as providing learning experiences for young people but that these are undervalued within current school structures and assessment mechanisms. These incidental out-of-school learning experiences incorporate a range of literacy-based activities which potentially overlap with in-school activities, such as writing and the production of multimedia texts. What characterises all of these out-of-school activities of choice is play and playfulness and, as Downes (1998) has suggested, 'the computer as an environment for learning by doing and exploratory learning emerges from the children's activity of playing games' (ibid, p204). Whereas we would argue that play is an important characteristic of any productive learning activity, it is this attribute of young people's out-of-school computer use which seems to be constructed by formal educational settings as in opposition to the work of learning. The fun of playing with the computer seems to disqualify any incidental learning this may engender from being considered proper learning.

Even if this incidental learning is currently not recognised by schools it is nevertheless a real experience for young people and constitutes real learning. The mainstream games industry could tap into this potential for incidental learning by developing rich and diverse environments for human expression and exploration. It could, however, be argued that the mainstream games industry is increasingly stagnating into pre-determined subjects and games mechanics. Jenkins (2001), for example, argues that computer games are currently at the same stage in their development as cinema in the 1920s, trapped perpetually in a series of chases and cop films. If games were to develop into as rich and diverse a medium for human expression as film or television, then there is potential for games to provide a wide range of intellectual and emotionally satisfying experiences incorporating design features and navigational strategies which could enrich young people's personal, intellectual and emotional development. Moreover, given the interactive quality of digital environments, the potential for young people to explore, simulate, develop strategies and explorations of different experiences and identities suggests that mainstream games could become a significant resource for young people *and adults* in their personal and intellectual development. But this is a long way off. Rather than trying to improve edutainment, a software category only tolerated by young people, it would be wiser to reinvigorate and regenerate the medium of mainstream games that is already enjoyed by millions around the world.

Redefining learning: getting to grips with cheating

The construction of an opposition between cultures of fun and learning discussed in this chapter suggests that a key element of fun which is absent from mainstream learning is the ability to play. Current discourses have succeeded in ghettoising learning as an activity to be endured at school rather than enjoyed and experienced through many aspects of life. How can schools begin to appreciate that it is the play of learning which is important and not the work of learning? What are the characteristics of this play of learning? Playing games at home points to the importance of subversive activities such as cheating and challenging sanctioned practices. It also points to the role that insider knowledge and expertise play amongst young people in generating motivation and interest. Interestingly, teachers are concerned about copying – ie cheating – when young people use the internet for homework. But copying existing material is a valid way to improve knowledge and skills (Davis *et al*, 2000). 'Getting inside the mind of a master' relates to the development of insider knowledge which appears to be motivating to games players. The emphasis is on participation in and not duplication of practices (Davis *et al*, 2000). Within pedagogy as a whole, and perhaps software design in particular, we may need to reconceptualise how we view cheating. Rather than seeing it as a way of avoiding the real difficulties of the problem, cheating could be conceptualised instead as giving access to a powerful way of solving a problem, how the expert would solve it. For example, when teaching mathematics, algebra could be reconceptualised as a cheat which under certain circumstances allows young people to transcend ineffective arithmetical approaches to solving a problem.

Young people harness a range of resources to support their fun at home and inevitably learn in the process, even if they do not construct it as learning. In this broader sense, all living can be conceptualised as learning. Although the concern of education is with particular sorts of learning, schools might do well to recognise the importance of play in learning.

> A key quality of all living forms is play – and conversely a likely indicator of an inert form is a lack of play. With such broadened appreciations of the importance of play in life, it's not surprising to note that playfulness is rapidly coming to be seen as a necessary element in the workplace, especially when creativity and problem solving are expected of workers. (Davis et al, 2000, p148).

Edutainment in the school setting

While the paradoxical nature of edutainment as both fun and learning may be problematic for its adoption in out of school contexts, it may be of benefit within the classroom. If we accept Draper's argument that fun is '*a relationship between that activity and the individual's goals at that moment*', the opportunity to access what might be seen within the school context as an unusual and potentially subversive activity (playing games in school is not the norm) may well be appreciated and received with pleasure in the classroom. The opportunity to access resources such as experiential edutainment environments may well feel liberating and so appeal to those actively in conflict with the practices and values of traditional school environments. The paradoxical nature of edutainment existing at the clash of cultures between fun and learning may be made to work *for* rather than against young people's goals and values.

What the analysis in this chapter demonstrates is that there will be no quick technological fix to the question of how education can be made enjoyable and interesting for young people either inside or outside school. Efforts to impose formal learning objectives on out of school cultures could and should be resisted by young people and parents, overriding, as these do, a recognition and proper appreciation of the different forms of learning experienced already by young people outside school. However, the opportunities offered by technological innovations such as edutainment software for different forms of learning experiences, and the growing gap between young people's digital out of school cultures and in-school paper based cultures are too great to ignore. If there is a place for fun within formal learning settings, and if technology offers a bridge between inside and out of school cultures, then an exploration not only of improved software design but the values, goals and aspirations of young people in school and out would be of primary importance. Only then could Atari's old claim that *'learning has never been more effective or more fun'* be achieved.

Acknowledgements

The authors would like to thank the ESRC for their support of the Screen Play Project from 1998–2000 (Ref: R000237298) which enabled the research and writing of this chapter.

Notes

1 This ESRC funded interdisciplinary project undertaken at the Graduate School of Education, University of Bristol and the University of Wales College, Newport, combined theoretical perspectives from the fields of education, sociology, cultural studies, psychology and media and visual culture. In order to expldore young people's digital technology use outside school, a questionnaire survey of 855 children in four different school communities in SW England and S Wales was conducted. Following this, 18 young people from 16 families were selected for detailed case studies in the home which involved visits to the families on five occasions, including in-depth interviews with all members of the family and observation and recording computer use. These case study young people were selected as being medium-high users of computer-based technologies and comprised nine boys and nine girls in years 6 (9-10) and 9 (13-14) from a wide range of family backgrounds in terms of geopgraphy, ethnicity, family make-up and parental occupation.

2 The survey was conducted in June 1998 in four communities in South West England and South Wales. The communities could be broadly characterised as: leafy dormitory suburb, multicultural city centre, ex-mining town, rural town. In each community two schools (one primary, one secondary) were surveyed, children from years 5 and 8 in each school completed a questionnaire probing their computer use in home and at school.

References

Choi, D., Kim, H., Kim, J. (1999) 'Toward the Construction of Fun Computer Gaes: differences in the views of developers and players' *Personal Technologies*, 3,3 pp92-104

Csikszentmihalyi, M. (1990) *Flow: the psychology of optimal experience.* Harper and Row, New York

Davis, B., Sumara, S., Luce-Kapler, R. (2000) *Engaging Minds, Learning and Teaching in a Complex World*, LEA, New Jersey

Downes, T. (1988) Children's Use of Computers in their Homes, unpublished D.Phil thesis, University of Western Sydney, Macarthur.

Draper, S. (1999) 'Analysing Fun as a Candidate Software Requirement' *Personal Technologies*, 3,3 pp117-122

Facer, K., Sutherland, R., Furlong, R., Furlong, J. (2001a) 'What's the point in using a computer: young people's constructions of the value of computer expertise' *New Media and Society*, Vol 3, No 2

Facer, K., Sutherland, R., Furlong, R., Furlong, J. (2001b) 'Constructing the Child Computer User: from public policy to private practices' *British Journal of Sociology of Education*, Vol 22, No 1

Green, C. and Bigum, B. (1993) 'Aliens in the Classroom' *Australian Journal of Education*, 37, 2, pp119-141

Jenkins, H. (2001) Keynote Speech given at 'Game Cultures'Conference, Bristol, UK

Johnson, C. (1999) 'Taking Fun Seriously: Using Cognitive Models to Reason About Interaction with Computer Games' *Personal Technologies*, Vol 3, No 3 pp105-116

Jones, M.G. (1998) *Creating engagement in computer-based learning environments*, ITForum (email list: invited paper posted 7 December 1998) and [WWW document] URL: http://itech1.coe.uga.edu/itforum/paper30/paper30.html

Livingstone, S.,and Bovill, M., (1998) *Young People: New Media,* London: LSE/BSC

McNamee, S. (1998) *Youth, Gender and Video Games: Power and Control in the Home* in Skelton, T. and Valentine, G. (eds) Cool Places: Geographies of Youth Cultures, London: Routledge

Nixon, H. (1998) 'Fun and Games are Serious Business' in J. Sefton-Green (ed.) *Digital Diversions: youth culture in the age of multi-media* London: UCL pp21-42

Selwyn, N. (2001) 'Learning to Love the Micor: The Discursive Construction of 'Educational' Computing in the UK 1979-1989' (draft paper in submission)

Smith, R., Curtin, P. and Newman, L. (1995) Kids in the Kitchen: the social implications for schooling in the age of advanced computer technology. Paper presented at the Australian Association for Research in Education conference, (Hobart)

Watterson, B (1997) *It's a Magical World: a calvin and hobbes collection*, London: Warner Book

Part IV:
Cultures Past and Present

Editors' introduction

In the final section of the book, we zoom in even more closely on life as it is being lived at the interfaces between conflicting cultural messages, opportunities and demands. What, these chapters ask, is the experience of a teacher, a lecturer or a counsellor as they struggle to keep their bearings, or to construct new ones, at the often turbulent meeting-point of different discourses? For many, the conflicts and difficulties are experienced as tensions between the familiar and the new; having 'learned the ropes' in one personal or professional culture, and come to see the world in its terms, there comes the cold wind of unfamiliar values and habits that feel dissonant and strange. The priorities and practices of an educational researcher may feel odd, even trivial or self-indulgent, to a hard-pressed school-teacher who has unwittingly absorbed attitudes that are pragmatic or even anti-scholastic, from her professional enculturation. Yet at a different level of her consciousness, the teacher may also feel somewhat attracted to the rigour and discipline of the research world. How is she to resolve the conflicts that new directives and opportunities stir not just in her professional practice but in her inner values and interests? Likewise, the discourse of education that a new physics lecturer, say, meets for the first time on a higher education induction course, may be both alien and repellent, and also intriguing. Surrounded by a culture that sees teaching as a necessary evil, and research as the proper business of a university academic, yet anxious about his untested and untutored ability to run a first-year practical class successfully, the lecturer may feel the plate-tectonics of different professional continents shifting under his feet. Or a student counsellor, still angry about the indignities of the assessment culture she experienced, and suffered, at school, and committed to a very different discourse of feedback that is much less judgmental, may nonetheless feel an ambivalent pride at the intensely 'summative' ritual of her degree ceremony. She too experiences the queasy sense of belonging simultaneously to two incompatible clubs.

These three examples are explored in greater detail in this part of the book. In Chapter 14, Peter John and Jayne Prior investigate the complex dynamics at work as school-teachers begin to familiarise themselves with the world of research. Their thoughts and opinions were sampled before and after they had grappled with research papers. While some were stimulated by the experience, a teacher who concluded that reading research was 'like wading through treacle and never getting to the point', and another who saw research as 'common sense dressed up in fancy words' were not untypical. John and Prior conclude that, if the gap is to be closed, the two cultures have to move closer together: the conduct of educational research has to change, as well as the receptivity of teachers.

In Chapter 15, Richard Brawn and Sheila Trahar present the thoughts and uncertainties of a group of new academics as they meet, many for the first time, an educational discourse that problematises teaching and learning – a discourse that, for some, is strikingly at odds with the values and preoccupations of their university department. While the university rhetoric may seem to value explicit discussion of, and even training for, their new role as teachers, their own colleagues and professors may act as if teaching were unimportant and/or unproblematic, and treat attempts to open up discussion with cynicism or disdain. New lecturers often feel caught between a rock and a hard place, and Brawn and Trahar unearth the range of strategies which they use to survive. They suggest that an informal system of cross-disciplinary mentoring would do much to ease these sometimes painful transitions.

Finally in Chapter 16, Jane Speedy, Jan Winter, Patricia Broadfoot, Judith Thomas and Barry Cooper explore their own experiences within a range of very different assessment cultures, past and present. Drawing on work in narrative therapy, the group told and retold significant aspects of their 'assessment stories' in the light of each others' experiences, and of their professional awareness of the literature of different assessment cultures and traditions. The chapter charts the shifts, insights and discomforts that accompanied their attempts to listen to and question each others' stories from a range of not-always-welcome-or-comprehensible perspectives. As the authors conclude, 'the art, perchance, is not to take an oppositional or a compliant stance, but rather to slip between these stories, to find the key points of entry that inhabit the liminal spaces and cultural interfaces.'

14

Conceptions, contentions and connections: how teachers read and understand different genres of educational research

Peter John and Jayne Prior

'*Only connect*' E.M. Forster

Government policy and professional guidance now insist that practice should be evidence based. The pressure is on for teachers to justify their patterns of practice by reference to a body of research evidence regarding efficacy and effectiveness (Blunkett, 2000; Hargreaves, 1996). Critics of this approach see it as a matter of practice by protocol – ways of working that are increasingly circumscribed and leave little room for discretion, experience, autonomy and judgement (Ball, 1990; Thomas, 1997; Hammersley, 1997; Atkinson, 2000). Others are excited by the prospect that custom and practice might be transformed and challenged by the application of high quality research findings (Reynolds, 1998; Hargreaves, 1997; 1999a; 1999b; Tooley and Darby, 1998; Smithers, 1999). Still others urge caution given the volume of research available, the different traditions from which it emerges, and the highly contextualised nature of teaching and learning (Edwards, 2000; Fitzgibbon, 1996; Bassey, 1998).

But there is still a large gap between rhetoric and reality. Evidence on what works remains under-used and many practice interventions have weak evidence bases. The literature on research utilization (Weiss, 1998) tells us that a great deal of research appears to have little or no impact on practice. Many reasons have been given but often the focus is on the cultural gap that is said to exist between researchers and teachers. They are said to live in different worlds; to have different interests, mindsets and concerns and consequently find it difficult to communicate with one another (Caplan *et al*, 1975; Husen, 1984). Furthermore, a great deal of research validated knowledge is necessarily imprecise, inconclusive, complex and contingent, whereas teachers it is argued, can only use such knowledge if it is accurate, gives clear guidance, and is formulated in simple enough terms to be directly applied (Merton, 1957; Lindblome and Cohen, 1979).

It is ironic that throughout this debate little time has been spent on investigating the processes that have been so hotly argued. Only a few studies cast light on the ways in which teachers understand and use research in their practice (Kennedy, 1984; 1997; Weiss, 1998, Fitzgibbon, 1998; Davies, 1999). In particular, we only have anecdotal evidence regarding the communication and reception of research. The purpose of this chapter is to find out how experienced teachers with differing levels of research acquaintance read different genres of research; and whether that acquaintance influenced their views on its credibility and utility.

The research reported in this chapter is part of an ongoing process of trying to strengthen the bond between professional teachers and various research communities, and encourage them to work together to improve practice. Both cultures are encouraged to engage with one another, to 'notice different things, organize themselves differently' perhaps, and 'value different kinds of experience and achievement' (Claxton, Sutherland and Pollard, 2002). This chapter invites them to ask what counts as evidence in their cultural habitats. It aims to help practitioners to be active in considering the quality and relevance of different types or genres of research to the practice in which they are engaged. It starts from the assumption that there are different ways of knowing, that no one way is better in all circumstances and that the kinds of research done and the evidence produced will largely depend on the questions being asked. The chapter also stresses context-dependency – because however sound the research may be in its own terms, its authority, persuasiveness and relevance will largely depend on its applicability to a particular set of cultural circumstances. There is also always a judgement to be made about the degree of fit which an idea, a piece of research evidence or a theory has with its surroundings; results from research cannot be simply transplanted from one setting to another. Thus there has to be active dialogue between researchers and practitioners, just as there has to be dialogue between teacher and pupil. Essentially then, the research reported here is an attempt to grapple with Bruner's (1996) supposition that 'the meaning of any proposition is relative to the frame of reference in terms of which it is construed.' (p13)

Method
The sample:
Following Zeuli (1996), two groups of teachers with differing experiences of educational research were chosen for the study. The first set, *the research-orientated group,* was composed of eight experienced teachers with upwards of five years classroom experience. Four of the group had been nominated by the DfEE as best practice scholars and had already engaged with research at a number of levels. The others were teachers enrolled on an MEd programme at a British university. The second set, *the practice-orientated group,* also comprised eight experienced teachers but had much less exposure to educational research. In each group there were two historians (one male and one female); three scientists (two male and one female); two English teachers (one male and one female); and a single mathematician (female). Since the sample is limited it is important to bear in mind that the interviewees' responses are only suggestive of the ways in which teachers might read different genres of research and the findings are not meant to be definitive.

The interviews were carried out in two distinct parts. In the first, each teacher was interviewed (semi-structured) about their teaching styles, ideals, and views on educational research, particularly its importance in their professional lives, its relevance, and its salience in terms of developing teaching as a profession. They were also asked about how research might relate to their teaching. In order to facilitate their answers, each teacher was given a collection of abstracts from various genres of research – experimental, statistical survey, case study, ethnography and action research – as a way of orienting them towards the issues. Before the second set of interviews, each teacher was given a pack of five research articles related to the genres outlined above. All of the sample were asked to read the papers and informed of the sorts of questions they would be asked during the interview.

The findings
Teachers' views about educational research

Analysis of the first data reveals an initial picture of teachers' beliefs about educational research and the relationship of research to their practice. Both sets had varying conceptions of the importance and relevance of educational research to their classroom practice. The *research-orientated group* responded with a more extended view of research. In the first instance they identified themselves as believing that the importance of research could not be seen simply in terms of its utility but that it should also raise general questions about their teaching and thereby offer them greater insights into their own classrooms and professional predicaments. They believed, typically, that the direct impact view of research was too narrow and that contextual relevance was helpful organizationally, both in aiding them to understand professional issues and in guiding them to improve their classroom practice.

Rebecca, a mathematician commented:

> Research is helpful; we would all like it to have a direct impact on what we do day to day but it's difficult because often there are too many issues in classrooms. Research should help us to see the complexity, our problems in a new light. It should seek to educate us and raise our standards of professionalism.

Matthew, an English teacher declared that:

> The value of educational research relates to where you are and what problems you have in your school. We're trying to develop literacy across the curriculum so I come into contact with other subjects so research might help there..... I suppose you could argue that all knowledge is potentially relevant even if it doesn't give you any final answers.

The *practice-orientated group*, on the other hand, had a more limited view of the value of research. Their responses tended to cluster around impact and practical relevance. They espoused the view that the findings of research should in some form or other be translatable into procedures that work in classrooms. Sara's views were typical. She pointed out that her only contact with educational literature came from ideas and articles in subject-based professional journals and observed that 'at least there are concrete ideas for teaching in them. Things I can try out in my classroom and the resources are there too, so I just have to read quickly and adapt. Research, from what I can gather from the abstracts you gave me, is long winded and full of jargon – it's like wading through treacle and some never get to the point.'

Another (Craig, a scientist) alluded to the notion that educational research was too ideological (although he never used those words):

> Research in universities is too vague and too biased. Every researcher in the social sciences has a pet way of doing things or believes things and that skews what they write. How can we believe them if they have an axe to grind, like they don't like a particular policy or a practice or whatever?

Some teachers from each group fell into what might be termed the uncertain category. They were often unclear in their responses to the abstracts and unsure about the role research should play and the impact it should have. They also had problems differentiating between the genres of research presented in the abstracts. Perhaps this reflects a lack of confidence about the role of a professional and the fear that research might undermine patterns of practice already well grounded in routine. This small group also tended to feel the pressure of the job more than the others and frequently complained about the intensification of their work; a process which appeared to inhibit them from reading more widely. Katrina, a mathematician, was typical:

> Well... I'm really not sure about research and how it should be used – if at all. I just want to be a good teacher of maths and I don't know whether research can help me... I'm a bit worried that when I think about it research might show up how little I knew about my work and that to be a professional I should read

more research. But it's hard to get hold of it in the first place and then it's the time – reading and thinking takes time – and I am rushed off my feet.

Teachers reading research

Substantive differences also existed in the data between the teachers from the two pre-selected groups in terms of how they read research. Those with a limited conception of research had difficulty in reading and understanding the articles, exhibited problems identifying their main points and often failed to link relevant evidence to substantive findings. Likewise they had problems with validity and the whole notion of evaluation. The main problem was associated with linkage; in other words, they could not wholly understand how the articles overtly connected with their practice. This affected how they read the articles and they often confessed to frustration and confusion over the language, credibility and usefulness of the research papers. Gary, a scientist, opined that some of the articles just did not fit with his experience:

> At the moment I'm concerned with getting my kids through GCSE and SATS – the articles didn't really help because it was hard to really come to any conclusions and they just... just didn't do anything for me. Reading them I felt cut off, my mind kept wandering back to Monday and there was very little in them. The explanations article was slightly helpful but again you need more time and I have some difficult kids – the research seems to have picked up the best bits – I mean there were no bloody inter-ruptions – that can't be right.

In general this group tended to look to the recommendations at the end of the articles for practice implications and this tended to influence the legitimacy they gave to the research paper. They showed little recognition that research might incorporate different conceptions of learning or educational aims that might be worth considering.

Many (from both sets) criticised the writing styles and jargon, claiming that too often it 'got in the way of understanding' and that it 'cut them off', making them 'feel small and stupid'. Philippa, a historian, came close to using the rhetoric of despair when she commented:

> That one about self-concept was totally confusing. The language and the symbols – it was...so...I don't know – irritating, in fact irritating makes it sound mildly acceptable. No it was confusing and pointless; I couldn't make any sense out of it. What the hell are 'step wise regressions' and 'present measures of accuracy of perceived ability ... to the explained variance of academic attainment'? It was like trying to crack the enigma code!

Katrina complained bitterly about the levels of theory that always seemed to get in the way of understanding. She pointed to the obsession with Vygotsky in the paper on explanations:

> The writer was clearly writing for someone else not me. I underlined some sentences because it took me three or more times to read them let alone understand them. All the 'instructional messages'...and the 'intrapersonal' and the 'interpersonal planes' and 'strategic predictions... and internalizing the predicting strategy'. Some parts of the article were really useful but having that at the start leaves a bad taste in the mouth, it's as if you know they aren't writing for you. It's almost patronizing so why should I struggle with that when I have a full timetable and marking and everything else.

In the *research-orientated group,* Mark expressed similar opinions. He cited the confusing language of social science and the ways in which extrapolations were drawn from statistical evidence. He felt that the writers were 'making the simple more complex' and that in the end 'most of it was common sense dressed up in fancy words'. The whole research culture reminded him of the Emperor's new clothes. On the other hand, Donal, a scientist with a doctorate who had been a medical researcher, was critical in a different way. He was suspicious of the ethnographic and case study material. He had a narrow view of research, believing that only quantitative studies represented 'valid research'. He also carefully cross-checked the validity and reliability of the findings of the survey and experimental study with their aims, hypotheses and methodology. When it came to qualitative work he was less than impressed and criticised the studies heavily, questioning their internal and more particularly external validity. He was a sophisticated reader but dismissed other genres as being too 'airy fairy and sociological'. For him they were 'empirically weak' and too ideological, since ethnography and case studies 'are only useful in terms of very general hints – no more'. And yet, somewhat ironically, he was also critical of experimental quantitative studies because they ignored context, maintaining that 'his classes were all different.'

Despite these anomalies most of the *research-orientated group*, read the articles in a more varied and extended way, always searching for insights and ideas that might inform their practice. Those studying for a higher degree or working on their dissertations recognised that research is shaped by the epistemological context in which it is constructed and that such considerations can shape and affect its internal and external validity. However, this did not stop them from being critical of the statistical papers because they had a greater affiliation to qualitative methods. As Joanna commented:

> I tended to read the articles in terms of the researcher's aims and questions. This helped me to see why they had chosen a particular framework, Ethnography in the Pollard piece and the experimental approach in the self-concept piece. I could then make sense out of their findings in terms of where they were coming from, even though I found the number crunching stuff heavy going and pointless at times, then I could make the links between what I do or want to do with my classes.

Susan, a scientist, added:

> Judging an article or chapter on its merits means going beneath the findings and making a connection between the research tradition and concepts that underpin the work. Even the experimental paper comes from a tradition and the methods fit with it. Without that understanding the research becomes just a set of recommendations or ideas for practice which you can take or leave. But don't get me wrong, the findings are still important and I found myself noting down ideas that might prove useful with my GCSE group.

Rachel also showed a sophisticated understanding and carefully linked the research to her school and professional concerns:

> At our school at the moment we are trying to improve motivation and attainment, so I was interested in the self-concept piece.

It seemed to be saying that the child's perceived ability and the teacher's evaluation of his or her ability can be skewed and this can lead to a lowering of motivation and achievement – I think. Too often in our school we label kids and we don't act on evidence or different forms of evidence. So I will use the research ideas to try to inform policy over the coming months.

Conclusions and implications

The research reported throws up a number of interesting issues that tie into the main themes of this book. First, a number of qualitative differences were apparent between the two groups of readers. This might be expected in light of the nature of their experience and acquaintance with educational research. Nonetheless, the receptivity of the *research-oriented group* and their ability, on the whole, to engage with the conceptual and methodological aspects of the research as well as the outcomes was marked in comparison to the *practice-orientated group*. Not only did they seek to connect the findings to their practice but they also perceived the purpose of reading as educative and enlightening. As a result they were able to draw conclusions from the research which might impact on their teaching, while *pari passu* using it to challenge their own conceptions of good practice. For this group the discourses of research had been imported successfully across cultural boundaries where, according to Wenger (1998), 'they were re-interpreted and adapted during the process of adoption'. (p128) So as a direct consequence of engaging with the unfamiliar, some 'reappraisal and amendments of existing habits and beliefs' had taken place (Claxton, Pollard and Sutherland, 2001).

The *practice-oriented group*, on the other hand, tended to exhibit a more consumerist approach to the research. They saw the process of reading and understanding in terms of procurement – the gaining of products that could be put to use directly in their classroom practice. They saw the purpose of research as providing answers to particular practical problems, and they had difficulties understanding the methodological underpinning and the way research emanates from different epistemological positions and traditions. They also had more problems with the language and the ways in which findings were expressed. Their version of adoption was therefore more *compartmentalised*, the ideas presented in the research only being taken on board when they related to certain contexts.

There are dangers however, in being both over-deterministic and perjorative about these findings. Narrow, ends-means instrumentality has been much maligned by educational academics and yet instrumentality is not inherently bad or wrong; on the contrary it is the *fons et origo* of everyday practice – the process that makes teaching acts possible. In fact both sets of teachers did look for answers and ideas that might be used in their particular contexts, but it was those with more experience of reading research who tended to blend instrumentality with a more educative approach. This is reminiscent of Schleiermacher's (1964) observation that 'the integrity of practice does not depend on theory... theory can only make room for practice once practice has settled' (p40). For both groups their practice had settled but the *research-orientated* teachers had begun to accommodate and assimilate (to use Piaget's twin terms) educational research mainly because they had been guided through their acquaintance to see the deeper purposes and meanings inherent within it.

In order to encourage this process it might be fruitful to consider the ways in which teachers connect the articles they read with their own classroom situations. It was clear from the research that both sets of teachers continually tried to forge analogies between the studies and their own situations and practices. This was done at different levels admittedly, but it was important that the responses nearly always returned to the key relationship between teaching and learning. New conceptualisations of research production (Gibbons *et al.* 1994), where experts and users are partners in the generation and utilization of knowledge through applied partnerships, are becoming more commonplace (TTA, 1999; DfEE, 2000; Bickel and Hatrup, 1996; Hargreaves, 1998). Here the centre-periphery model of research creation and dissemination is being challenged so that neither activity is seen as belonging to a separate domain of experts as opposed to users. All these innovations share similar goals and are committed to the bringing together of practitioners and researchers into new forms of discourse communities, where teachers can share their own knowledge of classrooms, children, subjects and pedagogy with researchers who bring their own methodological, critical and substantive expertise to the knowledge-building table of the profession. As Wenger (1998) points out 'Elements of discourse travel across boundaries and combine to form broader discourses as people co-ordinate their enterprises, convince each other, reconcile their perspectives and form alliances' (p128).

Finally, all the teachers expressed a preference for research that was easy to read and with clear messages. Hence their preference for reading professional journals rather than their more academic counterparts. This has implications for how research is communicated and received. For some – and this tended to cross both sets of teachers – the language used was a barrier to their understanding and interfered with their motivation to read. It was here that the idea of 'cultural clash' was at its most obvious. The academic use of a specialized vocabulary with its particular tropes, schemas and terminology became highly frustrating for some readers. The feeling that they somehow had to crack the code was pervasive – as Bourdieu *et al* (1994) have pointed out, 'effective learning implies engaging with both the knowledge itself and the code of transmission used to convey that particular body of knowledge'(p5). Too often the language used created a sense of *anomie* amongst the readers and there is a pressing need for us all to address this issue. If this is not forthcoming the feeling of distance between researchers and practitioners will continue unabated; in fact it might become as Bourdieu *et al* (1994) claim, '*E longinquo reverentia* – respectful distance and respect through distance' (p3).

Finally, Cohen (1996) and Eraut (1995) have argued that this cultural and linguistic gap inhibits receptivity and the deeper learning that is a pre-requisite for evidence based practice. Practitioners, they claim, develop procedural knowledge in abundance through the use of routines and case based knowledge. It is then stored as tacit or craft knowledge and is often used intuitively. Both argue that this 'process knowledge' is linked closely to the mode of communication in which it is initiated and received – in teaching usually through practice or oral communication. As has been shown, for many teachers integrating this type of knowledge with new forms, usually presented as a series of propositions, may continue to be problematic. However, the research reported here is optimistic in that it does indicate, however imperfectly, that if teachers are given opportunities to conjoin their understandings of research with their knowledge of practice then synergy can take place. This suggests that both the reading and use of research is not a matter of placing that research within the physical reach of teachers but rather of placing it within the guided conceptual domain of teachers. Because, as Kennedy (1998) puts it, 'the potential for research to contribute to practice depends ultimately on its ability to influence teachers' thinking' (p2).

References

Atkinson, E. (2000) In defence of ideas and why what works is not enough, *British Journal of the Sociology of Education*, 21, 3, p318-30

Ball, S. (1990) *Politics and Policy Making in Education*. London: Routledge

Bassey, M (1998) Fuzzy generalisations and professional discourse? *Research Intelligence*, 63, p24

Bickel, W. C. and Hattrup, R. (1995) Teachers and researchers in collaboration, *American Educational Research Journal*, 32, 1, p35-65

Blunkett, D. (2000) Blunkett rejects anti-intellectualism and welcomes.... *DfEE News*: London

Bordieu, P., Passenon, J. C. and De Saint Martin, M. (1994) *Academic Discourse*, London: Polity Press

Bruner, J. S. (1996) *The Culture of Education. Cambridge Mass: Harvard* University Press

Caplan, N., Morrison, A. and Stramburgh, R. (1975) *The Uses of Social Science Knowledge in Policy Decisions at National Level.* Ann Arbor MI: University of Michigan

Claxton, G., Pollard, A and Sutherland, R. (2002) Chapter 1 in this volume. Fishing in the fog

Cohen, M. D. (1996) Individual learning and organisational routine. In M. D. Cohen and L. S. Sproull (Eds) *Organizational Learning*. London: Sage

Davies, P. (1999) What is evidence based education. *British Journal of Educational Studies*, 47,2, p108-21

Department for Education and Employment (2000) *Best Practice Research Scholarships*. DfEE News: London

Edwards, T. (2000) Reasonable expectations of educational research. *Oxford Review of Education*, 26, 3 and 4, p300-14

Eraut, M. (1995) *Professional Knowledge and Competence.* London: Falmer Press

Fitzgibbon, C.T (1996) *Monitoring Education: indicators, quality and effectiveness.* London: Cassell

Fitzgibbon, C T. (1998) OFSTED: time to go? *Managing Schools Today*, 7, 6, p22-25

Forster, E.M. (1910) *Howard's End.* London: Penguin Books

Gibbons, M., Limoges, C., Nowotny, H., Schwatzman, S., Scott, P. and Trow, M. (1994) *The Production of Knowledge*. London: Sage

Hammersely, M. (1997) Educational research and teaching: a response to David Hargreaves. *British Educational Research Journal*, 23, 2, p141-61

Hargreaves, D. H. (1996) Teaching as a research based profession: possibilities and prospects (Annual Lecture). London: Teacher Training Agency

Hargreaves, D. H. (1998) *Creative Professionalism: the role of the teacher in the knowledge society.* London: Demos

Hargreaves, D.H. (1997) In defence of research for evidence based teaching: a rejoinder to Martyn Hammersley. *British Education Research Journal*, 23, 3, p405-19

Hargreaves, D. H. (1999a) The knowledge creating school, *British Journal of Educational Studies*, 47, p122-44

Hargreaves, D. H. (1999b) Reinvigorating educational research: lessons from the past and proposals for the future, *Cambridge Journal of Education,* 29,2, p239-49

Husen, T. (1984) Issues and their background. In T. Husen and M. Kogan (Eds) *Educational Research and Policy: How do they relate?* Oxford: Pergamon

Kennedy, M. (1984) Working knowledge. *Knowledge Creation and Diffusion*, vol.52, London: Sage

Kennedy, M. (1997) The connection between research and practice. *Educational Researcher*, 26, 7, p4-13

Lindblome, C. and Cohen, D. (1979) *Usable Knowledge: social science and social problem solving.* New Haven, CN: Yale University Press

Merton, R.K. (1957) The role of the intellectual in public bureaucracy In R K Merton (Ed) *Social Theory and Social Structure*, New York: Free Press

Reynolds, D. (1998) *Teacher Effectiveness: Better Teachers, Better Schools.* BERA dialogues, London: Paul Chapman

Schleiermacher, P. (1964) *Ausgewahlte Padfagogische Schriften.* Padderborn W. Germany: Ferdinand Schoning

Smithers, A. (1999) *Times Educational Supplement*, 22 January, 1999

Teacher Training Agency (1999) *TTA/CfBT Funded School Based Research Consortia: Annual Review.* London: TTA

Thomas, G. (1997) What's the use of theory? *Harvard Educational Review*, 67, p75-104

Tooley, J. and Darby, D. (1998) *Educational Research: a critique.* London: OFSTED

Weiss, C. (1998) Have we learned anything about the use of evaluation? *American Journal of Evaluation*, 19, 1, p21-33

Wenger, E. (1998) *Communities of Practice: learning, meaning and identity.* Cambridge: Cambridge University Press

Zeuli, J. (1996) How do teachers understand research, *Teaching and Teacher Education*, 23, 4, p39-51.

15

Supporting the learner teacher in changing higher education

Richard Brawn and Sheila Trahar

Give a person a fish and you feed them for a day.
Teach a person to fish and you feed them for life. (Confucius)

Introduction

A university may be viewed as a federation of educational institutions (departments/faculties) which share many characteristics but which often exhibit widely differing subject cultures (for example Becher, 1993; Thomas, 1990; Henkel, 2000). These cultures frequently reflect the professional culture for which the graduates, especially in vocational subjects, are preparing or the practices and modes of expression may arise from the nature of the subject itself. In addition, although a university may fiercely defend its independence, it is continually washed, eroded and re-shaped by the currents of accountability, wider community needs, commodification and globalisation. This setting – of relatively stable tacit beliefs (whether of individuals or subject groups) amidst the cultural turbulence generated by internal and external forces, provides an interesting area for debate and research.

Beginner teachers in this sector have much to learn and carry many impediments to progress as a result of the cultural baggage accumulated on their previous learning trajectories. Unlike teachers in other sectors, for whom there is considerable investment in training and preparation, teachers in higher education receive minimal induction into their role. For example, there is a clear framework which shapes the training and assessment of teachers in the primary, secondary and further education sectors and which leads towards a continuing professional development plan upon first appointment. No such framework exists for would-be teachers in the higher education sector, although the new UK Institute for Learning and Teaching (ILT) is likely to result in some degree of design convergence, if not specification, in terms of the learning objectives of support programmes. This is not to argue for the replication, nor even the emulation of such a framework, but the point is made to illustrate the differences between sectors in terms of the status attached to teaching, learning and assessment issues. At a time when the pressures for change in higher education have never been greater, how can those whose role is to support the learning of others best be supported in their own learning – in the remodelling of their perceptual and conceptual frameworks and the sharpening of their skills?

This chapter addresses the question posed above, and explores how the initial and continuing professional development needs of new academics might be influenced by subject and institutional cultures. It uses interviews with recently established (as opposed to newly recruited) academics in one institution to illustrate the discussion. Holding conversations with these academics about their teaching and learning experiences was an attempt to engage them in a critical dialogue, and centred around the following questions:

- What were the departments' attitudes towards teaching and learning?

- To what extent did they feel supported by their departments in developing their teaching?

- What did they feel they needed to retain their enthusiasm/ continue to develop their teaching?

Recruitment, induction, establishment

In universities – particularly the older ones – research is the dominant culture. Research profiles steer recruitment, research drives departmental finances, research dominates the discourse, activity and reward systems. New academics, whose research record is likely to have secured their appointment in the first place, find themselves immersed in environments which themselves may have dominant belief systems, traditions and practices – cultures, in short.

In the absence of any formal or structured induction system at departmental level and against the often vague grounding alluded to earlier, new appointees are, by and large, left to make sense of their working environment and to assimilate the important features of communal practice. The danger, well recognised in a number of training regimes – notably teaching and the police – is that by the time new recruits find their feet, many of the practices and beliefs have been accepted uncritically. This leads to an unconscious – or at best non-reflective – replication of the 'canteen culture' or, equally damaging in the context of the development of a critical perspective in this area, to a replication of their own teaching and learning experiences:

> When I was a student, whether it was at school or university, it was always sitting there and being lectured at. That was just the way things seemed to be ... so without having any training in teaching and learning and understanding what it was all about, I was just carrying on how I'd been taught. (Medical scientist)

> I'm sure a lot of people approach their teaching by reflecting on their experience of being taught. I'm not saying that's a good thing to do but I'm sure that's how a lot of people start out. (Arts faculty member)

> I'm not an educator. You've got a PhD and then all of a sudden you're a teacher. I mean I've never understood this business. You've been trained to do research, research, research. You're a great researcher and you've only ever been assessed on your research, not on your ability to communicate. And then you get thrown in at the deep end. (Computer scientist)

Furlong and Maynard's model of teacher development (Furlong and Maynard, 1995) provides a useful framework for analysing typical induction and development trajectories in a HE setting. Whilst the context is different, one might safely assume that the developmental processes are similar, and from these, infer the impact of local culture on progression through the stages they identify. These five stages: idealism, survival, dealing with difficulties, reaching a plateau and extension, can be seen in cross-sections of teaching staff in most HE departments.

Idealism

Early cynicism may be a better descriptor than idealism in the higher education context. Unlike teachers in other sectors, whose motivation and role construct centres around teaching and learning, new academics are often ambivalent, occasionally hostile, to these dimensions of their role. In common with many, the institution which formed the focus for this study requires new academics to attend a modular programme designed to deal generically with a number of important teaching, learning, assessment and course design issues. Ironically, when attendance was non-compulsory, a self-selecting, motivated group gained some kudos and personal reward from attendance. When mandatory, this kudos disappeared as did, to varying degrees, the personal satisfaction derived from attendance. The programme has been variously criticised as not being relevant to departmental context and/or subject, and an impediment to other more 'worthwhile' activity. Some on the course often resisted and opposed what they perceived to be a 'culture of education'; conversations revealed consternation and even fear at 'not knowing what other people were talking about':

> I seemed to be with engineers, vets and physicists and I did not have a clue what they were talking about. The teaching methods were completely alien; the situation was completely different to what I would be dealing with ... but I think by the end of the course I actually found that really useful, not fitting in anywhere but being able to learn from and get points of view from the scientists, engineers and the arts people.

> I didn't understand the education jargon. In my group there were lawyers, historians, philosophers. They seemed to have a lot to say that I couldn't connect with at all. The next day was fine because we had to process what we'd learnt from the day before, which I'm happy to do. The feedback for me was very positive. It was actually quite glowing from the people that I didn't understand in the first place. So that was a good reinforcing experience. I realised that there were a lot of people who could help me, even though I'd felt isolated in the department.

Perhaps this hostility that many new academics express towards the culture of teaching and learning masks a fear of their own inadequacies? After all, they have been appointed because of their research activity in an institution which without exception, each one viewed as not valuing teaching:

> ... in the department there's really quite an imbalance in the teaching. There's a huge imbalance in the teaching. And it's actually split the department politically into sort of two sides, one of which obviously are the people that do all the teaching, which is quite a small number of people, and the other side are the people that don't do any teaching at all, they only do research. Who have proper appointments, such as Senior Lecturer, Reader, Chair, whatever. Still don't do any teaching, who bring in large grants and beat everyone else with a stick because they haven't got major papers. So we have this split within our department... a research/teaching split which is not visible to anyone outside of the department because whenever there are reviews of the department it's pushed under the carpet if you like or it's ... the paperwork is announced in such a way that it doesn't look as if there's this overt split.

Participants in this study were clear that they wouldn't be promoted for being a good teacher, so do they enter the teaching and learning culture of an education department with all the resistance and resentment of the 2 year old being dragged in from the garden on a sunny day? This aversion applied equally to attendance on the Teaching and Learning Programme and to continued workplace-centred activities on teaching, learning, assessment and course design. It indicates that despite growing attention to such issues, the research cultural bias of the larger institution still exerts a powerful influence and that even when teaching and learning is considered at department level, subject cultures still shape teaching methodologies, assessment regimes and notions of effectiveness.

Survival

How to survive after having been 'thrown in at the deep end' was a theme that participants in the study returned to. They felt isolated in their department, isolated in the university, and isolated by their perceived lack of opportunity to engage in fruitful discussions with colleagues about their teaching. Each one considered that they had learned a great deal from the interdisciplinary structure of the induction programme. It gave them the opportunity to meet people from different disciplines and all had formed friendships that had continued beyond the course. These friendships led to informal discussions about anxieties around teaching. Participants appeared to feel more relaxed when talking with someone from a completely different subject area, almost as if they felt less pressure when away from their own hotbed of competitive research.

Every participant on the programme is required to have a mentor who is supposed to support the new teacher and observe her/his teaching and give constructive feedback. There was a wide variation in how people came to be mentors and whether the new teacher had any choice in who their mentor was to be. What happened in practice was that the new lecturer was intuitively drawn to others who were interested in teaching and would find ways of developing forums where their teaching concerns would be addressed. This informal method of sharing anxieties seemed to be rather more productive than a more formally designated mentor, although those who had mentors had mostly found them useful.

> There was a member of staff who I got on very well with. I guess she became an informal mentor as I could ask anything of her. The formal mentoring relationship that had been set up was fine but it was awkward. Unless something was very pressing, I wouldn't bother her.

> The best sort of teaching guidance I got was from people in the department who were not senior to me, but my peers. That was a wonderful way of learning to teach. There was another person in the department who again was someone who thought a lot about how to teach. We used to talk through how we were devising our lessons, seminars and tutorials and how we were going to try and get certain students to speak. That was fun.

Dealing with difficulties

Surviving the initiation into departmental cultures and dealing with the fallout from teaching often leads beginner teachers to seek a set of recipes, routines or teaching tips from more experienced colleagues and from one another. Agenda-setting exercises with participants in the early stages of the teaching and learning course often

reveal a concern for tried and trusted ways of dealing with difficulties. It can be hard to convince participants of the value of reflecting on why these approaches might be successful, yet eventually
most come to see that formulaic responses may be inappropriate.
Once again, the role of the mentor in continuing the reflective approach in the departmental context was flagged as critical to early
achievement of a repertoire of management and teaching approaches.

Reaching a plateau and extension beyond

Once early problems have been overcome, and a few successful
teaching and management strategies developed, there is the possibility that further development ceases, with new teachers operating
within a comfort zone of competence. This inertia may be most
apparent within departments where teaching and developments in
teaching are background activities:

> ... my teaching throughout the programme has improved and
> improved and improved. You know there's always room for
> improvements, but the plateau ... it's starting to plateau now. I'm
> constantly thinking of things that I can do but, you know ... and
> constantly thinking about ... constantly having ideas of new
> assessment styles, I'd quite like to just try that. But actually the
> reality for me is that I won't get promoted. Good on admin, good
> on teaching, I've got to be good at research... you know when I
> say I'm plateauing, what that means is I'm plateauing in terms
> of benefit gain to the department and to me. Not in terms of, you
> know, what the students' experience could be ...

High-order teaching skills allied to a more sophisticated notion of
learning don't come easily nor quickly. They require the investment
of time and energy and are promoted through guidance and support.
Development often requires taking risks, and in a conservative
culture – especially where the evaluation of teaching competence is
in fairly narrow terms – risk-taking on an individual basis is something to be avoided. In departments where there is corporate thinking on teaching development, and where action research is promoted, innovations are more likely. Once again, the value of the
teaching and learning course in exposing participants to different

teaching cultures and the value of the mentor in endorsing and validating experimentation was underscored in participant responses.

So what is it that motivates the new lecturer in higher education to continue to develop their teaching if there is widespread recognition that it is not particularly valued in their department, if they feel that only disastrous student evaluations will make anyone sit up and take notice and if, in spite of statements to the contrary, it will not make a significant contribution to their promotion prospects? It appears to be that believing oneself to be good at something, receiving regular affirmatory feedback, finding colleagues who are interested in similar issues, and enjoying teaching are the intrinsic rewards.

> I can already see that the first year of teaching is incredibly difficult but incredibly exciting and rewarding and you get to know the individual students very well.

Conclusion

Despite their trepidation about not knowing the language of education, each participant found real value in meeting people from other departments on the teaching and learning course. Friendships were forged and other common languages established. Moves to contextualise the more generic training courses by locating more of the teacher training in departments risk losing one of the great strengths of multi-disciplinary working – the opportunity to examine, contrast and compare the practices, beliefs and – if not too grand a claim – philosophies in different quarters of the learning village. All the participants interviewed identified as an important dimension of induction the opportunity to compare and contrast practices from other departments with one's own, the ability to share perceptions of teaching, learners and enterprise and to better understand the learning village in all its complexities. The challenge is to find ways of acknowledging the subject differences within a framework which guarantees parity of support, quality of experience and which, in a climate of accountability, preserves equity. Addressing the cultural entrenchment of academic departments by exposing people to different ways of doing things may be a way of engendering debate about teaching and learning. Redefining teaching as subject specific may be playing the multicultural game and could remove opportunities for learning from each other.

One of the most powerful pieces of learning for participants was that people learned in different ways and that active, discursive learning led to a much deeper and richer experience for both students and lecturer. The role of the mentor in maintaining focus, momentum, reflection and evaluation was endorsed in interviews, replicating findings from a wider survey in this institution reported elsewhere (Atkinson and Brawn, 1997). Establishing a system of mentoring which was cross disciplinary would also be an innovative way forward. People want to know how they are doing, what they are doing well and how they can improve. Removing the elements of judgement and competitiveness that may arise when the mentor is of the same discipline and recruiting as mentors people who are genuinely interested in teaching and learning issues, so that they can give constructive feedback on the teaching process, is crucial. This process is of a type that parallels the feedback most valued from students.

There are clear messages too as to the nature of personal and systemic support structures which might move beyond mere exhortations to develop thinking as well as technical skills in the realm of teaching, learning and assessment. The learning environment is as important for new academics learning new concepts and skills as it is for students. The irony is that whilst much thought and effort goes into improving for the latter, relatively little appears to go into helping the former. External inspections are having an impact on departmental cultures of teaching and learning, insofar as reviews force managers and course designers to examine rationales, purposes and practices. At the level of documentation at least, individuals and departments appear to have grasped the concepts and vocabulary, to be engaging in analysis of provision and perhaps to have embraced the educational philosophies driving change. Some may be thinking more actively about selecting teaching competence and supporting teaching development. Even if there is some evidence of rule-learning and game-playing in the context of teaching quality, reviews, institutions, departments and individuals appear to be accommodating some of the cultural shifts, albeit slowly and patchily.

Postscript

In writing this chapter, we have both drawn on our experiences of working on teaching and learning programmes for new academics and postgraduates who teach. We work with resistance, opposition and attempts to openly subvert a culture of teaching and learning – of 'education'. Where currents meet there certainly appears to be fog but is there also the best fishing? For example, learning that is deep rather than superficial; learning that is enriched by the confluence of subject cultures and the turbulence this generates? We ourselves experienced some of this turbulence in preparing this chapter. Our own subject disciplines of physics and social science may be considered to be diametrically opposed, and our approaches to writing were certainly different. At times it really felt as though we were fishing in the fog. By choosing to do so we acknowledged and respected each other's differences and, in the process, learned different ways of baiting our own hooks.

References

Atkinson, T. and Brawn, R. (1997) Perspectives on mentoring in one higher education context. Paper presented at ATEE Conference, Macerata, Italy

Becher, T. (1993) *Academic tribes and territories. Intellectual enquiry and the cultures of disciplines.* The Society for Research into Higher Education and Open University Press, Buckingham

Furlong, J. and Maynard, T. (1995) *Mentoring student teachers: the growth of professional knowledge.* London, Routledge

Henkel, M. (2000) *Academic identities and policy change in higher education.* The Society for Research into Higher Education and Open University Press, Buckingham

Thomas, K. (1990) *Gender and subject in higher education.* Society for Research into Higher Education, OUP.

16

Researching assessment cultures, re-searching our selves

Jane Speedy, Jan Winter, Patricia Broadfoot, Judith Thomas and Barry Cooper

Man is an animal suspended in webs of significance he himself has spun. I take culture to be those webs and the analysis of it to be therefore not an experimental science in search of law, but an interpretative one in search of meaning. (Geertz, 1973, p5)

A t the start of the 21st century, assessment is a hotly contested territory. The normalising gaze of some kind of assessment practice infiltrates virtually all aspects of our lives from the proliferation of school examinations to quality assurance procedures in professional practice, and the relentless quest for the evaluation of standards in our transport systems, health services and even leisure activities. We live in a measurement culture, but this exists alongside other cultures of assessment wherein participative, restorative, formative, diagnostic and intuitive assessment ideas and practices are equally, if not more, valued. As with all discourses, aspects of these competing cultures are privileged at different times by different social, professional and political groups, academic disciplines and even in the minds of individuals in different domains of their own life experiences.

We are a small group of white British writers and educators, all from different disciplines within the helping professions: social workers, teachers, counsellors and psychotherapists. We have been working together at the University of Bristol as a result of our shared interest in assessment practices and have found ourselves engaged in a series of conversations that seemed to go round and round in circles. We had been amongst the contributors towards a series of scholarly and professional critiques of the summative assessment age, from historical and cultural, sociological, political, professional and even therapeutic perspectives. Nonetheless, assessment as a means of monitoring, selection and accountability seemed to dominate and overshadow less categoric constructs of assessment, such as those that that identified, shaped and promoted children's learning needs. It was as if this 'one language had eaten all the others' (Atwood, 1986) and our critical voices seemed to have dropped like a stone into the pond without even causing a ripple.

Despite our strong commitments and best efforts, it seemed that we were all, from professors to PhD students, in the margins rather than in the mainstream conversations about assessment. We came from different disciplines, professions and positions within the academy, but our collective leanings were towards assessment practices that promoted learning, were participative, recorded strengths and achievements (Broadfoot, 1998a, Speedy, Hinett and Thomas, 1999), and formed part of a feedback culture and that shaped future learning opportunities. These leanings were definitely not where the smart money was going in terms of policymaking in statutory, tertiary or higher education.

We decided to place our 'circular assessment conversations' under closer scrutiny, to employ ideas borrowed from the narrative therapies to tell and re-tell our personal assessment stories to each other and explore the assessment histories and cultures we had inhabited in our lives in questioning ways and to critically examine the habitual assessment narratives we seemed intent on privileging in our group. As we went around in our circles of discontentment, we seemed to share a common critique of modernist perspectives on assessment and be united in our incredulity regarding policy makers. As one of us railed:

> But the policy makers are people like us, they are just like us. They've had educational experiences like ours and they have children like ours. What's their problem? ....

Were we experiencing commonalities or confluences? Were we glossing over the cracks and discontinuities in our exchanges?

Would such interfaces open up the space to move our conversations forward? Would these critical, deconstructing conversations open up points of entry to alternative or expanded versions of our traditional assessment narratives? What were the internal, local and personal narratives embedded in our broad-brush habitual descriptions? Could more vivid, reflexive, co-created texts emerge? How would our colleagues and readers assess this kind of re-search endeavour?

We decided to embark upon a small local archaeological dig or experimental narrative inquiry into our own constructions of assessment ideas and practices, present these explorations as narrative and juxtapose these conversations with the literatures of educational assessment, and see what might emerge.

Constructing a narrative inquiry across disciplines

Borrowing our interviewing stance from narrative therapists, we began by directing a glance of naive curiosity towards our own and each other's stories. We anticipated that a narrative inquiry might provide us with ways of researching our cultural practices that opened out into multistoried, thickly described versions of our texts, rather than collapsing our understandings into what Geertz (1973) would depict as uniform and thinly described conclusions.

In their attempts to deconstruct and explore the 'multistoried world' we create and inhabit in our public and personal conversations, Riessman (1993) and Angus and Hardtke (1994) documented three identifiable narratives: external stories or habitual narratives, local or personal narratives that are more specific, and reflexive emergent narratives that create new meanings out of the interplay between landscapes of context, action and identity. Intimate or therapeutic conversations often commence with a rehearsal of habitual narratives that shift into more vivid personal accounts that, may in turn invite new meanings in the re-telling. The proponents of narrative or post-structural therapies (see White and Epston, 1991) posit the use of a curious, questioning interview style to elicit the local knowledges implicit in more general narratives and to evoke 'externalising conversations' and the construction of alternative stories. These re-tellings often take place in the presence of a reflecting team, who also engage in questioning and re-telling in order to open up possibilities and thicken descriptions.

Drawing on these traditions, we produced this chapter by means of an inquiry that was akin to the feminist and narrative customs of 'collective biography' (Davies *et al*, 1997). It began with each author writing a short story, a slice of his or her assessment autobiography. We discussed these stories as a group and two of us presented some of the more poignant and powerful statements that emerged as 'work in progress' at a departmental research conference. We subsequently conducted a series of research conversations wherein each of us re-presented our story and the rest of the group engaged in a collective re-telling of that story, describing ways in which it resonated with their own experiences and with the literatures and cultures of assessment.

An anthropological dig into cultures of assessment

These conversations were also like anthropological expeditions in which, having previously voyaged out to explore, describe and classify the assessment events and practices of others, we were now turning our critical and curious gaze upon ourselves to 'make the familiar unfamiliar' and to describe our own cultural practices, rituals and events (Myerhoff, 1986). The principal researcher then analysed the conversations for habitual and local narratives, mutualities and discontinuities.

Certainly from an anthropological perspective, there does appear to be a series of arcane, disciplinary assessment rituals taking place throughout childhood and early adulthood. These rituals or 'definitional ceremonies' as we might call them (Myerhoff, 1986) seem designed to impart significant histories and mythologies that link the people of 21st century Europe to the past certainties that form their cultural heritage. At first glance these assessment ceremonies appear outmoded, contrary to the current rhetoric and no longer relevant to the lives of the population in future. They linger on, nonetheless, not merely as forms of theatre or recreational activity, but rather as central, publicly witnessed events of 'legitimate' socio- cultural significance. They form significant rites of passage that dominate and shape the contemporary landscapes of both action and identity and within the stories we tell ourselves about ability, potency, agency, creativity and hierarchy. We were curious. A powerful range of stakeholders seemed wedded to these assessment customs and practices. Were they merely 'habitual narratives' or did they have some other significance?

A constant refrain throughout our conversations was the fear that we would be assessed by our readers as self-indulgent and anecdotal in our approach, rather than rigorous in our methods. This fear had been expressed by other writers who had attempted to capture personal stories as a research endeavour (e.g. Ellis, 1995). Nonetheless, we were convinced that our narratives had something to offer. In contributing our personal stories to the discourses of assessment, we hoped, that our research might become more embodied.

Conversational habits and habitual assessment stories

We represent, as a group, an enormously successful professional, personal and academic profile. We come from a range of ethnic/ class backgrounds but are all white Europeans and, typically within the helping professions, perhaps, comprise five women and one man. We have not led charmed existences, but have somehow all managed to acquire the personal and professional adaptability and flexibility to overcome moments of academic and professional failure, childhood anguish and personal struggle and loss in our lives. Between us, we span the range of cognitive, practical and emotional intelligences that make, if government rhetoric is to be believed, for successful 21st century people (DfEE, 1997). We represent between us a mixture of professional portfolio and traditional academic career trajectories. We have all re-invented our professional identities at least once. Jane Speedy, for instance has, like many women, been on more of a career merry-go-round than a career trajectory and her list of past professional identity claims includes teacher, play therapist, education officer, parent advocate, student counsellor, head of sensory-impairment services and counsellor educator. Judith Thomas, who would have laughed at anyone who suggested that she might be an academic by the time she was forty, included houseparent, social worker, therapist, training officer and project manager in the list of identities she acquired en route to academia. Jan Winter was a teacher of mathematics in secondary schools and still sees that as her main interest – she has simply changed the way she contributes to it by now working in teacher education, both pre- and in-service.

Our written assessment stories were somewhat divergent and strongly reflected our professional and disciplinary cultures. The two social workers in our group both focused on the assessment and self-assessment of others in professional and adult educational contexts, the two educationalists both told stories from their experiences of schooling and the counsellor produced accounts from her personal and family life. There was some initial, unspoken awkwardness around these divergent understandings of assessment and some elaborate, overly polite negotiations took place around the 'unsaid' and the 'unsayable' within the group (Rogers *et al*, 1999).

Some of the counsellor's story, for instance, transgressed habitual sites of self-construction for educational researchers by including her own sexuality and sexual orientation. This difficulty was resolved by taking her story first, on the grounds that she was more used to doing this kind of thing, thus ensuring that the level of questioning established in the group maintained social distance and minimised potential conflict with convention (Brown *et al*, 1988).

Our conversations themselves represented something of a tug-of-war between preferred professional cultural practices and the possibly constraining influence of being in a research group in a university setting. The counsellor's questions were very direct and focused towards moments of emotional intensity or cognitive dissonance; the social work and teacher educators asked here-and-now clarifying questions about life and work experiences, the academic educationalists asked more speculative questions that led to a comparison with the literatures of assessment practices. But these were not fixed roles and most of the group could, and did, move between at least two of these positions. The following extract may illustrate some of these tensions and may indicate something about the circularity of our conversations:

Teacher educator: **The headlines in the Sun are never about participative processes ...there are other pressures on social workers...(wry laughter all round)**

Counsellor: So what sustains social workers in all this? How do you feel about your assessment role in people's lives?

Social worker A: Very rarely is it talked about although assessment is this omnipresent all-pervasive thing....

*Social worker B: **In the literature assessment is empowering, participative, in partnership... this is contradicted and constrained by resources...***

Social worker A: Yes, and by the ability of the two people to engage and forge a partnership...

*Academic educationalist: **I am intrigued with your speculation about how they were feeling. The literature of emotional intelligence comes to mind...***

Despite an initial determination to leave definitions of assessment ambiguous in our explorations, we all homed in, by silent agreement, on key experiences of formal, summative assessment. It was nonetheless clear from our narrative account, presented in sequence below, that these experiences had profoundly shaped our understanding of the assessment phenomenon. In our own explorations within the narrative metaphor we had come to understand and appreciate storytelling as a bridge between culture and agency and we therefore decided to present this chapter in chronological form as a 'collective biography' of our lives. This seemed somewhat counter-cultural in an academic environment in which many factors have distanced us from cherishing stories. As McLeod (ix, 1997) comments: 'many people, certainly those who control what takes place in the professions, have passed through an educational system that places little value on stories'. How then, will our chapter be assessed?

Assessment cultures of the 1950s and 60s: common experiences

As they went through the current English education system, our own children were well aware of the processes of assessment and categorisation they were subject to from a very young age. One of our own children, aged seven, had recently protested:

How come I'm in the 'derrh brains' group, when I got level three for English? That's so unfair

These kinds of understandings are paralleled repeatedly in the ways in which young children construct their school experiences. By way of contrast, as a group of people aged between 35 and 55, we had little memory of being formally assessed at primary school. We were acutely aware, both at the time and in retrospect, of the ways assessment crept up on us unawares. As we considered knowledge, power, structure and personal agency and their relevance to assessment practices we concluded that we had been a most powerless group of young children, who had little knowledge or control over assessment processes. Assessment was an operation of Lukes' (1974) third order of latent or disguised power. Summative assessment, at least, took place by stealth. If formative assessments were taking place, they were not overtly or transparently about promoting any sense of partnership in learning or self-evaluation:

> *I wasn't aware of any assessment processes that happened to me at primary school – they nevertheless happened fairly awfully really. Most of them only emerged after I had left. Like... When I discovered I'd passed the eleven plus, which I never knew I'd even sat...*
>
> **I had no idea why I didn't get into the school play. I supposed at the time I wasn't good enough, I have no idea...'**
>
> *I remember that I most wanted to sing... and I wanted to play the recorder... and somehow I didn't pass... in some way... I perhaps didn't pass... in any case, I didn't get into either group...*
>
> **I had a horribly inflated view of myself because people kept telling me I was clever... I realise I had no idea.... I hadn't really learned to assess the value of what I did myself at all....**

It was as if assessment were an absent but implicit assumption within the discourses of the primary schools that we had attended in the 1950s and 1960s. Given their absence and opacity, these assessment moments may well have been all the more difficult for us as young children to decode, however successful we were at the game we were not entirely sure we were playing.

As a group, we now share a strong our critique of the values and purposes of current assessment strategies and have voiced a growing concern that the present measurement culture is taking future citizens further way from the kinds of educational experiences that might encourage creative, flexible, emotionally intelligent life-long learners. Children in current English primary schools are acutely aware of the constant assessment pressures they are under. Assessment practice in contemporary primary schools is definitely present and explicit. If this transparency could be combined with a feedback culture, whereby overt assessment processes existed to promote and clarify future learning goals for pupils, students and teachers alike, we might have gone some way to cultivating school students as partners in their own learning processes and to promoting:

> '... the notion of lifelong education. Not only must it adapt to changes in the nature of work, but it must also constitute a continuous process of forming whole human beings – their knowledge and aptitudes, as well as the critical faculty and ability to act.' (Delors, 1997)

Learning the disciplines of the 'self' at home and at school

Cultures of home and school 'Assessment' took on completely different, highly transparent, dimensions for all of us in secondary education. Between us we attended the gamut of secondary modern, comprehensive, grammar and independent schools. Our social experiences were diverse. Some of us were self-confident, some shy, some good-at-going-out-with-boys, some socially inept. The assessment process uniformly defined us in transparent ways, regardless of whether we were successful at it, since it continually threw us into competition with ourselves, our friends and our siblings.

> *My headmistress felt I hadn't done well in getting a 2 for Latin. I can remember it. ...and I thought I'd done brilliantly. That was just typical. Surely more significant was that I'd only just scraped through English language*

> **and my mum said, well done, and it's especially good because you worked really hard for those results, not like your brother. It's much more to your credit than his, he's just naturally clever...**

> *No matter how well I did, Brenda always did better. The effect on me was not good, the effect on me was...that it systematically undermined my confidence in myself...'*

These comments emerged from different cultures in our lives, cultures of school, engendered family cultures and cultures of friendship, but the dominant discourses remained uniform. Regardless of our ability to pass or do well at exams, we seemed unable to self-monitor or self-evaluate. We were all involved in a process of selection and were keenly aware of it. This was a high stakes assessment culture in which almost nobody, it appears, felt prized, or able to develop a critique of the process they were engaged in.

I was socially self-confident, but when it came to assessments, well 'results'... I totally lost the plot.

I hadn't seen self-assessment as a useful skill. I hadn't learned to assess the value of what I did myself....

My assumption was that assessment was fair. Life was fair and the people at the top were good and there because they deserved to be.... the fact that they were all 'old', white and male was purely coincidental!

Perhaps the most glaring aspect of this process in terms of future assessment policies was how much these practices militated against our abilities to evaluate ourselves in meaningful ways. This bears out Heron's and Boud's (1998) observation that, within conventional educational systems:

Learners are seen as rationally competent to grasp the discipline taught by academic superiors, but are not seen as rationally competent to participate in determining [their] own academic destiny nor in assessing [their] own competence (p77).

If members of the 21st century learning society are going to be able to make informed and competent choices and decisions about their learning needs and strengths within communities and workplaces, clearly they will need to develop the self-monitoring skills purported to emerge from participative assessment practices (see Knowles, 1990, Boud, 1995, Speedy, 1998). It would seem advantageous that these skills and strategies be developed earlier rather than later in life and be actively encouraged in schools as well as within more participative adult learning environments.

Moving on to higher education

Our degree of enthusiasm for continuing into post-compulsory education was largely determined not by schooling but by whether we were sustained and supported by alternative cultures and traditions and in particular by customs and practices that contradicted the pervasive measurement culture. People who had difference strongly on their side, strong and positive differences of class or race or some other value system that distanced them from the values of schooling, seemed generally more robust:

> *my self-esteem, that was a strong feeling that I brought from my family really. I was the only one who stayed on at school. It was that, the family, or luck, that had helped me get through everything, being judged....*

> **being Jewish, stalwarts of the WEA, the Fabian society, the jazz club...all this somehow gave us a little bit of detachment from it all... perhaps we didn't take it so seriously...**

> *I just happened to have had a mother who had gone to university, which was quite unusual in those days, and it was that more than anything that made the difference.*

Those of us without a strong counterplot to the dominant story fared less well:

> *My experience of the entire education system was going to school and doing what I was told to do. My parents wanted me to get on in life and they didn't know any different. I wasn't challenged in any way at home or at school about how to think.*

> **I never got as far as higher education at this stage having failed the assessment hurdles and dropped out of the system to do something more real-any enthusiasm for learning had been assessed out of me.**

These experiences seem consistent with comparative educational research that presents French school children as more robust in the face of educational assessments than their English counterparts (Broadfoot, 2000). French society seems to have a wider understanding of legitimate forms of access to contemporary culture and therefore traditionally has far more limited expectations of its education system than Britain, with the result that classification via educational assessments has less personal and social impact. Perhaps our future life-long learners need to be encouraged to find ways of taking institutionalised learning and the normalising gaze of assessment with more of a pinch of salt and we need to place higher value on informal practices of learning, of cultural transgression (hooks, 2000) and even 'the wilful abandonment of the pursuit of adequacy'. Indeed, as one of us commented: '*It was when I failed to meet expectations that I was most successful*'.

Learning begins at forty

At some later point we all entered the 'helping professions'. One by one we drifted into higher education, some of us for the first time, some for a second round, for disparate reasons, such as not having the imagination to do anything else, or having our employers offer to pay our fees, or experiencing a curiosity about 'study' for it's own sake.

It seemed to be a common theme amongst us that the experience of studying for a higher degree was some kind of turning point in our understandings of ourselves as learners:

> *It was learning to suit my purposes; I was consciously critiquing the process.*

> **In many ways that masters degree was the first time I enjoyed learning. I was doing it absolutely for the intrinsic rewards.**

> *It wasn't until I got onto the M.Ed ...I thought, I can do this, I like this.... and I became empowered.*

> **What we seem to have in common is the resilience, the emotional survival skills to last until this point...**

For some of us this took place in early adulthood; others were in our thirties and forties. Middle age brought with it a certain robustness and an immunity to the vagaries of external assessment that gave many of us a sense of power in learning and has been highly influential in shaping future resolve.

> *As an adult leaner I experienced self-assessment in quite powerful ways. I realised how much I had covered up. How much less frightened I now am about being discovered.*

> **I'm very aware of the changeover time for our MSc students on the counselling programme, quite an exciting mid-course**

phenomenon that is almost visual, as assessment transforms from an extrinsic, 'done to me' process, to a process in partnership, a process that is restorative.

The whole discourse of self-assessed, intrinsically motivated, participatory learning sits comfortably with the rhetoric of 'the learning society' and with contemporary speculation that successful citizens of the future will be flexible, adaptable life-long learners conversant with participatory portfolio learning and assessment structures that cultivate portfolio career trajectories. Assessment strategies that encourage the evaluation of work in progress and that promote discovery and study skills rather than focusing on the acquisition of information would seem more conducive to society's stated future requirements.

Currently, assessment conversations that gave voice to more local knowledges seemed to be the preserve of older generations. As one of our number commented: *'we seem to have to wait until our forties in this society before permissions are granted and we are able to learn how to learn'*.

Definitional ceremonies and 21st century assessment practices

The secular eighteenth and nineteenth century educators who established the customs and practices we are now so keen to critique, did not overthrow their precursors but rather sought to legitimise their new, meritocratic educational principles within the traditions of the religious orders they replaced. Degree convocations and religious ordinations have much in common to this day. Perhaps we might have something to learn from our pragmatic, secular, 'modernist' forefathers after all.

It is perhaps in its quasi-religious uses of public ceremony that the enlightenment assessment traditions still have an appeal:

The other day I was at this gathering where people were being presented with cups and I whispered to my neighbour, with longing.... I've never ever had a cup in my whole life. Not in my WHOLE LIFE!

I know I'm going to feel a sense of achievement, ... And even though she's dead, I shall go to the degree ceremony that she'd have loved to come to, swirl around in my long red frock and think... look at me, mum, I'm a 'doctor'.... TARADA!

The anthropologist Barbara Myerhoff distinguished between day-to-day social dramas and the ceremonies that represented defining moments in the construction of cultural identities. These 'definitional ceremonies' were usually required to take place in the presence of 'outsider witnesses' of some kind:

> A kind of collective autobiography, a means by which a group creates its identity by telling itself a story about itself, in the course of which it brings to life its 'definite and determinate' identity. (Myerhoff, 1986, p40)

To some extent this is what we as a group have been doing, in this chapter. We have been trying to make sense of ourselves, for ourselves. This may or may not have some bearing on teaching, learning and researching where worldviews, or at the very least, professional cultures, meet. Our process of writing this chapter has not been as participatory as most of us would ideally have liked. The writing has been consensual rather than cooperative, with the principal researcher, Jane Speedy, also taking on the role of principal writer. Absent but implicit within this text lurk at least four other versions. This compromise has nevertheless gone some way towards researching beneath our habitual critique of the modernist discourse to capture some of the local knowledges that might shift us from structural to agentic positions in our descriptions. In exploring our alternative versions of either the dominant discourses of the policy makers or of our own habitual polemical narratives, we have been exploring identities for ourselves as co-creators of cultural practice, rather than as 'subjects' of cultural constraint (Davies, 2000). This has been a definitional ceremony that has unearthed strong commitments to transparency and participation in assessment processes, to resisting the established cultural practice amongst educators of privileging schooling and to valuing multifarious sites of learning.

In the wider context of British society, it seems possible that the passion for categoric assessment practices represents much more than a system of bench marking in educational settings, and that it also provides a series of contemporary definitional ceremonies that act as rites of passage from childhood to adolescence, from adolescence to early adulthood and so forth. An audience is recruited at each stage of this story and this sustains thickens its take on our sense of our selves and our cultural traditions.

The stakeholders in assessment practices throughout Europe, and indeed internationally, are many and various. Agendas concerned with individual educational opportunity and possibility and the 'ethical issues concerning the best interests of the candidate' (Torrance, 2000, p178) seem almost irrelevant in the maelstrom of political, cultural and almost numinous and quasi-religious expectations we seem to have of our assessment processes and ceremonies. Many of us have been calling for a or a 'storming of the Bastille' (Broadfoot, 1998a) or a 'deeper vision' (Heron, 1996) of assessment practices and have done much to communicate the possibilities of alternative assessment paradigms. In articulating our personal assessment stories in this chapter, we have contributed to these re visions with more embodied requests for transparency, participation, the encouragement of local knowledges and interests, and by casting doubts upon the habitual wisdom of privileging schooling as the font of contemporary cultural exchanges. We have also encountered the importance of ceremony and of audience in the embracing of new ideas and practices.

Perhaps we might now reconsider how to re-constitute these practices, which will in turn constitute us, in the future. Perhaps we might also consider emulating our pragmatic, modernist predecessors who did not so much overthrow or storm as surreptitiously maintain, the mysteries and adapt the traditional ceremonies of their own religious precursors to suit different purposes. Perhaps the architects of the modernist assessment project were more astute post-modernists than they are currently being given credit for. They certainly seem to have understood that they were living in a multi-storied world – a world in which traditional, modern, post-modern and future moments might all co-exist. The art, perchance, is not to take an oppositional or compliant position but rather to slip between these stories, find the key points of entry that inhabit the liminal spaces and the cultural interfaces, and – here's the tricky bit – re-author the text.

References

Angus, L. and Hardtke, K. (1994) 'Narrative processes in psychotherapy', *Canadian Psychology*, 35(2), p190-203

Atwood, M. (1986) Translation was never possible, cited (p81) in: Lather P, (1991) *Getting Smart: feminist research and pedagogy with/in the post modern*, London, Routledge

Boud, D. (1995) *Enhancing Learning Through Self-Assessment*, Kogan Page, London.

Broadfoot, P. (1998) Quality standards and control in Higher Education; what price life-long learning? in: *International Studies in the sociology of education* 892) 155-80

Broadfoot, P. (1998a) Records of Achievement and the Learning Society: a tale of two discourses, in: *Assessment in Education*, 5(3) 447-479

Broadfoot, P. (2000) *Promoting quality in Learning: does England have the answer? London,* Cassell

Brown, L. Argyris, J., Bardige, B., Gilligan, C., Johnston, K., Miller, B., Osborne, J., Ward, G., Wiggins, G. and Wilcox, D. (1988) *A Guide to Reading Narratives of Conflict and Choice for Self and Moral Voice,* Harvard Graduate School of Education, Center for the Study of Gender, Education and Human Development, Cambs, MA

Brown, S. and Knight, P. (1994) *Assessing Learners In Higher Education,* London, Kogan Page

Davies, B., Dormer, S., Honan, E., MacAllister, N., O'Reilly, R., Rocco, S. and Walker, A. (1997) Ruptures in the skin of silence: a collective biography, in: *Hecate: A Women's Interdisciplinary Journal* 23 (1) 62-79.

Davies, B. (2000a) *A Body of Writing 1990-1999*, Walnut Creek, CA., Alta Mira

Delors, J. (1997) quoted in: Learning for the 21st century: The first report of the National Advisory Group for Continuing Education and Lifelong Learning, on: http://www.lifelonglearning.co.uk

DfEE (1997) Learning for the 21st century: The first report of the National Advisory Group for Continuing Education and Lifelong Learning, on: http://www.lifelonglearning.co.uk

Ellis, C. (1995) *Final Negotiations: a story of love, loss and chronic illness,* Philadelphia, Temple University Press

Filer, A. (2000) (Ed.) *Assessment: Social Practice And Social Product*, Routledge Falmer, London.

Filer, A. and Pollard, A. (2000) *The Social World of Pupil Assessment: process and contexts of primary schooling.* London: Continuum

Geertz, C. (1973) (ed.) Thick Description; towards an interpretive theory of cultures, in: *The Interpretation Of Cultures*, New York, Basic Books

Heron, J. (1996) Helping Whole People Learn, in: Boud, D. And Miller, N. (Eds.) *Working with Experience: animating learning,* London, Routledge

Heron, J. (1998) in: Boud, D. (2nd ed.) *Developing Student Autonomy in Learning, London,* Kogan Page

Hinett, K. and Thomas, J. (eds.) (1999) *Staff Guide to Self and Peer Assessment*, Oxford Centre For Staff And Learning Development, Headington

Lukes, S. (1974) *Power: a radical view, studies in sociology*, London, Macmillan

McLeod, J. (1997) *Narrative and Psychotherapy, London,* Sage

Myerhoff, B. (1986) Life Not Death In Venice in: Turner, V. And Bruner, E. (Eds.) *The Anthropology of Experience*, University Of Illinois Press.

Riessman, C.K. (1993) *Narrative Analysis,* CA: Thousand Oaks, Sage

Rogers, A., Casey, M., Eckert, J., Holland, J., Nakkula, V. and Sheinberg, N. An Interpretive Poetics of Languages of the Unsayable, in: Josselson, R. and Lieblich, A. (1999) (Eds) *Making Meaning Of Narratives: the narrative study of lives, Vol 6*, Thousand Oaks, Sage

Speedy, J. (1998) Negotiated Learning And Assessment, in: Johns, H. (Ed) *Balancing Acts: studies in counselling training*, London, Routledge

Taylor, I. (1997) *Developing Learning In Professional Education: partnerships for practice*, Buckingham, Society for Research into Higher Education and Open University Press

White, M. (1999) Different Faces of Power, Course notes, Dulwich centre, Adelaide, SA

White, M. and Epston, D. (1991) *Narrative Means to Therapeutic Ends*, New York, Norton

17

Afterword
Dimensions of Culture-Clash

James Wertsch

The authors of this volume take up some of today's most complex and fascinating problems in education. Trying to understand these issues is highly ambitious now that education seems to be confronted with so many questions and demands. An Johnsson and his colleagues reminded us in Chapter 2, Bruner (1996) has summarized this situation thus:

> Our changing times are marked by deep conjectures about what schools should be expected to do for those who are compelled to attend them-or for that matter, what schools can do, given the forces of other circumstances. Should school aim simply to reproduce the culture, to 'assimilate' the young into ways of being little Americans or little Japanese? ... or would schools, given the revolutionary changes through which we are living, do better to dedicate themselves to the equally risky, perhaps equally quixotic ideal of preparing students to cope with the changing world in which they will be living? (pix).

In Bruner's quotation and in several chapters of this volume one witnesses a basic tension between schooling envisioned as a conservative force of socialization and schooling envisioned as an instrument of change. To add to this already complex picture, the authors recognise that they must address these issues in a context of ongoing social transformation and that this process has gained new momentum in an age of rapid globalization.

In their introduction Claxton, Pollard, and Sutherland emphasize that we can no longer assume a familiar, stable environment when we

273

discuss education-indeed such an assumption may have been dubious all along. The alternative, namely addressing complex issues of education in a rapidly changing world, is extremely ambitious, but Claxton, Pollard, and Sutherland boldly assert that this is our only option. Beginning with the assumption that analyses of schooling and learning cannot be limited to 'the mastery of skills or the retention of knowledge' (p10), they move into exciting new areas of inquiry. We owe a great deal to all the authors of this volume for their willingness to take on these issues and for bringing to them such intelligence and theoretical insight.

One of the points made by these authors is that education must come to terms with increasingly porous boundaries between instructional and non-instructional settings and between the disciplines that can be harnessed to provide insight into this issue. Indeed, it is increasingly difficult to identify settings that are not educational in one sense or another, and this raises a host of issues for understanding modern schooling and its place in a larger sociocultural context.

As Claxton, Pollard, and Sutherland point out, we are also confronted with an increasingly pluralistic and interwoven world in which 'we become enculturated into one group, and then find ourselves having (or choosing) to engage with people who do things in a very different way... We have to work alongside people from different disciplinary, professional, and national cultures' (p2). The increasingly common setting in which 'worldviews meet' is where much, if not most learning and teaching go on today, and the authors believe that we simply need to get on with dealing with this.

In their account of the culture-clash that characterizes so much of modern life and education, Claxton, Pollard, and Sutherland outline four basic ways that people can respond when confronted with unfamiliar ways of being. First, they can act in a defensive way by ignoring them, refusing to buy into them, or acting as if they did not exist. Second, an individual or group might 'more or less consciously decide to resist, oppose or subvert the other culture' (p10). Third, one can 'become more personally enculturated to the unfamiliar worldview' and 'adopt it wholesale, and update or abandon old values and practices in the light of the new, with the uncritical and pervasive enthusiasm of the naïve convert' (p10). And fourth, one can negotiate a process in which 'new and existing worldviews are redefined and allowed to resonate in a more delicate, but often more uncomfortable, fashion, perhaps over a longer period of time' (p10).

I know that the authors struggled with this list of alternatives and were concerned that the notion of culture they were presupposing in laying it out would be susceptible to the critique of naïve homo-geneity. To steadfastly ignore, consciously resist and oppose, or adopt another culture wholesale does sound like presupposing homogeneous cultures that stand in neat opposition to one another, and from this perspective the only theoretically satisfying alternative is the fourth path of negotiation.

At the same time, however, the *tendencies* identified in the first three alternatives are worth considering, and they shape several other authors' contributions to this volume in productive ways. While there is little attention by the authors to the possibility of simply ignoring other cultural perspectives or refusing to admit they exist (but see the discussion in chapter 9 by Brown and Coles about chickening out of engaging in math problems), the chapters do touch on all three of the other alternatives. Under the heading of more or less consciously deciding to resist, oppose or subvert another cul-ture, one can find several illustrations. In her discussion of overseas students' experiences, for example, Gilpin (chapter 4) writes of the problems of growing alienation and anomie. In this context 'students may withdraw into strategic or surface learning behaviours that enable them to pass their assignments adequately, but fail to engage with the culture of education in which they find themselves' (p64).

Or consider the insightful analysis by Pollard and Filer in chapter 12, of the various strategies parents may adopt as they deal with how schools assess their children. The authors propose a general model involving four dimensions of strategic action: conformity, noncon-formity, anti-conformity, and redefining. This model provides a means for discussing the complexities parents face as they strive to serve as both mediators and interpreters of their children's assess-ment and school experience, a prime site for culture-clash.

When reflecting on issues of this nature, I believe that adding an additional analytic dimension into the mix could help round out the picture. The dimension I have in mind arises most obviously in connection with resistance but is also relevant to the other alternatives. It is a dimension that exists on a separate analytic plane, one that could be called orthogonal to those considered by most of the authors in this volume. Specifically, I would argue that there is a need to take into consideration some distinction between private and public performance, something that can be grounded in the dramaturgical metaphor proposed by Goffman (1959).

From this perspective culture-clash may occur in public or on the front stage, but it may also take place backstage, in private performance regions. Instead of assuming that individuals either do or do not accept, reject, or negotiate over new cultural confrontations in general, it is useful to introduce additional nuance into the picture by asking what they are doing inside and outside the purview of public performance. This is an issue that forms part of the background assumptions for chapter 7, where Bond outlines various stances toward counselling. On the one hand, this is an activity that must preserve a private sphere of communication, but on the other, it should not be hidden from view as if it concerns something shameful and to be kept out of public sight. As a result of this tension, counselling is undoubtedly something that is sometimes openly embraced in private but resisted or rejected in public. Or consider the complex interaction of forces at work in the case of homework. In their analysis, Hughes and Greenhough (chapter 11) outline different spheres of activity-at school and at home, both of which involve public and private performance regions.

The very notion of what is to be performed on and off the front stage, how 'teams' are constructed and so forth may vary from one milieu to another, and this may play an essential role in understanding how students and teachers function in familiar and unfamiliar settings. Consider, for example, the observation that Lazarus and Tay make in chapter 5 that 'teachers who may already be overloaded with new initiatives may well buy into change on the surface but without any significant change in their practice' (p81).

The bottom line here is that the options for ignoring, rejecting, adopting or negotiating with new cultural contexts-as if it is done in an all-or-nothing manner for an individual-may not exhaust the possibilities. Instead, the main upshot of encountering a new cultural setting may be to create a new sort of differentiation between private and public spheres of performance. People may publicly accept certain aspects of a new cultural setting while resisting it in backstage performance regions. Furthermore, the issues raised by the dramaturgical metaphor may be expected to come into play as readily in the case of organizational cultures of the sort examined by Hoyle and Wallace (chapter 6) as in the case of national or ethnic cultures, which provide the cases usually considered.

When it comes to the alternative of adopting another culture, especially in public performance settings, institutions in modern society-especially schools-play an especially important role. They have been charged with the responsibility of socializing future citizens and are to some degree defined by this responsibility. This is an issue that Osborn, McNess, Planel, and Triggs take up in chapter 2. In their comparison of English, Danish and French school systems, they identify their different goals and tell us something about how well they have managed to attain these goals. The differences between the individual, child-centered pedagogy of the English system, the communitarian goals of the Danish system, and the republican ideal of the French system are interesting. These are differences in what it is that a state considers worthwhile, and the authors raise a host of issues to consider when thinking about how effective schooling may be at reaching them.

When thinking about the concrete means available to schools for pursuing its socialisation goals, I would like to propose that narratives play a particularly role. If Bruner (1990) is right, narratives and narrative thought must occupy a central place in cultural psychology, and this claim is nowhere more relevant than in the case of schooling. One of the most obvious ways that this plays out, and an issue that has been of particular concern to me (Wertsch, 2002), is in connection with narratives that formal schooling provides to students about their past. Such narratives, especially in the form of official, state-sponsored histories, are clearly intended to shape students' ideas about their current identity as well as what went before. The teaching of official history, which is perhaps more properly termed state-sponsored collective memory (Wertsch, 2002), is the most ambitious project in collective memory witnessed to date anywhere, and in taking up this issue, one is inevitably led to consider an essential means or 'textual resources' (Wertsch, 2002) involved in the socialization of thinking and identity.

To be sure, more than formal history instruction is involved in providing these textual resources and socializing young people into a collective memory community. For example, Wineburg (2001) points out the powerful role of film and other aspects of popular culture play in this process. However, there can be no doubt about the importance of formal instruction in this regard. It provides one of the central means that modern states have at their disposal to introduce their future citizens to a master narrative and to convince these citizens that they can find a place in it for themselves. Hence, an obvious site for socialization-and for culture-clash to occur – is history instruction. In totalitarian states, this process is carried to an extreme (Wertsch, 2002), but in one form or another it is to be found in every modern state in the world today.

At a general level, narratives should be understood as providing just one illustration of how 'cultural tools' (Wertsch, 1998) play a role in the culture-clash envisioned by Claxton, Pollard, and Sutherland. From this perspective it is important to distinguish the production of tools such as curriculum materials from their consumption, since one-sided analyses can provide partial, even distorted accounts. For example, it is possible to conduct an exhaustive analysis of the production of textbooks and films used in history instruction, but to know very little about how these cultural tools or textual resources are actually used or consumed.

This seems to have been the case during the Cold War years when it was common practice for western observers to examine Soviet history textbooks and go directly from that to making claims about what young people in the USSR actually thought. Such observations may have been accurate with regard to what was being presented to students, what they had to know in order to pass examinations, and what they had to say in public performance regions. As Tulviste and

Wertsch (1994) have demonstrated, however, this is not what at least some students believed or said in private.

In interviews conducted in 1992, for example, ethnic Estonians who were products of the official Soviet education system were able to provide not only the official history of certain key events, but an unofficial one as well. Specifically, when asked about the official history of what happened when Estonia became part of the Soviet Union in 1944, they were quite able to provide a version of what occurred that echoed what had been presented in Soviet textbooks and instruction. But when an interviewer then asked them to provide an unofficial version, they were equally prepared to do so, and in many cases were noticeably more enthusiastic in this performance. Furthermore, when asked what the difference between the two versions was, several interviewees stated that the official account was simply false and the unofficial one was accurate.

Had an analysis of the cultural tools for national identity been limited to textual production in this case, it obviously would have been missing a crucial part of the picture. During the Soviet period ethnic Estonians, as well as many other Soviet citizens, became quite adept at performing in public as they were required to by the state, but this clearly did not reflect what they said in private or what they appeared to believe at some deeper level.

Such dynamics may have existed in a particularly stark way in the Soviet context, but they can be found in one form or another virtually everywhere. When dealing with the issues of culture-clash, as this volume does, perhaps the most obvious place to look for them is in disenfranchised groups. For example, in the US it is not unusual for members of racial minorities to report that they know the official account of American history very well and had even studied it as part of an honours course in high school. When asked whether they believe what this account, however, it is also not unusual for them to respond flatly in the negative. Hence the need to consider what students and others actually *do* with the texts that are produced for them and not to stop at production studies alone.

It is precisely issues of consumption that are being raised when Claxton, Pollard, and Sutherland raise questions about ignoring other cultures, resisting them, adopting them, or negotiating with them. These are some of the most interesting and pressing issues we can address, but they are also the very ones most likely to be slighted, with the current overemphasis on how culture and text are produced, as opposed to consumed. An interesting take on this problem can be found in chapter 10, where Molyneux-Hodgson and Facer examine science textbooks as 'cultural artifacts.'

For the most part, this is an analysis of the forces reflected in the production of such textbooks and how these artifacts serve to create an image of what it is to be a scientist and to belong to the scientific community. For Molyneux-Hodgson and Facer, science textbooks do more than simply present the facts, however. In addition: 'central to the production of authoritative discourse... is the set textbook which is given legitimacy by its position as a pedagogical tool, re-cognised by existing members of the scientific community and proposed for purchase and use as an important artefact in the completion of a given programme of study' (p157). While most of this chapter is devoted to the production of these cultural tools, some space is given to discussing different reading strategies, including 'dominant, negotiated, and oppositional'. It is precisely such strategies that will need additional attention in the future to address issues of consumption as well as production.

As I noted earlier, virtually all instances of culture-clash involve negotiation of some sort or another and hence it serves as the master term for understanding how worldviews meet. At the same time, the way this negotiation is conducted can vary significantly and is consequently worth differentiating into categories such as Claxton, Pollard, and Sutherland propose. For example, it is not at all unusual for this to be a process that involves *both* resistance and acceptance. Furthermore, it is something that can go on in public, as well as private performance regions, and it can take place in both the production and the consumption of culture. With regard to production and consumption, negotiation is often envisioned as occurring as students use textual resources and other aspects of culture, but it can be an essential part of how cultural tools, artifacts and textual resources come into existence as well. This is a point made in chapter 13 by Facer, Furlong, Furlong, and Sutherland, where 'edutainment' software provides a ready example of cultures in conflict. Instead of assuming that learning can be equated with 'formal and involuntary educational experiences, while fun is often constructed as any voluntary activity that does not involve coercion' (p146), they outline a new form of negotiation that seems to be occurring between them.

Perhaps because I come to this issue from a perspective heavily influenced by the ideas of Bakhtin (1981, 1984, 1986) on 'dialogism' (Holquist, 1990), I believe that virtually any occasion on which worldviews meet will involve a form of what Claxton, Pollard, and Sutherland call negotiation. As I have emphasized, however, I believe the real task is then to differentiate the notion of negotiation and recognize the strikingly different forms it can take. This volume serves as a model for how to approach these issues, and for this reason it promises to inform educational thought and practice for years to come.

Acknowledgement

Support for the writing of this chapter was provided by a grant from the Spencer Foundation. The statements made and the views expressed are solely the responsibility of the author.

References

Bakhtin, M.M. (1981) *The dialogic imagination: four essays by M.M. Bakhtin.* Austin: University of Texas Press. (edited by M. Holquist; translated by C. Emerson and M. Holquist)

Bakhtin, M.M. (1984) *Problems of Dostoevsky's Poetics.* Minneapolis: University of Minnesota Press. (edited and translated by C. Emerson)

Bakhtin, M.M. (1986) *Speech Genres and Other Late Essays.* Austin: University Texas Press, pp60-102. (translated by Vern W. McGee; edited by Caryl Emerson and Michael Holquist)

Bruner, J. (1990) *Acts of Meaning.* Cambridge, MA: Harvard University Press

Bruner, J. (1996) *The Culture of Education.* Cambridge, MA: Harvard University Press

Goffman, E. (1959) *The Presentation of Self in Everyday Life.* Garden City, NY: Doubleday

Holquist, M. (1990) *Dialogism: Bakhtin and His World.* London, Rougledge

Tulviste, P. and J.V. Wertsch (1994) Official and unofficial histories: the case of Estonia. *Journal of Narrative and Life History,* 4(4), p311-329

Wertsch, J.V. (1998) *Mind as Action.* New York: Oxford University Press

Wertsch, J.V. (2002) *Voices of Collective Remembering.* New York: Cambridge University Press

Wineburg, S.S. (2001) *Historical thinking and Other Unnatural Acts: charting the future of teaching the past.* Philadelphia: Temple University Press

Index